The venerable Bede (c. 673–735) was one of the Middle Ages' most influential scriptural exegetes. In his commentaries he searches for the inner, spiritual meaning of scripture. He says of *Tobit*: 'anyone who knows how to interpret it historically (and allegorically as well) can see that its inner meaning excels the mere letter as much as the fruit excels the leaves.' Bede sees in *Tobit* 'the greatest mysteries of Christ and the Church', particularly in relation to the salvation history of Jews and Gentiles. Bede describes *The Canticle of Habakkuk* — sung in the monastic liturgy every Friday — as 'mainly a proclamation of the mysteries of the Lord's passion'. He also interprets it as 'a mystical account' of Christ's incarnation, resurrection and ascension, and sees in it another representation of Jewish and Gentile history. Both commentaries — here translated into English for the first time — are marked by Bede's concern for the spiritual welfare of contemporary believers. His approach to *Tobit* and *Habakkuk* deepens our understanding of his best-known work, *The Ecclesiastical History of the English People*, where he explores the extension of salvation to the Gentiles of the far west, the peoples of Britain and Ireland.

Seán Connolly graduated in Greek and Latin from University College, Galway. After his doctorate in Late Latin and Palaeography at University College, Dublin under the late Ludwig Bieler, he did postdoctoral research at the University of Munich under the late Bernhard Bischoff on unpublished eighth-century Hiberno-Latin scripture commentaries. He has written on St Augustine and Plotinus, edited and translated the earliest Latin Lives of St Brigit and translated Bede's *De Templo*. Formerly a Fellow in Indo-European Linguistics at the University of Pennsylvania, he taught at Villanova University and was a Visiting Associate Professor of Classical Studies at Loyola University of Chicago. He has until recently taught Medieval Latin, Greek and Palaeography at University College, Cork, and is currently working on an *editio princeps* of an anonymous eighth-century Hiberno-Latin scripture commentary known as the *Irish Reference Bible*.

Diarmuid Scully is a tutor in the Department of History, University College Cork. His principal research interest is Bede as historian and exegete.

Bede
On *Tobit* and on the
Canticle of Habakkuk

Seán Connolly

FOUR COURTS PRESS

This book is published by
FOUR COURTS PRESS LTD
55 Prussia Street, Dublin 7, Ireland
e-mail: fcp@ indigo.ie
and in North America by
FOUR COURTS PRESS
c/o ISBS, 5804 N.E. Hassalo Street, Portland, OR 97213.

A catalogue record for this title
is available from the British Library.

ISBN 1-85182-283-6 hbk
ISBN 1-85182-284-4 pbk

Printed in Ireland
by ColourBooks Ltd, Dublin.

For Tom McIntyre,
in grateful tribute and appreciation

Multi pacifici sint tibi
et consiliarii tibi sint unus de mille

amicus fidelis protectio fortis
qui autem invenit illum invenit thesaurum
amico fideli nulla est conparatio
et non est digna ponderatio auri et argenti
contra bonitatem fidei illius

Let those who are at peace with you be many,
but let your advisers be one in a thousand.

A faithful friend is a secure shelter;
whoever finds one has found a treasure.
Nothing can compare with a faithful friend,
and no weight of gold or silver
can balance the worth of his fidelity.

(Sirach 6.6;14–16)

CONTENTS

ACKNOWLEDGEMENTS

To my colleague and one-time student Diarmuid Scully who so readily agreed to write the introduction to this translation I owe a great deal. It was only fitting that he should have been given the opportunity to write it since he was instrumental in my taking a keener interest in the study of Bede and acquiring a deeper insight into his work than I might otherwise have done. I have to thank him for having so willingly, indeed enthusiastically, helped me with the task of drawing up a bibliography and checking the author's sources and a host of references. I have to thank him for adding some notes of historical interest as well as for having helped me with the task of checking the scripture references and the author's sources and for his inexhaustible patience with my repeated revisions and retouchings of the original rendering. Another of my colleagues to whom I am heavily indebted is Dr David Frendo, Head of the Department of Ancient Classics, where I first had the privilege of working at UCC. More than once, despite his heavy research schedule, he generously shared with me his knowledge of Hebrew and the benefits of his internationally recognized scholarship in the field of Byzantine Greek, helping me to a better understanding of textual *cruces* in the Septuagint.

My thanks are also due to Fr Gerard MacGinty, OSB of Glenstal Abbey for kindly looking at both the text and the translation of the *Canticle of Habakkuk* and shedding light on it by sharing with me his exceptional knowledge, ripened by a lifetime of experience, of the Rule of St Benedict and the history of the Divine Office. I am privileged to enjoy his collaboration in the work of producing the *editio princeps* of the 8th-century Hiberno-Latin encyclopedic compilation known as the *Irish Reference Bible* or *Das irische Bibelwerk* as it was referred to by my former teacher, the late Professor Bernhard Bischoff of the University of Munich. I owe more than I can say to his fellow-Benedictine, Fr David Hurst, of Portsmouth Abbey School, Rhode Island, who will already be well known to readers as the editor not only of the Latin text of Bede's Commentary on the Book of Tobit on which our translation is based but of several other of his works as well. Not alone has he read my translation of both works in the present volume but he has done so very closely and in more than one revision. In addition to offering invaluable suggestions on the interpretation of the text, he has taken the trouble to draw attention to the occasional oversight or misreading. Few scholars alive today can be better acquainted than he with Bede's Latin, given the number of the saint's works he has critically edited. As well as thanking him (which I do with warmth and sincerity) for his help towards improving the present translation, I am sure I speak for all students of the saint's writings when

9

I say that it gives me the greatest pleasure to acknowledge his prodigious contribution to Bede studies. *Euge, serue bone et fidelis!*

I am especially indebted to my Scots friend and colleague of long standing, Tom McIntyre. One envies his pupils at St Richard's School, Bredenbury, Bromyard, Herefordshire, where he is at present teaching. A classicist of long experience in the English Public School system and a scholar who deserves to be more widely known, his judgement, based on his outstanding knowledge of classical Latin and Greek, was of inestimable value throughout this entire enterprise. His observations quoted or referred to in a number of footnotes were made in private communication to me, as were those of Fr Hurst and Fr MacGinty. Like them he has, despite his onerous personal commitments, generously devoted a huge proportion of his time to reading my translation and making me, as a result, more aware of the finer shades of meaning in Bede's Latin. For this I shall be forever in his debt.

For the typesetting of the book I owe everything to Peter Flynn of our Computer Centre at UCC who is our expert in the arcane but elegant program TEX which was used in the process.

To end on a more personal note, I want to thank my wife, Cláirín, who not merely by helping with the wearisome but indispensable work of confirming myriads of references, but also by reading the text and improving the wording, by her cheerful forbearance with my sometimes unsocial hours of research, as well as by her unfailing assistance, encouragement and support, made it possible for me to complete this undertaking.

Seán Connolly

Department of English
University College Cork, Ireland.
31 October 1996

ABBREVIATIONS

CCM	*Corpus Consuetudinum Monasticarum*
CCSL	*Corpus Christianorum Series Latina*
CSEL	*Corpus Scriptorum Ecclesiasticorum Latinorum*
DEB	Gildas, *De Excidio Britanniae* (*On the Ruin of Britain*)
Douay	*Holy Bible* Douay version
DTab	Bede, *De Tabernaculo* (*On the Tabernacle*)
DTemp	Bede, *De Templo* (*On the Temple*)
EHD	*English Historical Documents*
HA	Bede, *Historia Abbatum* (*History of the Abbots*)
HE	Bede, *Historia Ecclesiastica Gentis Anglorum* (*Ecclesiastical History of the English People*)
Hom	Bede, *Homilies on the Gospels*
InHab	Bede, *In Canticum Abacuc* (*On the Canticle of Habakkuk*)
InTob	Bede, *In Tobiam* (*On Tobit*)
JB	*Jerusalem Bible*
Knox	Mgr Ronald Knox's version of the *Holy Bible*
L&S	*Lewis and Short: A Latin Dictionary*
LXX	*The Septuagint*
Moral	Gregory, *Moralia in Iob* (*Morals on the Book of Job*)
MGH	*Monumenta Germaniae Historica*
NIV	*New International Version of the Holy Bible*
NJB	*New Jerusalem Bible*
NJBC	*New Jerome Biblical Commentary*
Nom.	Jerome: *de Nominibus Hebraicis*
OLD	*Oxford Latin Dictionary*
PL	*Patrologia Latina*
RB	*Rule of St Benedict*
RCR	*The New Testament: Revised Challoner-Rheims Version*
RSV	*The Holy Bible: Revised Standard Version*
Sit.	Jerome: *de Situ Locorum*
Vg	*Vulgate*
VL	*Vetus Latina* or *Old Latin* versions of the Bible

My first serious encounter with the writings of St Bede was the study of his two books *On the Temple* when I was conducting a Latin course for our Medieval History students and was asked by my colleague, Diarmuid Scully, to take *De Templo* as the Latin text. Encouraged by him and others, especially his teacher Dr Jennifer O'Reilly, I then went on to translate the text into English for the Liverpool University Press series, *Translated Texts for Historians*. I was struck by Bede's preoccupation with the unity of the Church, understood as the community of believers, even before the incarnation, and his keen awareness of the enormity of the Christian debt to the Jewish people. He sees Jewish history as relevant to the Church of his own times. For him everything that happened in salvation history is recorded not merely for Jewish readers but for his own contemporary fellow-Christians as well. A convinced disciple of St Paul, he is at the opposite pole from Marcion who was for total repudiation of the Old Testament, and who argued that the true God, the Father of Jesus Christ was not the deity of the Old Testament. To those early Christians who were unsure of their Jewish heritage, Marcion set out to furnish a way to transcend that heritage. Paul, on the other hand, even after his revelatory experience near Damascus (Gal 1.12,16) never changed his commitment to the one God of Abraham, Isaac and Jacob. Rather he was left with the abiding conviction of the unity of the economy of salvation. This conviction Bede not only shared, but seized every opportunity to hammer home in chapter after chapter of his exegetical writings. In terms of content, this is what prompted my choice of the two texts I have translated here, his commentaries on the *Book of Tobit* and on the *Canticle of Habakkuk*. In them, it is true, one senses a difference in feel from the *De Templo* where one sees the author's developed thought, but the underlying themes are already evident.

However, as a classicist, my first fascination was with the author's style of writing which possesses a kind of holy clarity that comes across very powerfully. There is a sublimity about Bede's mind and outlook on life which is uplifting to anyone who not only reads but ruminates on what he says, after the fashion of the ancient monks. His repeated references to our heavenly homeland, the heavenly Jerusalem, the mother of us all, and the angels as our heavenly compatriots, show where his heart lies. Few writers could more truly echo the words of St Paul to the Philippians (3.20) which he had made his own: 'For us our homeland is in heaven, and from heaven comes the saviour we are waiting for, the Lord Jesus Christ, and he will transfigure these wretched bodies of ours into copies of his glorious body' (*JB*). As in the translation of *De Templo*, it is my aim not only to be faithful to Bede's meaning but also to adhere, as far as English usage allows, to the structure of his sentences. On the advice of my Latinist colleagues I have made considerably greater concessions to the reader than I did in translating *De Templo* by way of breaking up the author's very lengthy sentences into more manageable units of sense. This will sometimes be obvious. Where I think it needs explanation I try to let the Latin learner or the one whose Latin is rusty from disuse see what it is I have done while endeavouring to safeguard the author's meaning. Where I have had to depart from the literal rendering, I try as often as possible to let the reader know this by giving the original Latin followed by its literal equivalent. In a word, my aim has been to make the translation process as transparent to the reader as I reasonably could. Occasionally it has been necessary to add explanatory words or phrases, subjects or objects of verbs, as well as adjectives, adverbs, pronouns or prepositions which can be omitted in the Latin. This has had to be done more than once where, for instance, the pronoun alone would have left the referent ambiguous or unclear. Here and there I have used the passive instead of the active where it suited the English sentence structure better without materially affecting the meaning. No one who has attempted to translate Bede needs reminding of the dictum: *Traductores traditores*. The responsible translator always has misgivings about being faithful to the author's intentions. The translator of Bede confronts a more than usually daunting challenge, given the care the author takes in choosing the *mot juste* and in view of the fluctuations the chosen word is apt to undergo, (like Proteus, the Old Man of the Sea), while one is wrestling with it to make it yield up its true contextual meaning. Add to this the fact that few writers seem to enjoy word-play so much. One is seldom altogether sure whether Bede is punning or not.

If I have commented at some length on certain Latin expressions or on matters not directly to do with Bede's discussion it is (a) because I am not writing for the benefit of scholars who already know Latin well; they should not be relying on a translation anyway; (b) because I am not writing primarily for professional Bede scholars; it is assumed that they already know Latin well enough to read the original text. The readership I *am* writing for is (a) those for whom, not knowing any Latin, Bede would otherwise be a closed book; (b) those who have only the little Latin they learnt at school or college and have, perhaps, to a greater or less extent forgotten; (c) those to whom the writings of Bede are either totally or relatively new. This was my brief from Liverpool University Press for the translation of *De Templo*. I have also had an eye to the needs of those who might choose or be required to read either of the two books as a text for a course in Medieval Latin, whether self-taught or taught by others. Some of the footnotes on the Latin will seem elementary to those already competent in the language of the period. Others assume a sound knowledge of the classical language. It would be temerarious to choose either text (indeed any but a few of Bede's works) for an introductory reading course in Latin. A century ago in the preface to his edition of Bede's *Historia Ecclesiastica Gentis Anglorum* (I, liii–liv), Charles Plummer wrote: 'Bede's command of Latin is excellent, and his style is clear and limpid, and *it is very seldom that we have to pause to think of the meaning of a sentence*' (my italics). With the first part of this statement there is no argument. The words in italics, however, must be taken as referring to the *Historia* or such works, and also, no doubt, understood in the light of Plummer's own command of Latin. They simply do not reflect this translator's experience of reading and translating Bede's *exegetical* writings. The plain truth is quite often the reverse.

In the Latin editions of our two commentaries (*CCSL* 119B), the translator's difficulties have been compounded by a number of textual errors (some of them, I daresay, typographical rather than attributable to the individual editors) which have not been noted in the corrigenda. Some of these were so obvious as not to pose a problem; others less obvious were somewhat disconcerting. For the user's convenience and to save space, I am giving a list of these errors here according to the page and line number of the *CCSL* Latin edition. In the Tobit commentary on page 3 line 22 (3.22): for *peregrinatione* read *peregrinationem*; 5.8: for *caecitas* read *caecatus*; 9.8: for *tradixit* read *traduxit*. In the Habakkuk commentary: 391.297: for *nomina* read *nomine*; 398.489–90: for *accepiatis* read *accepistis*; 404.644: for *non* read *nos*; 399.504: for *impletus* read *impletum*; 399.508 I suspect that for *patri*, (wrong case and most probably wrong word, even though it appears in the apparatus also), one should read *patria* with Migne; 407.716: for *caelesti* read *caelestis*; 407.727: for *carnem* read *carmen*; 409.768: for *Pater* read *Patet*; 409.776: for *meribimur* read *merebimur*. It might be noted that one of the corrigenda, viz., 13.61: *praeminentia* has been miscorrected to *pareeminentia*. The more problematical of these emendations I have checked against several of the collated codices as well as the *PL*.

Regarding the layout of the present version a few explanations are due to the reader. I have given the page numbers of the Latin text in the outer margin for the convenience of those wishing to refer to the original. In both commentaries the text is divided (usually by lemmata) into sections and each section into numbered sub-sections or verses according to sense-units for ease of reference on account of the great length of Bede's sentences. Before the lemma commented upon in each section are given the relevant chapter and verse of the book in question. In the Indexes I have labelled the references *T* for *Tobit* and *H* for *Habakkuk*.

In the translation of biblical quotations, where this has not been done by me, I have generally followed the *Douay* version with occasional modifications where the language was archaic or the rendering seemed inappropriate. The latter translation, of course, sometimes happens to coincide with that of the *RSV* (which I rarely use here since it is not based on the Vulgate) or is only minimally different. At other times my own translation may coincide with or closely resemble one or the other or both. In several instances the meaning was so obvious as not to require consulting any of the standard translations.

I follow *RSV* in the spelling of proper names and in its system of abbreviation for books of the Bible, (except e.g. for 3 Kings), e.g. Gen for Genesis, Jn for John etc. Regarding references to the Psalms, since Bede and his editors follow the *Vg* numeration, I give, as occasion arises, the *Vg* Psalm and verse number first, followed by those of the *RSV* in parentheses e.g. Ps 67.20(68.21). Scriptural and patristic references which are allusions or reminiscences rather than direct quotations are marked with an asterisk. The + sign before a scriptural or patristic reference indicates that the reference (not noted in the *CCSL* edition) has been added in our edition of the translated text. In the Index of Names and Selected Themes I have (a) chosen what appeared to me the more significant or interesting topics, (a choice on which, of course, I have consulted others but which is ultimately a purely personal one, and therefore unlikely to win the approval of all readers) and (b) as far as feasible, I have retained substantially the wording of the translated text. Often for purposes of compression it was necessary to modify this e.g. by omitting the definite or indefinite article, rephrasing, abridgment or other means. The ‖ sign is meant as shorthand for a parallel or figural meaning and can be understood either actively or passively as e.g. 'parallels/represents/symbolizes/typifies' or 'is paralleled/represented/symbolized/typified by' depending on context. In the headwords, where the expression does not occur in the text at all, but the corresponding event or reality is alluded to or indicated, I have used italics, e.g. *Transfiguration, Annunciation, Septuagint* and the like. Italics are likewise used for a few Latin expressions retained in the translated text. The numbered marginal arrows in the Introduction are page references to the translated text; the similar arrows in the translated text refer the reader back to the place in the Introduction where the reference was made.

INTRODUCTION BY DIARMUID SCULLY

I

At the age of seven, Bede (c. 673-735) entered the monastery of St Peter and St Paul at Wearmouth-Jarrow in Anglo-Saxon Northumbria. He remained in that learned and civilized community for the rest of his life, devoting himself 'entirely to the study of the scriptures' and producing many commentaries on the word of God (*HE* 5.24).[1] Bede recognizes scriptural exegesis as an ancient endeavour, sanctioned by the authority of scripture itself. He says that 'there are many hidden mysteries of the divine tidings that the minds of ordinary people do not grasp. There are some that those less learned are unable to assimilate on their own, but which they are able to understand once they are explained by teachers' (*Hom* 2.2). Concerning these teachers Bede comments:

> They are ordered both to gather up by meditating ⟨on them⟩ the obscure points of the scriptures which the crowd is unable ⟨to understand⟩ on its own, and to preserve the results of their meditation and ⟨the Lord's⟩ commandments in their writings for their own use as well as that of the crowds. This is what the apostles themselves and the evangelists did, by including quite a number of mystical sayings of the law and the prophets in their works, with the addition of their own interpretation. This is what a large number of their followers, guides of the Church throughout the entire world, have done by scrutinizing complete books of both testaments of the scriptures in very diligent explanations, and although they have been despised by men, yet they have been fecund with the bread of heavenly grace. (*Hom* 2.2)

In effect, Bede here describes his own purpose and approach in commenting on scripture. The care of souls is always his first exegetical concern. He is anxious to deepen spiritual teachers' knowledge of scripture in order to prepare them for the exercise of pastoral care.[2]

He reserves a modest place for himself in the history of scriptural exegesis, writing that 'I have made it my business, for my own benefit and that of my brothers, to make brief extracts from the works of the fathers on the holy scriptures, or to add notes of my own to clarify their sense and interpretation' (*HE* 5.24). His commentaries are profoundly influenced by the Church Fathers, in particular by Ambrose, Augustine, Jerome and

---

1 All quotations from the *HE* are taken from Colgrave and Mynors (ed. and tr.) 1969.
2 Holder 1994, xiv. But Bede emphasizes that 'it is not only bishops, presbyters, deacons and even those who govern monasteries who are to be understood as pastors; but also all the faithful who keep watch over the little ones of their house, are properly called pastors' (*Hom* 1.7).

Gregory — above all, Gregory. But Bede's writings are not collections of other men's flowers. He combined earlier insights into scripture with his own, and his greatness as an exegete was immediately apparent. From the German mission of the 740s, Boniface hungrily sought his commentaries for use in his own evangelizing work. He wrote to Archbishop Egbert of York: 'I beseech you to copy and send me some treatises from the work of the teacher, Bede, whom lately, as we have heard, the divine grace endowed with spiritual understanding and allowed to shine in your province, so that I may benefit from that candle which the Lord bestowed on you.'[3] By the twelfth century, Bede's reputation was such that the *Glossa ordinaria*, the standard biblical commentary of the age, could rely massively on his work for its entries on Tobit and Habakkuk, among other books.[4]

II

The primary objective of this introduction is to examine a single aspect of Bede's commentaries on Tobit and the Canticle of Habakkuk, namely, his approach to the salvation history of Jew and Gentile. Bede was the first exegete to devote an entire, detailed commentary to Tobit.[5] Although Jerome included Tobit in the Vulgate, he did not consider it to be a canonical work. Instead he reckoned it among those books suitable for edification but not for the confirmation of Church teaching.[6] However, the western Church generally accepted the work's canonicity.[7] Concerning Habakkuk, as Bede notes at the beginning of his commentary (*InHab* 1.2), the Canticle (Hab 3.2–19) is a liturgically important text. Indeed, the text of the Canticle employed by Bede reflects its liturgical use.[8] Habakkuk's Canticle features in the monastic morning office of Lauds, and also in the readings for Good Friday.[9] Jerome commented on Habakkuk as a whole, and in the sixth century Verecundus Iuncensis discussed the Canticle in his *Commentaries on the Ecclesiastical Canticles*.[10] Bede's commentary on the Canticle owes something to Augustine's compressed discussion of the text in his *City of God*.[11] Commenting on Tobit, Bede briefly calls upon Augustine again, and in both commentaries he makes extensive use of Jerome.[12] Jerome's investigation of the allegorical meaning of scriptural names and places helped to reveal their spiritual significance. His work was therefore an essential exegetical tool, since, as Bede observes,

⇒65

---

3 *EHD* I, 824 4 Ward 1990, 144. 5 Ambrose's *On Tobit* is an attack on usury and the misuse of wealth. 6 *Biblia Sacra* 1984, 957. 7 Ackroyd 1970, 534. 8 Marsden 1995, 214–5. On Bede's text of Tobit, see ibid. 215–17. 9 For a discussion of the liturgical use of the Canticle in the light of patristic exegesis, see Ó Carragáin 1986, 383–88; 1987, 118–19; 1988, *passim;* 1994, 422–26. 10 Jerome,*Commentarium in Abacuc Prophetam ad Chromatium, CCSL* 76A, 618–54; Verecundus Iuncensis,*Commentarii super Cantica Ecclesiastica, VI, Habbacuc, CCSL* 93, 124–47. His comments on Hab 3.1–3 are lost. 11 Sanford and Green (ed. and tr.) 1965, 481–91. 12 Augustine, *Serm* 105, and *Quaest. Eu.*; Jerome, *Sit.* and *Nom.*; see index of patristic citations.

everything in scripture, every detail it records, is charged with spiritual importance. Bede quotes St Paul's words: 'all these things happened to them in figure but were written down for us' (*DTab prol.*; 1 Cor 10.11). Gregory's understanding of the complexity and interpretative variety of scripture also shapes Bede's approach here. It is Gregory who lies behind Bede's statement in the Tobit commentary that sometimes in scripture, 'typologically speaking, men's good deeds have a bad meaning and their bad deeds a good meaning' (*InTob* 5.2).

⇒41

Bede does not tell us when he wrote his commentaries on Tobit or on the Canticle of Habakkuk. Both works appear in the list of his writings appended to the *Ecclesiastical History of the English People*, which was completed in the early 730s (*HE* 5.24). Bede dedicates the Canticle commentary to his 'dearly beloved sister and virgin of Christ' (*InHab* 38.26; cf. 1.1). Bede's writings, the correspondence of Boniface and his friends and other sources including Aldhelm's *On Virginity*, dedicated to the nuns of Barking, indicate the existence of a learned female monastic audience in Anglo-Saxon England.[13] Aldhelm speaks of the Barking community studying scriptural exegesis, grammar, orthography, metre and 'the old stories of the historians and the entries of the chroniclers', all of which were essential for a thorough understanding of scripture. The Barking programme of study closely resembles Bede's own scholarly pursuits. As *HE* 5.24 indicates, he produced works on the same subjects in order to prepare the reader for an encounter with the challenging and often mysterious text of scripture.

⇒95

Ever reticent with personal detail, Bede does not explain his connection with the dedicatee of the Canticle commentary or identify her further. Friendships between men and women in the religious life certainly existed at that time. Bede speaks of the 'deep affection' felt by Abbess Aelfflaed for St Cuthbert (*VCP* 23), and he says of 'the sacred virgin and bride of Christ' Aethelthryth, that 'there was none whom she loved more than Wilfrid', another of the great saints of the period (*HE* 4.19). According to Petrus Comestor, Bede said that the serpent in Eden had a woman's head, 'because like attracts like.'[14] Bede never made this remark, and the view of women it represents is alien to his thought. He insists that all believers, 'quite removed from each other though they may be in space, time, rank, status, sex and age, are linked together by one and the same faith and love' (*DTemp* 18.9). In the *Ecclesiastical History*, he presents the virtues of women such as Aethelthryth and Abbess Hild of Whitby (*HE* 4.23) as timeless and universal. He envisages an active pastoral role for lay-women too. Through their way of life and preaching they may help those who work to build up the temple of the Lord.[15]

---

13 Hollis 1992 *passim*. **14** Henderson 1980, 22; O'Reilly 1992, 168. **15** *In Ezram et Neemiam*, *CCSL* 119A, 257, 650–55.

Inclusivity is the hallmark of Bede's work. A great scholar himself, he emphasizes the place of the simple along with the learned in the Church. He notes with approval that because the monk Owini 'was less capable of the study of the scriptures, he applied himself more earnestly to manual labour' (*HE* 4.3). But, with guidance, the Bible need not be a closed book to the unlearned. Gregory compares scripture to a river, both shallow and deep, in which a lamb may walk and an elephant swim. Its mysteries occupy the wise and its outward meaning helps the simple.[16] Bede himself comments on Tobit and on Habakkuk in a way that reveals both the simple and mystical meaning of those books, and he may therefore be included among the 'holy preachers, inwardly filled in their heart with a deep knowledge of the truth, ⟨who⟩ outwardly exercise the ministry of the word for their hearers, revealing gradually and partially, according to the capacity of the weak, the insights both many and rich that they themselves inwardly possess' (*InHab* 24.6–8).

⇒81

Bede opens his commentary on Tobit with the remark that the book is 'clearly of saving benefit for its readers even in its superficial meaning inasmuch as it abounds in both the noblest examples and the noblest counsels for moral conduct' (*InTob* 1.1). Earlier, Cassiodorus made the same point in his *Institutiones*, where he wrote that Tobit and the other books of the Hagiographa, (Job, Tobit, Esther, Judith, 1 and 2 Ezra, 1 and 2 Maccabees) 'on account of their most excellent moral character... were written to impart to our minds in becoming fashion patience, hope, charity, fortitude, even in women, a life on God's account contemptuous of the present, and other kinds of virtue which under the guidance of the Lord flourished in them.'[17] Commenting on the *Seven Catholic Epistles* — 1 Pet 3.17 — Bede says that the outward, simple meaning of Tobit serves an immediate edificatory purpose; Tobit temporarily lost his sight 'for the reason that the virtue of his patience might shine more widely for all as an example.' Rembrandt's *Anna and the Blind Tobit* (c. 1630) quietly conveys a sense of that patience, a virtue to which Bede attaches great importance. In the *Ecclesiastical History*, he comments on the exemplary patience of such figures as the nun Tortgyth and Hild, both of whom suffer so that their strength might be made perfect in weakness (*HE* 4.9; 23; 1 Cor 12.9). The example of Tobit and other scriptural figures may help those who are in pain. When Abbot Benedict Biscop of Wearmouth-Jarrow lay dying, he would 'call upon one of the monks to read aloud the story of Job, that model of patience, or any other passage of the Bible which might bring consolation to a sick man and lift him out of his depression to think cheerfully of higher things.' (*HA* 12).

⇒39

Bede's respect for the basic, outward reading of scripture is matched by his belief in the literal truth of its narratives. Thus, he believes in the

16 Gregory, *Moral.*, *CCSL* 143, 6, 173–8.   17 Jones (tr.) 1966, I. vi. 4–5. I owe this reference to Dr Jennifer O'Reilly.

reality of scriptural miracles, saying, for example, that 'our Lord through the miracles he wrought in the flesh showed the Jewish people from whom he had taken flesh that he was the Son of God' (*InTob* 8.3). However, those 'who read or listen to the signs and miracles of Our Lord and Saviour properly do not receive them in such a way that they pay attention to what in them produces outward astonishment, but instead they consider what they themselves ought to be doing inwardly, following the example of these ⟨signs⟩, and what mystical truths they ought to be pondering in these ⟨stories⟩' (*Hom* 2.12). The literal truth of Old Testament miracles likewise contains a spiritual lesson. In his prose *Life of Cuthbert*, Bede follows the Anonymous *Life* in using the Archangel Raphael's cure of Tobit's blindness to validate a modern miracle, the healing of Cuthbert's knee by an angel (*VCP* 2; *VCA* 1.4). But, as Sr Benedicta Ward observes, the historical fact of these cures contains a deeper significance; 'in his commentary on Tobit, Bede consistently sees Raphael as a representation of Christ, healing Tobit, the devout Jew, that is, giving salvation to those who were already devout but not yet wholly given to Christ. Here the 'healing' of Cuthbert is also a preface from a good life to a more devout one: 'for from this time the boy was given wholly to God.'[18]

⇒45 (margin, at line "he had taken flesh...")

Bede outlines the deeper, spiritual meaning of Tobit and The Canticle of Habakkuk in his introductions to those works, and goes on to demonstrate that, important though the literal sense is, this spiritual meaning 'excels the mere letter as much as the fruit excels the leaves' (*InTob* 1.2). Understood spiritually, Tobit 'is found to contain within it the greatest mysteries of Christ and the Church' (*InTob* 1.3; cf. *HE* 5.24). Tobit's faithfulness symbolizes the faithfulness of the Jewish people of the old dispensation, his blindness symbolizes the spiritual blindness of those among the Jews who rejected Christ, and his cure denotes their eventual conversion. The Canticle of Habakkuk 'is mainly a proclamation of the Lord's passion.... But it also gives a mystical account of his incarnation, resurrection and ascension into heaven as well as of the faith of the Gentiles and the unbelief of the Jews' (*InHab* 1.1,3).

⇒39

⇒39

⇒65

III

The interest that Bede displays in Jew and Gentile in his commentaries on Tobit and Habakkuk is characteristic of his exegesis as a whole. His scriptural commentaries again and again investigate the profound spiritual significance of Jewish history and ritual for contemporary believers. They emphasize the continuity of Old Testament Jewish and present Christian belief. That continuity is further — if obliquely — expressed in Bede's historical works. They too are works of exegesis, unveiling the spiritual meaning of past events among Bede's own people and beyond. Their

---

18 Ward 1990, 99.

concerns illuminate his approach to Jewish and Gentile history in the Tobit and Habakkuk commentaries. Those commentaries in turn deepen our understanding of Bede's approach to the history of the peoples of Britain and Ireland, the Gentiles of the far west.

Bede emphasizes that Jesus was a Jew. Tobit gave his own name to his son 'because he learnt that Christ was to be born of his own kin as Moses had said: *Your God will raise up for you a prophet like me from among your brethren; to him you shall listen;* (Deut 18.15; Acts 3.22)' (*In Tob* 3.3–

⇒40 4). Habakkuk's promise that God will come from Teman or the south, as
⇒71 Hab 3.3 says 'in the Hebrew scriptures' (*InHab* 7.12), was literally fulfilled when Christ was born in Bethlehem which 'is situated to the south of
⇒71 Jerusalem' (*InHab* 7.13). When Christ was brought to the temple to
⇒71 be circumcised, 'God did indeed come from the south' (*InHab* 7.14). If Hab 3.3 is read as 'God will come from Lebanon' then Jesus' Jewish origin is likewise indicated. The temple in Jerusalem was built with cedars from Lebanon, and so God comes from Lebanon because 'the Lord when he appeared in the flesh scattered the first seeds of the gospel in the temple itself and from there filled the whole world with the shoots of his faith and truth. Which is why Isaiah says: *out of Zion shall go forth the law, and*
⇒70 *the word of the Lord from Jerusalem* (Is 2.3)' (*InHab* 7.5–6). So, scattering water on the way — one variant reading of Hab 3.10 — God 'will dispense waters from the springs of Israel far and wide among the nations of the whole world, when he says to his disciples: *Go and teach all the nations, baptizing them in the name of the Father, and of the Son and of the Holy*
⇒82 *Spirit* (Mt 28.19)' (*InHab* 24.13–14).

These, and many other passages in Bede's exegesis, not only affirm Jesus' Jewishness but also teach that the faith preached by the apostles at his command is the same faith held by Jewish and Gentile believers throughout the ages. Indeed, the fact that the temple was entirely covered in Lebanese cedarwood, symbolizing spiritual perfection (*DTemp* 8.3), means that 'all the elect are joined to each other by the most beautiful bond of charity so that though the multitude of the faithful is innumerable, they can nevertheless, with good reason, be said to have one heart and one soul on account of the community of faith and love they share (cf. Acts 4.32)' (*DTemp* 11.1). Before the incarnation, the community of faith was called the Synagogue, now it is called the Church (*In Cant.*, CCSL 119B, 190, 1–7). The scripture and values of the Old Testament Synagogue foreshadow those of the Church, since 'from the time when the law was given until the Lord's incarnation and the revelation of grace there was no lack of people who were grounded in the law and observed evangelical perfection in all things in outlook and action; and there was no lack of scripture to intimate by its prophetic words the grace of the New Testament in the old' (*DTemp* 5.2). Thus, commenting on Tobit, Bede refers to Old Testament Jewish faith in 'the Lord's incarnation or of the Synagogue

⇒41 as an institution' (*InTob* 4.4). The Church is rooted in the spirit of the Mosaic law as taught in the Synagogue; 'in whatever direction the Church has been spread throughout the world, among diverse nations and tribes and tongues (Rev 5.9), it stands completely firm in the single love of God and neighbour which was contained in the decalogue of the law' (*DTab* 2.2). The Church on earth thereby joins the Church in heaven, where 'the angelic powers keep with unfailing devotion the law of God which is written in five books, that is, by loving the Lord their God with all their strength and loving their neighbours as themselves (cf. Lk 10.27). *For love is the fulfilling of the law* (Rom 13.10)' (*DTemp* 13.2).

⇒39 Under the law, 'the people of Israel...served God when all the Gentiles were given over to idolatry' (*InTob* 1.4). But Bede does not exclude the possibility that salvation was also available to the Gentiles of that period. 'For not only Jeremiah and Isaiah and the other prophets of the circumcision but also blessed Job with his sons who were of the Gentiles, afforded teachers of the succeeding age the greatest example of lifestyle and patience, and the greatest proclamation of salutary teaching' (*DTemp* 4.2). Nevertheless, the Jews of that time were God's chosen people, 'as he says of the people themselves: *Israel ⟨is⟩ my first-born son*

⇒40 (Ex 4.22)' (*InTob* 3.7–8). As Maccabees records, they held firm under the
⇒41 devil's persecuting assault (*InTob* 4.4; 2 Mac 6–7). The Jewish people thus became part of a continuing tradition of witness to God in time of adversity. Some of their spiritual descendants appear in the *Ecclesiastical History*, for example the faithful Christian Britons under pagan Roman persecution and pagan English attack. Trusting in God and hiding in 'woods and deserts and secret caverns' (*HE* 1.8) and among 'the mountains and woods and forests (*HE* 1.14; cf. 15–16), they recall the Jews of Maccabees who withdrew into deserts and mountains (2 Mac 5.29; cf. 1 Mac 2.8) and the believers whose wanderings in mountains and caves and caverns of the earth Hebrews celebrates in its history of the power of faith (Heb 11.37–38).[19]

⇒40 Bede attributes Jewish steadfastness to the influence of the 'many holy teachers who made provision for their life and salvation' (*InTob* 4.3). The Jews 'earnestly took care to correct...through all their more learned and chosen ones and turned to imploring God's mercy to obtain eter-
⇒43 nal life' (*InTob* 5.15). Their teachers stood in contrast to the teachers of the Gentiles who 'knew about life in this world only ...⟨but⟩ were unable to say anything about eternal life. And so they were all carried off by the devil inasmuch as they were given over to idolatry
⇒43 until the true bridegroom, Our Lord, came' (*InTob* 6.2–3;
⇒51 cf. *InTob* 19.3–4). As Coifi, the Northumbrian pagan priest enlightened by God, acknowledges in the *Ecclesiastical History*, 'our religion is worthless;

---

19 Here Bede follows Gildas' *DEB* 11.2 and 25.1; cf. *DEB* 72.4.

for the more diligently I sought the truth in our cult, the less I found it' (*HE* 2.13).

Bede praises the pastoral care exercised by Jewish teachers of the old dispensation. They 'ministered the alms of God's word not only to the unlettered audience of their own nation but also to those of the Gentiles who wished to convert to the religious observance of their way of life' (*InTob* 2.4). Commenting on the construction of Solomon's temple, Bede speaks of the significance of these proselytes, 'the Greek term for those who were of other nationalities by birth but accepted circumcision and converted to the fellowship of the people of God' (*DTemp* 3.4). Their involvement, and that of King Hiram of Tyre, in helping Solomon to build the temple signifies that 'the Jews and proselytes and Gentiles converted to the truth of the Gospel build one and the same Church of Christ whether by upright living or by teaching as well' (*DTemp* 3.5; cf. *DTab* 2.1). Before the incarnation, Israel's gifts to the Gentiles included the translation of scripture into Greek. Through the Septuagint, 'the people of God entrusted to the Gentiles the knowledge of the divine law which is contained in the decalogue' (*InTob* 3.12; cf. *InTob* 25.6). They thereby 'gave a certain portion of their saving knowledge (*scientia salutaris*) even to the Gentiles' (*InTob* 2.6). This phrase connects Old Testament Jewish instruction to the sharing of knowledge in the present Church. Archbishop Theodore of Canterbury (669–90) and his companion Hadrian established a school at Canterbury and 'attracted a crowd of students into whose minds they daily poured the streams of *scientia salutaris*' (*HE* 4.1).[20]

The Jews' generosity in sharing their faith with the Gentiles mirrors the Gentiles' generosity in sharing the word of God with one another after the incarnation. Bede interprets Raguel's servant and camels in Tobit as 'preachers chosen from the Gentiles through whom the Lord gathers in others too.... These with Raphael's help bring Gabael to Tobias' wedding when holy preachers bring new peoples together into the unity of the Church of Christ with his assistance' (*InTob* 26.2–5; cf. *InTob* 25.1–6). In the *Ecclesiastical History*, Bede presents the triumph of the faith among the Gentiles of Britain and Ireland as the work of people from various nations. He depicts papal Roman involvement in the conversion of the Britons (*HE* 1.4) and Irish (*HE* 1.13). A Briton, Ninian,

⇒39

⇒40
⇒55
⇒39

⇒55
⇒54

---

20 Colgrave in Colgrave and Mynors (ed. and tr.) 1969, translates this phrase as 'wholesome learning.' At Canterbury, one of Theodore's students was named Tobias; he afterwards became bishop of Rochester (*HE* 5.8 and 23). In the *HE*, Bede gives a number of instances of English people taking spiritually significant names; the first English-born archbishop of Canterbury was Deusdedit (*HE* 3:20), while Willibrord, archbishop of the Frisians, was given the name Clement by Pope Sergius (*HE* 5:12). The symbolic importance of name-change is illustrated by the Roman epitaph of King Cædwalla of the West Saxons who, on baptism, 'laid aside his barbarous rage and shame/And, with changed heart, to Peter changed his name' (*HE* 5:7).

and an Irishman, Columba (Colum Cille), later appear as the apostles of the Picts (*HE* 3.4). Columba's Irish followers, along with Gregory's Roman missionaries, convert the English, a process that dominates the narrative of the *Ecclesiastical History*. The Roman missionaries are helped by Frankish interpreters (*HE* 1.25) and an English convert, King Oswald of the Northumbrians, acts as an interpreter for the Irish missionary, Aidan (*HE* 3.3). A Burgundian bishop, Felix, comes to preach to the English (*HE* 2.15) as does another Continental bishop, Birinus (*HE* 2:7). Archbishop Theodore is a native of Tarsus, in Cilicia, and Hadrian is an African (*HE* 4.1). Once converted, the English themselves evangelize the Continental Germans (*HE* 5.9–11,19), while the English exile for Christ, Egbert, 'brought much blessing... to those among whom he lived in exile, the Irish and Picts' (*HE* 3.27). Tracing Bede's account of Egbert and the Continental mission, Alcuin clearly articulates its message in his *York* poem:

> This race of ours, mother of famous men,
> did not keep her children for herself,
> nor hold them within the confines of her own kingdom,
> but sent many of them afar across the seas,
> bearing the seeds of life to other peoples.[21]

Bede's interest in Jewish pastoral care recalls his commitment to pastoral care in the Church of his own day. In a letter to Bishop Egbert of York, he says: 'keep safe the flock entrusted to you from the audacious attacks of ravening wolves... remember that you have been appointed not as a hireling but as a shepherd.'[22] Jewish instruction of the unlearned and use of translation in spreading the word of God parallels the work Bede demands of modern teachers. In the same letter to Egbert, he calls for the translation of the essential statements of Christian belief — the Apostles' Creed and the Lord's Prayer — from Latin into English; 'the unlearned, that is, to say those who only know their own language, must learn to say them in their own tongue and to chant them carefully.... For thus the whole community of believers may learn of what their faith consists, and how they ought in the strength of that belief to arm and defend themselves against the assault of evil spirits.'[23] He himself 'frequently offered an English translation of the Creed and the Lord's Prayer to uneducated priests.'[24] Furthermore, in the *Ecclesiastical History*, he links pastoral care and translation in several places, most notably in his account of Caedmon, divinely gifted with the power of song, 'who turned scripture into English verse for the benefit of his listeners' (*HE* 4.24).

---

21 Godman (ed. and tr.) 1982, 83. **22** McClure and Collins (tr.) 1994, 353. **23** ibid., 345–6. **24** ibid., 346. The monk Cuthbert writes that Bede, on his deathbed, was engaged in a translation of John's gospel, ibid., 301.

Bede describes Caedmon as ruminating on scripture before composing his songs, 'like some clean animal chewing the cud' (*HE* 4.24). Clean animals are those which the Mosaic law permits Jews to eat, namely ruminants with cloven hooves (Lev 11.3). Patristic exegetes compare these animals to discerning readers of scripture, and to people who can distinguish between right and wrong. Bede himself discusses the symbolism of clean animals in his exegesis.[25] In his commentary on Genesis he says that in the present age 'were born not a few holy men of God's people who learn to imitate clean animals by ruminating over the word of God and treading their way by a sure foot, carrying the yoke of the divine law in good works and keeping the poor from the cold by pelts of their own sheep.'[26] Chief among them is Christ, he says, and he elsewhere names the Virgin Mary too as a clean ruminant.[27] The Jews of the old dispensation were also clean animals. Bede compares the Jews and Gentiles of that time to the ox and ass of Is 1.3; the ass represents the Gentiles, 'who remained always unclean with the stains of idolatry' while the ox 'designates the people of the Jews who were accustomed to carry the yoke of the law and ruminate upon its words' (*Hom* 1.6).[28]

Commenting on Habakkuk's Canticle, Bede identifies the ox specifically with Jewish teachers: 'sheep (were reflected) in those who humbly listened to the voice of the supreme pastor; oxen, on the other hand, in those who, by assiduously bearing the yoke of the law, were preparing to produce the fruits of good works by zealously teaching and chastening the hearts of their hearers, as if ploughing the land of the Lord' (*InHab* 37.11–12). This comparison again aligns Old Testament Jewish teachers with Christian teachers in the age of the incarnation.

⇒91

> For that by oxen we must understand the apostles and evangelists and indeed all the ministers of the Word we know from the teaching of the apostle. Expounding the commandment of the law in which it is said: *You shall not muzzle the mouth of the ox that treads out the grain*, he says, *Is it for oxen that God is concerned? Does he not speak entirely for our sake? This is written for our sakes; because the one who ploughs should plough in hope, and the one who threshes in the hope of receiving fruit.*
>
> (*DTemp* 19.5; 1 Cor 9.1–10)

---

25 Crépin 1976; West 1976; Wieland 1984. West, 22 n.20, and Wieland, 195, attribute the authorship of *In Pentateuchum Commentarii*, PL 91, to Bede. 26 Crépin 1976, 188. 27 ibid., 188. 28 Bede adds: 'From both peoples a great many turned to the grace of the gospel and recognized the Owner by whom they were created, and were seeking by means of his heavenly nourishing fare to grow toward perpetual salvation' (*Hom* 1.6).

The teachers of the Gentiles in Bede's commentary on Tobit may therefore be likened to cattle: 'these are indeed the cattle because they bear the light yoke of the gospel (cf. Mt 11.30) for by preaching they beget and nurture those also who would advance further towards bearing the same yoke' (*In Tob* 23.3).

⇒53

IV

In *The Pilgrim's Progress*, Talkative represents the antithesis of scripture's clean animals; 'he cheweth the cud, he seeketh knowledge, he cheweth upon the Word; but he divideth not the hoof, he parteth not with the way of sinners; but, as the horse, he retaineth the foot of a dog or bear, and therefore he is unclean.'[29] Jerome would characterize such a man as a camel, a ruminant that does not part the hoof (*In Zach.* 893, 592–6). He compares the camel with Jews of the present age who reject Christ. 'They too meditate upon God's law and ruminate upon it and turn it over in their heart but they do not have cloven hooves so as to believe in the Father and the Son and they are unclean in this respect that they do not separate letter from spirit or shadow from reality and bear the burdens of the law and hear through the prophet, *Woe ⟨to you⟩ sinful nation, people laden with iniquity*' (*In Zach.* 893, 596–602; Is 1.4).[30]

⇒93 Among the Jews who reject Christ, says Bede, there are no clean animals left in 'the stalls of heavenly scriptures' — 'those who bear the sweet yoke of the gospel are not there' (*InHab* 37.30–31). Unbelieving Jews may still study scripture, but their studies are useless. Before the incarnation, the work of the oxen bearing the yoke of the law caused 'the very extensive fields of the divine scriptures' to produce 'spiritual food'

⇒91 for the Jews (*InHab* 37.13). Now, the fields 'do not produce food when this people, on opening the pages of the divine scriptures, is unable, for

⇒92 lack of proper understanding, to find the pastures of truth' (*InHab* 37.25). Habbakuk's prophecy of a famished and empty landscape where sheep starve in the fields and the fig-tree, vine and olive-tree produce no fruit,

⇒91 represents the unbelieving Jews' spiritual sterility (*InHab* 37.1–31). As Augustine writes, Habakkuk saw that 'the nation which was destined to kill Christ was to lose its rich harvest of spiritual good, which is figuratively described in prophetic fashion in terms of the fertility of the earth.'[31] The

⇒92 circumstances of the 'masses of the Jews' (*InHab* 37.18) now parallel those

⇒43 of the 'mass of the Gentiles' (*In Tob* 6.1). For Bede the barren desert is a symbol of 'the people of the Gentiles, who were once separated from the

---

29 Bunyan, *Pilgrim's Progress* 66; cf. *Grace Abounding to the Chief of Sinners* 21–22. 30 However, for Bede, Raguel's camels symbolise preachers chosen from among the Gentiles by God. These preachers are camels 'because with the deference of brotherly love they also carry the burdens of their ⟨converts'⟩ infirmity' *In Tob* 26.3. 31 Sanford and Green (ed. and tr.) 1965, 491.

worship of God, uncultivated by the preaching of the prophets' (*Comm. on Acts* 8. 26b). So, Raphael binds the demon in the desert of upper Egypt because 'Both 'desert' and 'Egypt' refer to the hearts of unbelievers which are both deserts, i.e. forsaken by God of whose indwelling they are ⇒52 unworthy' (*In Tob* 21.4).

Tobit's blindness also symbolizes the Jews' spiritual failure. 'The white film which had obstructed his eyes denotes the folly of self-indulgence. For *they have a zeal for God but ⟨it is⟩ not based on knowledge*, and as he (Paul) says again, *seeking to establish their own righteousness they* ⇒58 *did not submit to the righteousness of God* (Rom 10.2–3)' (*In Tob* 34.3–5). Bede elsewhere explains Rom 10.2 thus: 'at the preaching of the apostles in Judea the Synagogue produced many who had a zeal for God but not based on knowledge, since they wanted to hold on to the still imperfect and, so to speak, unripe observance of the letter of the law rather than accept the sweetness of spiritual meaning ⟨contained⟩ within it' (*In Cant.* 223, 465–69). But since the incarnation there are many things 'that the law commands to be made, or that it predicts must be done or celebrated forever, which have in fact ceased to be observed according to the letter. However, they will never cease to be observed spiritually observed by the saints in accordance with the the typic understanding, for the one who comes not *to abolish the law, but to fulfil it* bears witness that not one iota, not one stroke, will pass from the law until all is accomplished' (*DTab* 3.14; Mt 5.17–18). Some early Jewish converts to Christianity wished to continue the literal observance of Mosaic customs, a situation that Bede, in the *Ecclesiastical History*, compares with Irish adherence to outmoded Easter observances in the modern Church. Far worse, the unenlightened zeal for God of other Jews prevented them from recognizing Jesus as Lord. Indeed, it led them to crucify him, thinking that they were thereby doing a service to God (*Hom* 2.16; Jn 16.2; cf. *In Sam.* 219, 300–06). Realizing this, Jesus on the cross asked his father to forgive those 'who having a zeal for God but not based on knowledge, did not realize what they were doing' (*In Luc.* 403, 1592–93; Lk 23.34).[32] Failing to recognize Jesus as God incarnate and as *the one mediator between God and men* (1 Tim 2.5) — a quotation Bede repeatedly cites in his exegesis — Jewish unbelievers sever themselves not only from present believers but from the faithful Jews of the old dispensation:

---

32 When Jesus asked his Father to forgive those who crucified him, he did not, however, mean 'those who, inflamed by the promptings of malice and pride, chose to crucify him whom they understood to be the son of God rather than profess belief in him' (tr. S. Connolly from *In Luc.* 403, 1590–92). Bede believed that some of those who demanded the crucifixion knew that Jesus was truly the son of God. See Cohen 1983, 10–12. Nevertheless, Bede believes that the Jewish people generally were not aware of Jesus' divinity.

If the salvation of the world is in no other, but in Christ alone, then the fathers of the Old Testament were saved by the incarnation and passion of the same Redeemer, by which we also believe and hope to be saved. For although the sacramental signs differed by reason of the times, nevertheless there was agreement in one and the same faith, because through the prophets they learned as something to come the same dispensation of Christ which we learned through apostles as something which has been done. For there is no redemption of human captivity (to sinfulness) except in the blood of him who gave himself as a redemption for all. (*Comm. on Acts* 4.12)

Long before the incarnation, Habakkuk had 'showed what he himself would do, together with the faithful ones of this same people, indeed with the brotherhood of the entire Church which was to be or had been assembled in Christ all over the globe, when he said: *I on the other hand shall rejoice not in my own uprightness but, in my belief in God's protection, I shall rejoice in the Lord, my Jesus*, i.e. 'Saviour, because it is not in myself but in him that I reckon salvation to be' (*InHab* 37.33–36).[33] But resistance to belief in Jesus was not confined to Jews. So too, 'the Gentiles were agitated, some to believe and receive the mystery, but others to argue against or even persecute the heralds of this faith' (*InHab* 32.4). At the same time, many of the Gentiles, convinced by the miracles of Jesus or the apostles, embraced the faith, while among the Jews 'many of the people were inspired to believe in the Lord' by those same miracles (*InHab* 30.7–10).

⇒93

⇒87

⇒86

Bede emphasizes that Jewish spiritual blindness is limited in extent and duration. He quotes Rom 11.25: *blindness has come upon a part of Israel.* (*InTob* 5.5.) Tobit's commitment to pastoral care even when blind indicates that the Jewish race in the age of the incarnation contains both believers and unbelievers: 'Nor should it seem absurd that this Tobit, blind as he was and preaching God's word, is said to signify both reprobate and elect alike. For the patriarch Jacob too, while wrestling with the angel, was both lamed and blessed, signifying, that is, by his limping the unbelievers of his nation, and by his blessing the believers' (*InTob* 5.16–17; cf. 28.5). Moreover, 'the divine mercy remembers that the believers among the Jews experience great sadness and continual grief of heart at

⇒42

⇒43

---

33 Bede writes that 'the prophets were in agreement that this ⟨Jesus⟩ would be the name of the Christ. Desiring to be saved through his grace, Habakkuk says *I will glory in the Lord; I will rejoice in God my Jesus* (*Hom* 1.17).' Habakkuk is not overwhelmed by a misguided zeal for the law. His statement, *The just person lives from faith* (Hab 2.4; cf. Rom 1.17; Gal 3.11; Heb 10.38) leads Bede to include him among those who 'learned to hope for salvation from the gift of the Lord Jesus and not from the justice of their own works' (*Hom* 2.19). Bede writes that love of God 'is perfected through sincerity of faith and purity of life, *for without faith it is impossible to please God* (Heb 11.6) *for faith without works is dead* (James 2.26). The prophet ⟨Habakkuk⟩ sums up both of these ⟨truths⟩ in one little verse when he says, *But my righteous one lives by faith* (Hab 2.4 via Heb 10.38) openly suggesting that the only way that anyone will enter into life is by combining works of righteousness with true faith' (*DTab* 3.11).

the blindness of the unbelievers, their relatives according to the flesh, who
⇒56 are Israelites' (*InTob* 29.4). Jewish believers 'console themselves and their
own folk that there will really come a time when the Lord will come back
⇒56 to them and that then all Israel will be saved' (*InTob* 28.3–4; Rom 11.26).
Just as God restored Tobit's sight, says Bede, so too he will enlighten
Jewish unbelievers and they 'will recognize that Christ has already come
⇒59 and redeemed the world with his blood' (*InTob* 34.16).

At present, Jewish unbelievers 'suffer from mental blindness in the
very fond and futile hope of a Christ who is to be born in the flesh
and set them free and give them a great kingdom throughout the world'
⇒59 (*InTob* 34.15). Commenting on the *Seven Catholic Epistles* — 2 Jn 5.7 —
Bede says that those who still wait for the Messiah 'wait for the antichrist
who is to come for their destruction.' Even in this world, God punishes
Jewish unbelievers. Not long after the crucifixion, 'the Roman army
attacked them and, with the sole exception of those who had seceded to
the faith of the gospel, they suffered an overwhelming defeat and were
moreover deprived of their very kingdom and fatherland' (*InHab* 29.4–
⇒85 5). Like other Christian commentators, Bede interpreted the collapse
of Jewish power as a sign of the end of the Mosaic dispensation and as a
symbol and consequence of spiritual crisis. He says that spiritual blindness
triumphed over 'the people of Israel especially as the coming of the Lord
in the flesh was imminent, when they were both being oppressed by the
yoke of Roman slavery and transgressing the precepts of the divine law by
⇒42 very immoral living' (*InTob* 5.11).

The temporal ruin of Jewish unbelievers matches the 'eternal death'
⟨sent⟩ by God 'to those did not take the trouble to be anointed with his
⇒84 grace' (*InHab* 29.2). They now meet the 'spiritual death' from which good
⇒40 teachers had saved their ancestors (*InTob* 4.3). Tobit — symbolizing the
pastor — was blinded when he was tired and sleeping, 'because the one who
tirelessly perseveres in good works is never deprived of the light of faith'
⇒42 (*InTob* 5.6). When Jesus came, Jewish teachers and spiritual leaders were
deprived of that light because of their sins: 'because of their earlier faults,
they themselves were the cause of God's closing their eyes' (*Comm. on
Acts* 28.27b). So, 'the heads of the mighty, i.e. the chief priests and elders
⇒86 were cut off by their unbelief from the destiny of the faithful' (*InHab* 30.8).

Bede's interest in this Jewish spiritual crisis reflects his concern for the
welfare of the Church in his own day. His letter to Egbert, several remarks
in his exegesis, and some discreet references in the *Ecclesiastical History*
indicate that he feared for its spiritual health.[34] He speaks of complacent
believers facing the death of the soul (*HE* 5.12). He holds corrupt pastors
to be responsible for the people's waywardness, and compares them to the
Pharisees.[35] Bede knew that God had once devastated Britain because

---

34 Plummer, 1896, i, xxxv. **35** McClure and Collins (ed. and tr.) 1994, 356.

of the sins of its people and their evil kings and priests. His authority was *The Ruin of Britain*, written by the sixth-century prophet-historian Gildas.[36]

Gildas parallels the Britons' ruin with that of sinful Old Testament Jews at the hands of their foreign enemies. Bede compares the English conquest of the Britons to the victory of Nabuchednezzar of Babylon; it 'was not unlike that fire once kindled by the Chaldeans which consumed the walls and all the buildings of Jerusalem' (*HE* 1.15; 2 Kgs 25. 8–10). For Bede, Gildas' central question retained its urgency and power. Gildas asked: 'when they strayed from the right track the Lord did not spare a people that was peculiarly his own among all nations, a royal stock, a holy race, to whom he had said: *Israel is my first-born son* (Ex 4.22).... What then will he do with this great black blot on *our* generation?' (*DEB* 1.13). But Bede has hope. Ultimately, God liberated the Jews of the Babylonian captivity and restored them to Jerusalem. Their experience is a symbol of humanity's spiritual journey: 'For in our first parent we were removed from our heavenly homeland and brought into the Babylon, i.e. the confusion, of this world, but by the bounty of the Lord Jesus Christ, our king and high priest of whom Zorobabel and Joshua were a type, we were recalled once more to the homeland and vision of supreme peace, which is what
⇒90   the name "Jerusalem" means' (*InHab* 36.11–13).

V

Bede emphasizes the role of Jewish believers in constructing the Jerusalem of the present Church. He sees the fig-tree as a symbol of the
⇒91   Synagogue (*InHab* 37.8–9;16–17). Commenting on the Canticle of Canticles, he says that according to Apponius the verse *The fig-tree has put forth its green figs* (Song 2.13) refers to the apostles' origin in the Synagogue: 'the fig-tree put forth its green figs when the Synagogue begot the apostles who after they were begotten of it would administer the most delicious food of the teaching to believers' (*In Cant.* 222, 470–2; cf. *Apponii In Cant.* 104, 413–20). Bede declares in his Tobit commentary that Christ 'preached through the apostles to the people and Synagogue from which he had taken his human origin, the joys of heavenly salvation and peace; and to those who were willing to believe and accept them, he granted them of himself, and so in these teachers of his he came for the salvation of the
⇒46   Gentiles' (*InTob* 10.4–5). So, 'the Lord gathered to the faith from Judea just as many as would serve as an example of ⟨virtuous⟩ living or for the ministry of preaching until he should lay the foundations of the Church
⇒50   among the Gentiles too' (*InTob* 16.8).

---

36 Winterbottom (ed. and tr.) 1978. On Bede's use of Gildas, see Hanning 1966; Goffart 1988, 299–303; O'Reilly 1995, xli n. 27; Higham 1995, 15–40.

In his *Greater Chronicle*, Bede further records the work of Jewish believers in building up the Church. There, for example, he notes that the first fifteen bishops of Jerusalem, over the course of one hundred and seven years, were all Jews.[37] The city's first bishop, James the brother of the Lord, ordained by the apostles, was martyred.[38] Simeon (Simon), the son of a later Jewish bishop, Cleophas, was also martyred.[39] So too was Alexander, a Gentile bishop of Jerusalem.[40] Jewish and Gentile believers, then, bore a common witness to Christ.

Bede records the persecution of believers across the world. The Gentile martyrs — symbolized by Raguel's slaughtered cattle in Tobit ⇒53 (*InTob* 23.1,6–7) — included Alban, Aaron and Julius 'together with many other men and women' in Britain.[41] The conversion of Britain was ultimately due to Christ's commands to his followers. Commenting on Tobit, Bede says that when 'the Lord came to save the Gentiles, holy preachers followed in his footsteps because they carried out what he had commanded: ⇒46 *Go and teach all the nations* (Mt 28.19)' (*InTob* 11.2). Then, as he says on Habakkuk, the apostles' '*voice went out through all the earth, and their* ⇒70 *words to the ends of the world*' (*InHab* 7.8; Ps 18.5(19.4); Rom 10.8). Following the *Book of Pontiffs* Bede dates the conversion of the Britons to the reigns of Pope Eleutherius and the apocryphal British King Lucius in the second century.[42] Britain was under Roman rule at that time. In common with other Christian exegetes and historians, Bede believed that God ordained the rise of the Roman empire, 'since it bestowed on the preachers of his word the capability of travelling over the the world and spreading abroad the grace of the gospel wherever they wished, and this would have occurred to much less an extent if the whole world had not been under the rule of one empire' (*Hom* 1.6).

Bede connects Britain's entry into the empire with a critical episode in the history of the early Church. Claudius secured Britain for Rome 'in year of our Lord 46, the year in which occurred the very severe famine throughout Syria, which, as is recorded in the Acts of the apostles, was foretold by the prophet Agabus' (*HE* 1.3; Acts 11.28). Agabus prophesied at the time of Peter's vision of a linen sheet containing all the animals of the earth and all the birds of the sky (Acts 10.11–16). That vision sanctioned the evangelization of the Gentiles. The creatures in the sheet were 'all the nations, unclean in their error, but cleansed... by the mystery of the Holy Trinity in baptism' (*Comm. on Acts* 10.12). The linen sheet was lowered by its four corners from heaven, designating 'the four regions of the world to which the Church extends' (*Comm. on Acts* 10.11b) just as Raguel's four slaughtered rams symbolize 'the flock of Christ throughout ⇒54 the whole world which is divided up into four quarters' (*InTob* 23.9).

---

37 McClure and Collins (ed. and tr.) 1994, 312. **38** ibid., 309. **39** ibid., 311. **40** ibid., 315. **41** McClure and Collins (ed. and tr.) 1994, 319; cf. *HE* 1.7; *DEB* 10–11. **42** Davis (tr.) 1989, 6; *HE* 1.4.

Thus, Britain entered the divinely favoured empire 'in the days when the Church's sphere began to increase, as the gospel came to be preached throughout the outlying provinces, islands and cities, not only to the Jews, but also to the Gentiles' (*Comm. on Acts* 11.19).

Centuries after the Britons received the gospel, their English conquerors received it too. Bede also regarded the conversion of the English as part of the providentially ordained conversion of the whole Gentile world. In *On Tobit*, he speaks of the Lord enlightening 'the hearts of those whom he has predestined to eternal life' (*InTob* 40.3; cf. Rom 8.29; Eph 1.5). The English were a people foreknown to God who did not desert them (*HE* 1.22; cf. Rom 11.2). [43] In Northumbria, as many 'as were foreordained to eternal life believed and were baptized' (*HE* 2.14; cf. Acts 13.48). The missionaries themselves and their sponsors believed that the conversion of the English was part of the unfolding history of salvation. Bede includes in the *Ecclesiastical History* letters from Pope Boniface V (619–25) and Pope Vitalian (657–72) which explicitly state that their conversion represents the fulfilment of scriptural imperative and prophecy. Boniface writes to the missionary Justus:

> Almighty God has not failed either to uphold the honour of his name or grant fruit to your labours, in accordance with his faithful promise to those who preach the gospel, *Lo, I am with you always, even unto the end of the world* (Mt 28.20). This promise he has in his mercy specially fulfilled in the ministry he has given you, opening the hearts of the Gentiles to receive the wondrous mystery of the gospel you preach. . . you will receive the reward of a finished task from the Lord and giver of all good things: and indeed all nations will confess having received the mystery of the Christian faith and will declare in truth that *their sound is gone out into all the earth and their words unto the end of the world* (Ps 18.5(19.4); Rom 10.18).(*HE* 2.8)[44]

The prophets foretold the conversion of the world. So, according to Augustine, when Habakkuk says that *The tents of Ethiopia will be terror-stricken, and the tents of the land of Midian* (Hab 3.7), he indicates that all the Gentiles, even those outside the Roman empire, will become part of the Christian people — a comment pregnant with meaning for the English, who had never known Roman dominion. [45] Bede interprets Habakkuk's words thus: 'all the nations of the Gentiles, which, on hearing the gospel preaching, were stricken with a wholesome fear. . . began to serve the Lord in fear and rejoice with trembling before him' (*InHab* 18.3,6). The Midianites' conversion indicates the salvation of 'the Mediterranean

⇒61

⇒77

---

43 These words have sometimes been taken to mean that Bede regarded the English as the new chosen people, but O'Reilly 1995, xxxviii, comments: 'The new people of God in the *HE* are not the Anglo-Saxon race but all members of the universal Church of which the Anglo-Saxons form but a tiny part at the ends of the earth.' 44 See further O'Reilly 1995, xxxiv–v. For Vitalian's letter see *HE* 3.29. 45 Sanford and Green (ed. and tr.) 1965, 485.

⇒78 peoples' (*InHab* 18.11), but Habakkuk 'does well to mention first the Ethiopians who are at the ends of the earth, so as to intimate in mystical terms that the voice of preachers would go forth over the entire world and their words to the ends of the earth... let the Ethiopians be awestruck at the name of Christ, so that faith in him which is to reach the ends of the ⇒77 earth may be sealed' (*InHab* 18.7,10; cf. Ps 18.5(19.4); Rom 10.8).

In antiquity and beyond, if Ethiopia symbolized the eastern ends of the earth, then Britain and Ireland represented its western edges. In the ninth century, celebrating the universal triumph of Christianity, Walahfrid Strabo wrote that the name of the Lord was praised from the rising of the sun in Ethiopia and India to its setting among the Britons and Irish[46]. Ethiopians and Saxons — the English — could also represent the eastern and western ends of the earth. As George Henderson observes, Bede was familiar with this convention and with Gregory the Great's proclamation in his *Moralia* that the conversion of the English joined the boundaries of east and west in one faith.[47] The English now share in the Gentiles' wholesome fear of God. Recognizing that God was indeed with the missionary Paulinus, Edwin of Northumbria 'began to tremble and would have thrown himself at the bishop's feet' (*HE* 2.12). Justly rebuked by Aidan, King Oswine of Deira took off his sword and knelt to ask forgiveness. Aidan wept and said: 'I never before saw a humble king' (*HE* 3.14). Erring more gravely, King Sigberht of the East Saxons, confronted by Bishop Cedd wielding his episcopal staff, 'leapt from his horse and fell trembling at the bishop's feet, asking his pardon' (*HE* 3.22). As Gregory, quoted by Bede, says of the English, 'he who as an unbeliever did not flinch before troops of warriors, now, as a believer, fears the words of the humble' (*Moral., CCSL* 143B, 1346, 74–6; *HE* 2.1)

Gregory declares that 'the proud Ocean has become a servant, lying low now before the feet of the saints', proof indeed of the triumph of Christ (*Moral., CCSL* 143B, 1346, 71–2; *HE* 2.1). When Habakkuk asked the Lord was *your indignation against the sea?* (Hab 3.8), says Bede, he referred to 'the hearts of unbelievers... (they are called) the sea because they are inwardly darkened by disordered and bitter thoughts and exalt themselves above the rest by the swollen waters of boasting' (*InHab* 19.2– ⇒78 3). In the *Ecclesiastical History*, God's victory over paganism and other forms of sin is symbolized by his servants' literal power over the sea. The sea around Britain becomes calm at the word of Germanus, defender of orthodoxy against the Pelagian heresy (*HE* 1.17), who thereby imitates Christ's calming of the storm on Lake Galilee (Mt 8.24–27).[48] Later, the sea is calmed by Aidan, leader of the Irish mission to the pagan English

---

46 Krusch (ed.), *Vita Galli* 282, 20–22; cf. Ps 112.3 **47** Henderson 1980, 9–13; cf. Santoro 1992 on images of Britain in classical and late antique literature. **48** Bede records that Habakkuk's remains were discovered by divine revelation in the year that the Briton Pelagius began his heretical teachings; McClure and Collins (ed. and tr.) 1994, 323.

(*HE* 3.15) and by Oethelwald, Cuthbert's successor as hermit on Farne Island (*HE* 5.1), a place which Bede depicts as a spiritual battleground against the powers of evil (*HE* 4.28; *VCP* 17). The saints have brought to life Gregory's words on the British ocean: 'its barbarous motions, which earthly princes could not subdue with the sword, are now, through the fear of God, repressed with a simple word from the lips of priests' (*Moral.*, *CCSL* 143B, 1346, 72–4: *HE* 2.1).

Once again, nature mirrors man's spiritual state. Opening the *Ecclesiastical History*, Bede depicts the islands of Britain and Ireland, united in the Christian faith, as fertile, temperate and filled with good things — an image of the garden of paradise, the promised land, and the restored creation at the end of time (*HE* 1.1). [49] This physical fruitfulness is an appropriate metaphor for an spiritually fruitful community, just as the flourishing fig-tree, vine and olive-tree, were 'the Synagogue of the Jews, when in its dedication to God it preserved the sweetness of good works and the ardour of love (and) produced the rich abundance of a compassionate disposition' (*InHab* 37.8–9). Indeed, in the opening chapter of the *Ecclesiastical History*, Bede explicitly connects the Christian peoples of Britain with the Jews of the old dispensation, writing that the study of scripture unites the languages of the island, and that five languages exist there — English, British, Irish, Pictish and Latin — 'just as the divine law is written in five books' (*HE* 1.1).

⇒91

VI

Paradoxically, the Christian unity of the peoples of Britain also connects them to the Jews of the new dispensation who reject Christ. On the authority of scripture, Christians believed that those Jews would be converted only at the end of time. As Marvell says:

> And you should if you please refuse
> Till the conversion of the Jews.[50]

Their conversion will follow that of the Gentiles. Throughout the world, says Bede, God 'incorporates new peoples into the Church every day' (*InTob* 25.5). The incorporation of the English is particularly significant — with the complete conversion of Britain and Ireland the ends of the earth acknowledge their creator. Scriptural prophecies concerning the evangelization of the entire Gentile world are therefore moving toward final fulfilment.[51] However slowly, the time of Jewish conversion is approaching. For Bede, scripture's prophecies regarding the conversion

⇒55

---

49 Kendall 1978, 164; 1979, 180–82. **50** 'To His Coy Mistress', Donna (ed.) 1972, 51. **51** Kendall 1979, 17–18; Davidse 1982, 664–5; Ward 1990, 112. However, as Davidse notes — 665, n.97 — Bede rejects any attempt to predict the time when Christ will come again.

of the Jews are symbolized by the Archangel Raphael's promise to take Tobias to Rages — a Gentile city — and then to return him to his father Tobit.

> The Lord promises the believers among the Jewish people (although this same people is largely blinded) that he will reveal the mysteries of his incarnation to the Gentile people, and again at the end of our times he will make them known more widely to his own people from whom he had taken flesh, when faith in his divinity will both accompany him everywhere and accomplish everything. Of the 'bringing' to the Medes he says: *And I have other sheep which are not of this fold; these too I must bring*, and so forth (Jn 10.16); of the 'bringing back', the Apostle says: *Until the fulness of the Gentiles should come in, and so all Israel should be saved.* (Rom 11.25–26).

⇒45 ■   (*In Tob* 8.7–10)

⇒60 ⇒56 ⇒40 ⇒57 ⇒60 ⇒44

With the conversion of the unbelieving Jews, 'the knowledge of the scriptures too which they once used to lend to the Gentiles is then returned to them' (*In Tob* 35.8). Then, 'in their writings they recognize that Christ is true God and man. And so at last, after acknowledging the true faith... they join the holy Church, which has been assembled from among the Gentiles, by sharing in the heavenly mysteries' (*In Tob* 29.9–10). The Gentiles now repay their great spiritual debt to the Jewish people. The Jews once shared their faith with the Gentiles, and the Gentiles 'pay back the creditor when they receive into the unity of the Church the Jews who believe at the end of the world (cf. Rom 11.25–26) and, as well as entrusting to them the mysteries of Christ for their salvation, they also unlock for them the secrets of the scriptures,' (*In Tob* 3.15–16). Taught by Gentile teachers who 'rejoice that by means of their ministry Judea is to be brought together again by the Lord' (*In Tob* 30.9), the Jews will once again fulfil their ancient role; the 'Jewish people when converted to the faith at the end of the world will have many teachers and prophetic men to set the minds of their neighbours on fire with heavenly desires when by frequent proclamation they make the everlasting joys of their heavenly homeland resound in their ears' (*In Tob* 37.3). God's providential design is at last accomplished, for Christ 'was sent into the world to redeem both the Jewish people from the darkness of unbelief and the Gentiles from the bondage of idolatry' (*In Tob* 7.2).

Events in the history of Britain and Ireland prefigure the universal reconciliation which Bede describes here. Just as God rewards the generosity of the Jewish people, so too he rewards the generosity of the Irish who 'had always been most friendly to the English' (*HE* 4.26). He rescued them from the error and disunity caused by their Easter observances because 'they were not lacking in grace and fervent love' (*HE* 3.5). The Irish followed those observances since, like the Jews, they clung to 'the deep-rooted tradition of their ancestors to whom the apostle's words apply: *They had a zeal of God but not according to knowledge*' (*HE* 5.22; cf. 3.3; Rom 10.2). In the dramatic climax of the *Ecclesiastical History*, Bede tells how God sent the English spiritual exile, Egbert, to convert Iona, home of the Irish missionaries to the English, and the last outpost of Irish particularism. Egbert won the Irish of Iona to the true Easter and 'the grace of unity.' Bede comments:

> It is clear that this happened by a wonderful dispensation of divine mercy, since that race had willingly and ungrudgingly taken pains to communicate its own knowledge and understanding to the English nation; and now, through the English nation, they are brought to a more perfect way of life in matters wherein they were lacking. (*HE* 5.23)

The conversion of Iona offers a foretaste of the unity to come at the end of time when Jew and Gentile alike join together 'so that there may be *one fold and one shepherd* (Jn 10.16) and one house of Christ supported ⇒60 upon one cornerstone (cf. Eph 2.20; 1 Pet 2.5–6)' (*InTob* 35.4).[52]

---

52 On Bede's understanding of the Insular Easter controversy in the light of Jewish and early Christian history, see Olsen 1982, 524–5; Ray 1986, 79–81; O'Reilly 1995, xxxv–ix, and xliii–xl. I would like to thank Dr Jennifer O'Reilly for her help and encouragement in the preparation of this introduction. I would also like to thank Ms Catherine Ware, Ms Claire O'Halloran and Mr Bob Harris for commenting on an earlier draft.

1

20⇐ [3]

[1]The book of the holy father Tobit is clearly of saving benefit to its readers even in its superficial meaning inasmuch as it abounds in both
21⇐ the noblest examples and the noblest counsels for moral conduct, [2]and anyone who knows how to interpret it historically (and allegorically as well) can see that its inner meaning excels the mere letter as much
21⇐ as the fruit excels the leaves. [3]For if it is understood in the spiritual sense it is found to contain within it the greatest mysteries of Christ
23⇐ and the Church; [4]inasmuch as Tobit himself denotes the people of Israel which alone served God with true faith and acts of virtue when all the Gentiles were given over to idolatry, [5]as one reads of Tobit: *when everyone was going to the golden calves which Jeroboam king of Israel had made, he alone fled the company of all and went to Jerusalem and there adored the Lord, the Lord God of Israel.*[1] [6]Jeroboam, since he made himself golden calves to mislead his subjects, represents the authors of idolatry.

2

1.2 [1]And indeed Tobit was **taken captive in the days of Shalmaneser king of the Assyrians but when he was in captivity he did not forsake the way of truth.**[2] [2]This captivity at the hands of the king of the Assyrians denotes the captivity of the human race whereby, through the king of all the perverse, i.e. the devil, it was banished from the abode of its heavenly homeland and deported to its sojourn in this exile.

[3]Tobit shared all he could get every day with his captive brethren who
24⇐ were of his own kin, but also gave tithes to strangers and proselytes.[3] [4]And the people of Israel through their teachers ministered the alms of God's word not only to the unlettered audience of their own nation but also to those of the Gentiles who wished to convert to the religious observance of their way of life. [5]For whatever natural good thing they could get that was not confiscated by the enemy who held them captive, they showed
24⇐ it all to their own folk as an instance of virtue. [6]But also they always gave a certain portion of their saving knowledge even to the Gentiles. [7]Which explains the significance of Tobit's assigning a tithe of his property to strangers.

---

1 Tob 1.5–6.   **2** Tob 1.2.   **3** Tob 1.3,7.

3

1.9 ¹When Tobit became **a man he took as his wife Anna from his own tribe.** ²And this people, after they had grown up and increased in Egypt, espoused the Synagogue which had been established by Moses with legal ceremonies.

22⇐   ³**By her he begot a son and gave him his own name** because he learnt that Christ was to be born of his own | kin as Moses had said: *⁴Your* [4] *God will raise up for you a prophet like me from among your brethren; to him you shall listen;*⁴ *⁵and the Lord ⟨said⟩ to David: ⟨One⟩ of the fruit of your womb I will set upon my throne.*⁵ ⁶He gave him his own name
23⇐ believing and confessing what the Father says of him: *⁷And I will make*⁶ *him the first-born,*⁷ as he says of the people themselves: *⁸Israel ⟨is⟩ my first-born son.*⁸

       ⁹**He taught him from his infancy to fear God and refrain from all sin,**⁹ ¹⁰believing and confessing that he would commit no sin and that no deceit would be found on his lips¹⁰ but that the spirit of the fear of the Lord would fill him.¹¹ ¹¹To Gabael his fellow-kinsman who was in
24⇐ need, Tobit gave ten silver talents in trust.¹² ¹²And the people of God entrusted to the Gentiles through the seventy translators the knowledge of the divine law which is contained in the decalogue¹³ in order thereby to free them from the indigence of unbelief; ¹³but they gave it in trust, i.e. on condition that it be repaid after they themselves got wealthy or the one who had given it asked it back. ¹⁴On the other hand, the Gentiles received the word of God from the people of Israel through the medium of translation because now after the Lord's incarnation they also understand
36⇐ it spiritually and work at acquiring the riches of the virtues; ¹⁵but they pay back the creditor when they receive into the unity of the Church the Jews who believe at the end of the world;¹⁴ ¹⁶and, as well as entrusting to them the mysteries of Christ for their salvation, they also unlock for them the secrets of the scriptures.

4

1.22–23 ¹Orders were given by the king that Tobit be killed and **all his property** confiscated on account of the good deeds he had done, ²but he **with his son and wife fled naked and went into hiding because**
30⇐ **many people loved him.** ³And the devil did his utmost to bring about

---

4 Deut 18.15; Acts 3.22.   **5** Ps 131(132).11: upon my throne: *super sedem meam.* Bede's text *as received by the editor here*, follows the Hebrew and differs from the Vulgate which reads *super sedem tuam.* Three codices have the Vulgate reading. **6** I will make: *ponam.* For this meaning of the verb *pono* (very common in the Vulgate) see *L&S* s.v. II.B,4. Compare Greek τίθημι. **7** Ps 88.28(89.27). **8** Ex 4.22. **9** Tob 1.10 **10** cf. 1 Pet 2.22. **11** cf. Is 11.3. **12** cf. Tob 1.17. **13** cf. *infra* §25.6 (Tob 9.3). **14** cf. Rom 11.25–26.

the spiritual death of the people of God through idolatry and strip them of all the riches of their virtues but could not because there were many holy teachers among them who made provision for their life and salvation. [23⇐] [4]However he fled with his son and wife because the enemy could not rob them either of belief in the Lord's incarnation or of the Synagogue as an institution[15] however ferociously he persecuted them, as became evident in the tortures of the Maccabees.[16]

[5]But when the king was assassinated by his sons, all Tobit's belongings were restored to him[17] because often after the devil had been overcome and condemned by reason of his crimes which he spawned like a thoroughly wicked brood, prosperity returned to the people of God. [6]In these vicissitudes we can see the Church too as an institution[18] being tossed to and fro like the waves after the Lord's incarnation.

5

2.10–11 [1]**Wearied with burying,** Tobit **came to his house** and when [5] **he had thrown himself down by the wall and fallen asleep, hot droppings from a swallows' nest** fell down into **his eyes** and he be- [19⇐] came **blind.** [2]Do not be surprised, reader, that sometimes, typologically speaking, men's good deeds have a bad meaning and their bad deeds a good meaning; [3]that *God is light* would never have been written in black ink but always in bright gold if this were not permissible;[19] [4]but even should you write the name of the devil in pure white chalk,[20] it

15 See note at §4.6 below. 16 cf. 2 Mac 6–7. 17 cf. Tob 1.24–25; *restituta sunt cuncta sua Tobiae*: lit. 'all his goods were restored to Tobias'; the sentence has had to be rephrased in English to avoid the ambiguity of the pronoun 'his'. 18 the Church... as an institution: cf. the earlier expression 'the Synagogue as an institution' at §4.6. The Latin has *statum sinagogae... ecclesiae statum*. It is difficult to find a rendering that fits both contexts. There is clearly an intended parallel though one feels *status* is being used in rather different senses. One could almost say 'the very existence of the Synagogue' and 'the current condition of the Church'. 19 1 Jn 1.5 20 in pure white chalk: *in calculo... candido*: Literally 'with a pure white stone'. (a) The meaning 'chalk' for *calculus*, which seems to be the only meaning that will fit here is one I have not found in the standard Latin dictionaries. It is clearly a later semantic development. *Calculus* is fundamentally 'a pebble'; it then acquired the sense of 'a marker or counter'. The meaning 'chalk' may be due to the fact that *calculus* came to be regarded by the Latins as a cognate of *calx* which was 'limestone or lime' (slaked or unslaked) though this etymology is questioned by the best Latin scholars. The phrase may have originated from a confusion of two or more ideas. The normal word for chalk is *creta*, and *creta scribere,*'to write with chalk', is opposed to *carbone scribere*, 'to write with charcoal', in a metaphorical sense. *Creta notare* is used of marking a *faustus dies* ('a lucky day' as opposed to a *dies ater* an 'unlucky' or 'black' day) in the calendar. More common in that sense is *calculo candido notare*, but that does not mean using a pebble as chalk. It means sticking a white pebble in the wall or into the ground. *Calx* in the sense of the finishing line in the Circus was a white mark (replaced later by *creta* according to Seneca). Bede who had had a fine training in Latin might well have met some of these usages without, perhaps, knowing the full background. (b) One may assume that he was giving full weight to the distinction between *candidus* 'pure or shining white' and *albus* 'dead or lustreless white'.

29← still means deep darkness.[21] [5]Tobit's being blinded, therefore,[22] denotes *that*, as the Apostle says, *blindness has come upon a part of Israel.*[23]
30← [6]He was wearied with burying and blinded, because the one who tire-lessly perseveres in good works is never deprived of the light of faith; [7]the man who neglects to watch and stand firm in the faith and act manfully and be strengthened,[24] spiritually lies down and sleeps from fatigue. [8]The apostle's saying fits him well: *Rise you who sleep and arise from the dead, and Christ will enlighten you.*[25] [9]Because of their swift flight, swallows are a figure of pride and volatility of heart,[26] since their uncleanness immediately blinds those over whom it holds sway. [10]For the one who recklessly enslaves his soul to the volatility of li-centiousness and pride, sleeps, as it were, lying down beneath a swal-
30← lows' nest. [11]Now this blindness got the better of the people of Is-rael especially as the coming of the Lord in the flesh was imminent,

---

21 'But should someone be concerned as to why I have ventured to interpret the acts of the wicked king (Saul) allegorically as referring to Christ who is king of kings, let him know that it is the practice of commentators, indeed of the scriptures, to apply an allegory favourably to a wicked person or unfavourably to a good person when occasion demands. Otherwise one should never write in black ink but always in bright gold or some other beautiful medium that *God is light and in him there is no darkness,* (1 Jn 1.5), in case black should incongruously mean brilliant white. Finally the blessed Pope Gregory had no hesitation in applying figurally not only the anointing of this same Saul to the kingship of Christ, but even his very death which resulted from his sin to the innocent death of Christ'. (Tr. Seán Connolly from *In Primam Partem Samuhelis, CCSL* 119, 91–92, 993–1005; cf. 92–93, 1031–1049; Greg. *Moral.* (*CCSL* 143, 161, 117–18; see also Henderson 1980, 8–9). **22** Tobit's being blinded, therefore: here Hurst's Latin text reads: *Caecitas ergo Tobias....* Circumstances did not permit an inspection of the codices, but there is surely an error of some kind: if *caecitas* were correct, then we should have to read *Tobiae.* In view of the fact that Migne too has the nominative, *Tobias,* and Hurst's apparatus shows no variant for *caecitas,* one has to suspect that what the exemplar had was not *caecitas* but *caecatus* as Migne has. **23** Rom 11.25: The Greek of this text reads: πώρωσις ἀπὸ μέρους τῷ 'Ισραὴλ γέγονεν. This the Vulgate renders: *Caecitas ex parte contigit in Israhel* which is the same text as Bede follows here. What the original Greek means is put simply and clearly, if somewhat freely, in the *JB* translation: 'One section of Israel has become blind.' What it does not mean is that Israel was affected by *partial* blindness, i.e. a blindness that was partial in nature or severity, a fairly common interpretation following the *RCR* version: 'a partial blindness only has befallen Israel.' The phrase 'blindness in part' refers not to the nature or severity of the blindness but to its extent among the people of Israel. All modern translators (basing their version on the original Greek) so understand this text. The *RSV* renders it: 'a hardening πώρωσις [pōrōsis] has come upon part of Israel'; πώρωσις means 'a process of hardening or becoming insensible'; metaphorically it is used for 'blindness'. Likewise *Knox:* 'Blindness has fallen upon a part of Israel'. In the Greek text there is no single word corresponding to the Latin preposition *in.* Instead the dative of the noun *Israel* is used together with the definite article. The *Douay* in its zeal for almost slavish fidelity, like most translators of its time, adheres rigidly not only to the wording but to the word-order of the Vulgate. In the process it links *ex parte* with the word *caecitas* instead of with the verb *contigit,* giving the rendering: 'Blindness in part has happened in Israel.' **24** cf. 1 Cor 16.13. **25** Eph 5.14. **26** and volatility of heart: *cordisque leuitatem*; here Bede is playing on the various senses of the word *leuis,* which, as well as meaning 'light' in weight, can mean 'light in motion' and therefore 'swift' just like the Greek κοῦφος hence the tropological meaning 'flighty, capricious, volatile, inconstant'.

when they were both being oppressed by the yoke of Roman slavery and transgressing the precepts of the divine law by very immoral living.

*12*Tobit's relatives taunted ⟨him⟩, and even his wife upbraided ⟨him⟩ as if he had served God in vain. *13*But he rebuked and instructed them and turned to God in prayer.[27] *14*There were some among that people who with foolish temerity treated with derision the misfortunes of his people[28] because they were already far from the original happiness of their holy ancestors who once nobly served God in their midst. *15*But the same people earnestly took care to correct these through all their more learned and chosen ones and turned to imploring God's mercy to obtain eternal life. *16*Nor should it seem absurd that this Tobit, blind as he was and preaching God's word, is said to signify both reprobate and elect alike. *17*For the patriarch Jacob too, while wrestling with the angel, was both lamed and blessed,[29] signifying, that is, by his limping the unbelievers of his nation, and by his blessing the believers.

6

3.7–8 *1*Sarah, Raguel's daughter, in a city of the Medes, who had been given to seven husbands whom a demon killed[30] as soon as they went in to her, figurally denotes the mass of the Gentiles.[31] *2*Their teachers all knew about life in this world only, which runs a course of seven days, ⟨but⟩ were unable to say anything about eternal life. *3*And so they were all carried off by the devil inasmuch as they were given over to idolatry until the true bridegroom, our Lord, came. *4*He overcame the enemy and through faith united them (i.e. the Gentiles) to himself,[32] as Tobias took Sarah to wife after tying up the devil on the instructions and with the aid of the archangel. *5*By the latter,[33] quite appropriately, the divinity of our Saviour is signified, just as his humanity is by Tobias. *6*And the fact that we say that by two persons, i.e. an angel and a man, the one person of the mediator between God and men[34] is denoted figurally, *7*will be no surprise to the one who reads in the commentaries of the venerable Fathers that in Isaac who was offered up by his father on an altar, and in the ram which was immolated,[35] was denoted figurally the one person

[6]

---

27 cf. Tob 2.15–3.6. **28** cf. ibid. **29** cf. Gen 32.24–29. **30** whom a demon killed: *et daemonium eos occidebat*: lit. 'and a demon killed them'. **31** mass of the Gentiles: *turbam nationum*: 'Gentile throng'. **32** united them...to himself: *sibi...coniunxit*: The *hanc* here in our Latin text agrees with the *turbam nationum* ('mass of the Gentiles') mentioned above. **33** ...with the aid of the archangel. By the latter:...*cooperante archangelo per quem...*: lit. 'with the aid of the archangel, through whom....' **34** cf. 1 Tim 2.5. **35** cf. Gen 22.10–13.

of him who suffered for the world's salvation.[36] [8]He in his humanity was slaughtered like a sheep, ⟨but⟩ in his divinity remains with God the Father incapable of suffering, just as Isaac came back home alive with his father. [9]For if the ram aptly represents the humanity of Christ, and the man his godhead, why should not a man much more aptly signify his humanity and an angel his divinity?

7

3.25 [1]The reason why **the Lord's holy angel Raphael** (which means 'the healing of God') **was sent** was to rid Tobit of blindness and Sarah

of the demon.[37] [2]The Lord who says of himself: *It is not those who are well that need the physician but those who are ill,*[38] was sent into the world to redeem both the Jewish people from the darkness of unbelief and the Gentiles from the bondage of idolatry. [3]And of him the prophet said: *And his name shall be called the angel of great counsel.*[39]

[4]An angel appeared to Tobias and offered himself as a companion[40] through whom he might perform wonders for the people to whom he had been sent. [5]And the Son of God assumed ⟨the nature of⟩ a human being so that, thus visibly spending his life with human beings, he might save the human race.

8

5.11–13 [1]Tobias brought the angel in to his father and he (the angel) **greeted him** with the words: **Joy be to you always.** [2]And when he (Tobit) replied: | **What kind of joy shall I have who am sitting in darkness and do not see the light of the sky?** he (the angel) said: [7]

---

36 This patristic understanding of the Abraham and Isaac story was visually reinforced for Bede by the pictures displayed in the monastery and church of St Paul at Jarrow. In his *History of the Abbots*, Bede says that Benedict Biscop, Wearmouth-Jarrow's founder, 'put up a set of pictures 'consisting of scenes, very skilfully arranged, to show how the Old Testament foreshadowed the New. In one set, for instance, the picture of Isaac carrying the wood on which he was to be burnt as a sacrifice was placed immediately below that of Christ carrying the cross on which He was about to suffer'. (*HA* 9). Bede assigns such pictures an important teaching role, 'since the sight of these things often tends to elicit great compunction in the beholders and also to make available to those who are illiterate a living narrative of the story of the Lord'. *DTemp.* 19.10; cf. *HA* 6. 37 Gregory writes: 'Archangels are distinguished by personal names to indicate by the word the service they are able to perform.... Raphael means "the healing of God".... Raphael is interpreted "the healing of God", as I have said, because when he touched Tobit's eyes, as if in performance of a healing service, he wiped away the darkness of his blindness. One who was sent to heal deserves to be called "the healing of God" '. *Homilies on the Gospels*, 34. Gregory took his cue from Jerome's commentary on Daniel (*CCSL* 75A, 857, 930–31). 38 Mt 9.12. 39 Is 9.6. The Latin text which Bede is using here is, unlike the Vulgate, a direct translation of the *LXX* which reads: καὶ καλεῖται τὸ ὄνομα αὐτοῦ Μεγάλης βουλῆς ἄγγελος. The Vulgate has *et uocabitur nomen eius Admirabilis consiliarius, Deus fortis, Pater futuri saeculi, Princeps pacis.* 40 cf. Tob 5.5–8.

Have courage; your cure from God is at hand. *3*And our Lord through the miracles he wrought in the flesh showed the Jewish people from whom he had taken flesh that he was the Son of God and the angel, i.e. the messenger, of his Father's will. *4*He also announced to them the joy of eternal salvation saying: *Do penance, for the kingdom of heaven will draw near;* **41** *5*and to those who despaired of obtaining heavenly light he said:*I am the light of the world; the one who follows me will not walk in darkness but will have the light of life.***42**

*6*The angel promises Tobit to bring his son to Rages, a city of the Medes, and bring him back to him.**43** *7*The Lord promises the believers among the Jewish people, (although this same people is largely blinded), that he will reveal the mysteries of his incarnation to the Gentile people, *8*and again at the end of our times will make them known more widely to his own people from whom he had taken flesh, when faith in his divinity will both accompany him everywhere and accomplish everything. *9*Of the 'bringing' to the Medes he himself says: *And I have other sheep which are not of this fold; these too I must bring,* and so forth.**44** *10*Of the 'bringing back' the Apostle says: *Until the fulness of the Gentiles should come in, and so all Israel should be saved.***45**

9

5.18 *1*When Tobit asked the angel where he was from, he said: **I am Azarias, son of the great Ananias.** *2*Azarias means 'the Lord is ⟨my⟩ helper', Ananias 'the favour of the Lord'.**46** *3*And the Lord intimates to those who believe in him that he is the one whom the prophet longed for when he sang: *Lord, you are my helper and liberator; do not delay;***47** *4*and of him too the evangelist ⟨says⟩: *And we saw his glory, the glory as it were of the only-begotten of the Father, full of grace and truth.***48**

10

5.22 *1*Then when everything that was to be taken on the journey had been made ready, Tobias bade farewell to his father and mother, and they both set off together. *2*When the Lord appeared in the flesh everything had been made ready that had to do with the redemption of the world, and everything with which the faith and life of the holy Church might be nourished and strengthened until it should end

---

41 Mt 4.17; will draw near: the reading received in our text here is *adpropinquabit.* The apparatus criticus gives the variant *adpropinquauit,* attested by three codices, which corresponds to the received Vulgate reading and means *'is at hand'.* The apparatus of *Biblia Vulgata* shows *adpropinquabit* as the variant. **42** Jn 8.12. **43** cf. Tob 5.14–15. **44** Jn 10.16; these too I must bring: *et illas oportet me adducere:* note the verb *adducere* corresponding to *ducere* in v.5 above and to *ductu(s)* here in v.7. **45** Rom 11.25–26. **46** cf. Jer., *Nom.* (*CCSL* 72, 114, 16; 125,12). **47** Ps 69.6(70.5). **48** Jn 1.14.

its journey in this world, *³*i.e. his works of power, his teaching, tempta-
tion, passion, resurrection, ascension, the sending of the Holy Spirit, the
31⇐ faith of believers, the persecution by unbelievers. | *⁴*And when these had   [8]
been accomplished in Judea, he, *the mediator between God and men,*⁴⁹
preached through the apostles to the people and Synagogue from which
he had taken his human origin, the joys of heavenly salvation and peace;
*⁵*and to those who were willing to believe and accept them, he granted
them of himself, and so in these teachers of his he came for the salvation
of the Gentiles.

11

32⇐ **6.1** *¹***Tobias then set off and his dog followed him.**   *²*When the
Lord came to save the Gentiles, holy preachers followed in his footsteps
because they carried out what he had commanded: *Go and teach all the
nations.*⁵⁰ *³*Finally the Lord himself filled the home of Cornelius with the
Holy Spirit and so Peter baptized ⟨them⟩ with water.⁵¹ *⁴*On the other
hand, the teachers are called dogs because they defend their founder's
spiritual home, property and sheep from thieves and beasts, i.e. from
unclean spirits and heretical men.⁵²

12

6.1–2 *¹*Having set out with the angel as guide, Tobias **paused by the
river Tigris for the first break in his journey, and went out to wash
his feet, and, lo and behold, a huge fish came up to devour him.**
*²*Here again the mystery of the Lord's passion is quite obviously signified.
*³*For the huge fish, which, since he wanted to devour him, was killed by
Tobias on the angel's instructions, represents the ancient devourer of the
human race, i.e. the devil. *⁴*When the latter desired the death of humanity
in our Redeemer, he was caught by the power of the divinity. *⁵*The river
Tigris which, because of its swift current, takes its name from the tiger,
a very swift animal, intimates the downward course of our death and

---

49 1 Tim 2.5. **50** Mt 28.19. **51** cf. Acts 10.44–48. **52** *infra* §30.3; in *Homilies on the
Gospels*, 40, Gregory writes: 'Sometimes in scripture dogs represent preachers. . . .Holy
preachers were chosen from among the unbelieving Jews. When they declared the
truth, coming out against thieves and robbers, they were barking loudly on the Lord's
behalf, if I may say so. On the other hand, some are condemned in these words: *They
are dumb dogs, and cannot bark*' (Is 56.10). Commenting on Job 30.1, Gregory again
compares dogs to preachers. Ps 67.24(68.23) says, *the tongue of your dogs ⟨is⟩ from
your enemies*. Gregory explains that the tongue of the Church's dogs comes from its
enemies because the Lord made preachers of the converted Gentiles. He says that the
prophet rebukes his fellow Jews who are slow to speak for God as *dumb dogs that
cannot bark*. *Moral. (CCSL* 143A, 1014, 10–23). Gildas wrote his account of Britain's
history and the accompanying denunciation of the country's corrupt kings and priests
because he did not wish to be known as a dumb dog that could not bark. *DEB* 36.4.
For Gildas' influence on Bede see Intro. p.14–15.

mortality.[53] [6]In it lurked a huge fish inasmuch as the invisible seducer of the human race held the power of death.[54] [7]Tobias stopped over by the waters of the Tigris because the Lord, when he appeared in the world, spent his life among sinners and mortals; [8]but the water of sin did not touch him, nor did the prince of darkness, when he came, find in him anything of his own. [9]On the other hand, Tobias went out into the river to wash his feet; [10]and the Lord embraced death to which he was under no obligation, in order to wash all the faithful, i.e. his members, free from the contagion of sin and death. [11]The fish rushed at Tobias eager to devour him; [12]and when the Lord had suffered on the cross, the devil, who had ordered him to be crucified, came to see if perhaps he could find any sin on his soul.

13

6.3 [1]Tobias **being very frightened of** the fish **shouted aloud saying: Sir, he is coming at me.** [2]And the Lord as the critical moment of death was upon him *began to tremble with fear and | be deeply dismayed,*[55] not   [9] that he was greatly afraid of the devil but, through the natural frailty of the flesh, dreaded death which *entered the world through the devil's envy.*[56] [3]This is why *he also prayed that, if it were possible, the hour might pass from him, and said: 'Abba, Father, all things are possible to you; remove this cup from me, but not what I will but what you will.'*[57]

14

6.4 [1]**The angel said** to Tobias: **Take** the fish **by the gill and pull him towards you.** [2]The Lord seized hold of the devil and by dying caught and conquered the one who wanted to catch him in death. [3]Moreover he seized him by the gill so that, with the right hand of his power, he might separate his most wicked head from his entrapped body, [4]i.e. that he might remove the wickedness of the ancient enemy from the heart of those whom he had wickedly allied to himself and had made, as it were, one body with him, [5]and that, as a merciful redeemer, he might graft them into the body of his Church. [6]For a fish has a gill at the joining of its head and body. [7]Now, just as our Lord is the head of his Church and the Church is his body,[58] so the devil is the head of all the wicked and all the wicked are his head and members.[59] [8]The reason why the Lord seized the very savage fish by the gill, dragged it towards him and cast it up on dry land was that, [9]in smashing them to pieces, he openly and boldly exposed the

---

53 cf. Jer., *Sit.* (*PL* 23, 923 C).   **54** cf. Heb 2.14.   **55** Mk 14.33.   **56** Wis 2.24. **57** Mk 14.35–36.   **58** cf. Eph 1.22–23; 5.23.   **59** cf. Greg. *Moral.* (*CCSL* 143, 487, 23–26).

devil's capabilities in public,[60] and rescued from the power of darkness[61] those whom he foreknew[62] to be children of light.[63]

[10]**And when he had done so**, he says, **it began to thrash about on dry land at his feet.**[11]Although the Lord on overcoming the wickedness of the malicious enemy brought him forth into the light and exposed him to everyone, [12]⟨the latter⟩ was still arrogant and contrived to instigate persecution against his (the Lord's) elect who are his feet because by their means the Lord who is king in heaven over all things walks upon the earth.[64]

---

60 exposed: *traduxit*. This Latin verb is open to several interpretations here. One suspects that in choosing it (in preference, for example, to *transtulit* with which it is often synonymous: cf. *L&S* s.v. *traduco*), Bede is engaging in some subtle word-play. Its literal meaning is obvious from its composition: *trans+duco*: 'lead/bring across', and, taking *quos filios...* as object, one might render the phrase *traduxit... eruitque* as: 'led across... and rescued...' (an apt reminiscence of Moses and the Exodus which fits the present 'river' context). However, *L&S* s.v. B.2 gives the meaning 'make a show of, expose to public ridicule, disgrace.' Taking *potentiam diaboli* as object, the merits of this sense of the verb in the present context (brought to my attention by Tom McIntyre) are significant: (a) it explains *palam* and (b) this in turn makes a nice effect with *eruit de potestate tenebrarum* and *filios lucis*; (c) the meaning of the derivative noun *traductio*, 'leading a prisoner in a triumph' lends colour to this interpretation which moreover appears to be paraphrased at §14.11: *nequitiam maligni hostis superans proferret in lucem* and explains the comparative *latius* at §15.2 *nequitiam diaboli latius sanctis aperuit*. Besides, given Bede's exquisite choice of words, one must ask: Why does he choose e.g. *traduxit* rather than *transtulit* or *potentiam* ('capabilities/powers/capacity') rather than *potestatem* ('power/dominion/control/authority'), even allowing for some semantic overlap between the latter pair? Hardly for stylistic reasons alone. Fr Hurst, however, makes a compelling case for rendering *traduxit* as 'transferred', 'brought over' or 'removed' on the basis of Col 1.13 which reads: *qui eripuit nos de potestate tenebrarum et transtulit in regnum Filii dilectionis suae....* In favour of this (a) he could point to §16.2 (still in the 'fish' context): *qui de membris diaboli in Christi membra transferuntur* and (b) *traduxit* in the sense of 'brought over/carried across', *inter alia*, takes account of the 'river' context: 'carried across (the dangerous river of life)', so to speak. His version then, would run somewhat like this: 'after smashing to pieces the devil's might, he openly and undauntedly brought over and rescued from the power of darkness those whom he foreknew to be children of light.' The whole passage is strikingly reminiscent of St Leo the Great's Sermon for Christmas in which, speaking of Christ and also citing Col.1,13, he says: 'Recognize, O Christian, the dignity that is yours, and now that you have *become a partaker of the divine nature* (2 Pet 1.4), do not relapse into your old habits by a degenerate way of life. Bear in mind whose head and whose body it is that you have been made a *member* of. (cf. 1 Cor 6.15). Remember that you have been rescued *from the power of darkness and translated* into God's *light* and *kingdom*.' *Agnosce, o christiane, dignitatem tuam, et diuinae consors factus naturae, noli in ueterem utilitatem degeneri conuersatione recidere. Memento cuius capitis et cuius sis corporis membrum. Reminiscere quia erutus de potestate tenebrarum translatus es in Dei lumen et regnum.* (*Tractatus* 21, (*CCSL* 138, 88, 70–74); and *In Natiuitate Domini Sermo I SC* 22,72). Note the parallel with Bede's allusion to Christ as the head of his Church and the Church as his body. Significantly, we know from Bede himself (*Hom* I.5) that he was familiar with this sermon of St Leo's. 61 cf. Col 1.13. This text reappears in *DTemp* at 3.3 where he writes: 'those of us *preordained to life*' (Acts 13.48) 'by God's grace... were transferred from the mountain of pride to the mountain of the house of the Lord, and rescued from the power of darkness....' cf. *InHab* 15.2 n. 62 cf. Rom 8.29. 63 cf. +Lk 16.8; +Eph 5.8; +1 Thess 5.5. 64 For a more detailed discussion of preachers as the Lord's feet, see Bede's comments on Hab 3.6 (§13.1): 'His feet stood and the earth moved'.

15

6.5 *¹Then the angel of the Lord said to him: Gut the fish and put away for yourself its heart and gall and liver*. *²The Lord gutted the fish when he exposed more extensively to his saints the devil's wickedness and tore from their flesh, as it were, the secrets of his snares.*[65] *³He put away his heart for himself because he wanted to point out in the holy books his cunning, of which it is written: ⁴Now *the serpent was more cunning than any of the beasts of the earth*;*[66] *⁵and of this heart Paul too says: *For we are well aware of his intentions*.*[67] *⁶He also put away the gall, since, in his concern for caution he wanted the extent of the malicious fury with which he raged against the human race to be written about and put on record.* *⁷The liver too he put away because he deigned to make known to us through the teachers of the truth the mischievous maturity of his intrigues against us.* *⁸For they say that it is by the heat and power of the liver the hidden properties of the food which is eaten are 'cooked out'*[68] *and reach the system.*[69] *⁹But when with careful consideration we seek to find in what order the things we propose to do | are to be carried out, we,* [10] *as it were, 'cook out' by the heat of the liver the foods received in the stomach.*

*¹⁰***For these are (in practical terms) necessary for medications**[70] *¹¹***The astuteness and cunning of the ancient enemy's trickery which are known to us are beneficial for healing because the more thoroughly we investigate them, the more cautiously we avoid them.**

6.6 *¹*Tobias **broiled the flesh** of the fish **and they took it with them on their journey; the rest, as much as would serve their needs,**

---

65 tore from their flesh, as it were, the secrets of his snares: *quasi archana insidiarum eius euiscerauit*. The plural noun *uiscera*, from which the denominative verb *euiscerare* is formed, commonly means, among other things, the flesh, especially the soft tissue to which the inner parts of the body are attached. I purposely retain Bede's striking metaphor for 'revealed, laid bare, exposed'. **66** Gen 3.1. **67** 2 Cor 2.11. **68** are cooked out: *excoquantur*. **69** reach the system: *ad digestionem peruneiant*. The noun *digestio*, like its parent verb *digero*, implies the same dual process of 'forcing apart, dissolving' on the one hand, and 'distributing and assimilating' on the other. One might translate Bede's phrase as: 'go on to be digested' or more literally as: 'attain digestion'. **70** For these are (in practical terms) necessary for medications: *Sunt enim haec necessaria ad medicamenta utiliter*. '…necessary for useful medicines' is the *Douay*'s inadequate rendering of this syntactically puzzling sentence. Taken in its normal sense of 'usefully' *utiliter* resists satisfactory syntactical explanation. Translated as an adjective, as in the *Douay*, it is not only tautologous but makes little sense. In classical Latin *utiliter* is used in legal language to mean 'in practical effect or terms'. It is on this that our version is based. The *JB* version simply says: 'for the gall and heart and liver have curative properties.' The clause is missing in the *RSV* and, regrettably, the *LXX* can throw no light on the problem, since it does not contain the corresponding clause.

they salted.²The amount of the fish they took for themselves signifies those who are changed[71] from members of the devil into members of Christ, i.e. are converted from unbelief to the faith; ³but the amount they left represents those who, on hearing God's word, prefer to remain behind among the dead and decaying members of their deceiver rather than return to the companionship of the saviour. ⁴He broiled its flesh in those whom he found carnal but rendered spiritual and strong again by the fire of his love. ⁵Finally the Holy Spirit came down upon the apostles in a vision of fire.[72] ⁶*The rest*, he says, *they salted*, which is particularly applicable to teachers to whom it is said: *You are the salt of the earth.*[73] ⁷Now they, i.e. Tobias and the angel, salted ⟨it⟩, because the same *mediator between God and men*[74] both humanly taught the apostles by word, and divinely gave them the salt of wisdom in their hearts.

31⇐   ⁸Now **they took with them what would serve their needs till they got to Rages the city of the Medes** because the Lord gathered to the faith from Judea just as many as would serve as an example of ⟨virtuous⟩ living[75] or for the ministry of preaching until he should lay the foundations of the Church among the Gentiles too.

⁹The angel suggests to Tobias that on entering Raguel's house he ask for his daughter Sarah for himself in marriage.[76] ¹⁰Raguel stands for the people of the Gentiles whom the Lord deigned to visit through his preachers in order to take himself a bride from their stock, i.e. make of the Gentiles a Church for himself. ¹¹Also Sarah's name befits the Church because of Sarah, the patriarch Abraham's wife, who bore Isaac the son of the promise,[77] i.e. the free people of the Church. ¹²Raguel's name too, which means 'God is his sustenance' or 'God is ⟨my⟩ friend'[78] denotes the people who, after overcoming the devil's deceit, unite themselves and their folk to the community of the Lord and can say:¹³*The Lord is my shepherd and I shall want for nothing,*[79] and earn the reward of hearing: [80] ¹⁴*I shall no longer call you servants* but *friends.*[81]

17

6.12 ¹**To you,** he said, **all my property is due.** ²And the Father ⟨said⟩ to his Son, *Ask me and I will give you the Gentiles for your inheritance,* and so forth.[82]

---

71 cf. *supra* §14.9 on *traduxit.*   **72** cf. Acts 2.3.   **73** Mt 5.13.   **74** 1 Tim 2.5.   **75** as an example of ⟨virtuous⟩ living: *ad exemplum uiuendi:* lit. 'for an example of living'.   **76** cf. Tob 6.10–13; that... he ask for...in marriage: *ut... petat sibi uxorem* lit. 'that he ask for himself as wife'.   **77** cf. +Gal 4.28.   **78** cf. Jer., *Nom.* (*CCSL* 72, 71,29; 77, 21–22).   **79** Ps 22(23).1.   **80** earn the reward of hearing: *audire meretur:* lit. 'merit to hear'.   **81** Jn 15.15.   **82** Ps 2.8.

7.1 *¹They went in to Raguel who welcomed them with joy.* ²The   [11]
Lord went to the Gentile people through the teachers of his word and they
gladly received it in a great many places as the Acts of the Apostles testify.

19

7.11 *¹When* asked for his daughter, Raguel at first **got very alarmed
knowing what** had happened **to the seven husbands,** but when the
angel told ⟨him⟩ that the unclean could not have her, whereas Tobias, who
feared God, could, he agreed forthwith to give her away.⁸³ ²The Gentile
people on hearing the message of the faith and being admonished by the
apostles to form the Church of Christ from their progeny throughout the
world, were able (but only after reliable investigation) to undertake the
obligations and rules of the new religion.⁸⁴ ³For they knew that⁸⁵ in former times they had had many teachers who all (comprised, as it were, in
the number seven) knew about the joys of this life alone ⟨but⟩ had nothing
reliable to say about eternal joys; ⁴and consequently the destruction of
eternal death would have snatched them away without hope of immortal
life. ⁵But, thanks to Truth itself teaching within them which outwardly
made itself heard through the mouths of teachers, they eventually understood that it was inevitable that foolish people should say foolish things,
and that those who did not know the true God should perish. ⁶On the
other hand, ⟨they⟩ rightly ⟨understood⟩ that the creator of the world on
coming into the world undertook the world's way of life; ⁷and ⟨so⟩ they
confessed belief in Christ and rejoiced that they were sanctified by his
sacraments.

23⇐

---

83 cf. Tob 7.10–16.   84 (a) but only after reliable investigation: *non sine certa
exploratione*: lit. 'not without reliable investigation'. Note Bede's use of this litotes,
non sine, which Roman poets were so fond of. For the reader less familiar with Latin
stylistic usage it may be worth noting the much stronger force of Latin litotes. It is in
a sense a different idiom in English where, e.g. 'not often' is elegant understatement for
'rather seldom'; in Latin the corresponding *non saepe* is vigorous irony: 'hardly ever'.
(b) Here Bede resumes a favourite theme: belief in the true God alone brings certainty.
Addressing King Edwin of Northumbria's pagan council on the spiritual future of the
kingdom, a divinely inspired speaker says: 'If this new doctrine (Christianity) has
brought us more certain information, it seems right that we should accept it – *si haec
novit a doctrina certius aliquid attulit, merito esse sequenda videtur*' (*HE* 2.13). The
spiritual progress of Edwin himself as described by Bede in *HE* 2.9 illustrates *InTob*'s
statement that the Gentiles accepted Christianity, 'only after reliable investigation'.
In the *HE*, as here in *InTob*, Bede emphasizes the role of teachers in promoting love
of eternal, over earthly, joys; see his account of the work of Bp Jaruman among the
East Saxons and St Cuthbert among the Northumbrians in time of plague. (*HE* 3.30;
4.27; cf. *VCP* 9).   85 For they knew that: *sciens quod*...: lit. 'knowing that ...'

20

8.2 ¹When Tobias had been brought into the bedroom to Sarah **he produced from his satchel part of the liver and laid it on the live coals.** ²And the Lord, as he is about to receive the Church from the Gentiles ⟨as his bride⟩, bids it at first betrothal (in the person of each individual believer)**⁸⁶** to renounce Satan and all his works and all his pomps, ³and then to confess its faith in the holy trinity for the remission of sins, which is the significance of burning up with live coals the innermost entrails of the fish.

21

8.3 ¹When this was done the angel caught the **demon and bound him**, because after the renunciation of the devil, after the confession of the true faith follows the remission of sins when the demon has been driven out by means of the water of baptism. ²Moreover he bound him because he restrained him from harming the faithful, whom, although he is allowed to tempt occasionally that they may be tested, he is still forbidden to overcome lest they fall away from the faith.

28⇐ ³**He bound him**, he says, **in the desert of upper Egypt.** ⁴Both 'desert' and 'Egypt' refer to the hearts of unbelievers which are both deserts,**⁸⁷** i.e. forsaken by God of whose indwelling they are unworthy; ⁵and according to the meaning of the name 'Egypt',**⁸⁸** these same ⟨hearts⟩ are, plunged into shadow by the darkness of their own unbelief. ⁶And not without reason is the one who is deserted by the grace of divine light filled by the prince of darkness. ⁷The reason why the angel got hold of the demon that wanted to kill Tobias and bound him in the desert of upper |Egypt is that, the devil while restrained from snatching away the faithful [12] who are members of their redeemer, is allowed by this Lord and redeemer of ours to have dominion over unbelievers only. ⁸And even in their case he (the Lord) holds him bound because even the wicked, the very ones of whom he is master, he is not allowed to harm as much as he longs to in his insatiable rage.

22

8.11 ¹Meanwhile **about cock-crow** Raguel, fearing lest by any chance Tobias had been killed by the demon, dug a grave with his servants, but,

---

86 at first betrothal: *in primo desponsionis eius initio*: lit. 'at the first beginning of its betrothal'. In the context of the baptismal ritual in which the phrase is set one might even say: 'at the very first exchange of vows'. Bede is connecting baptism of the individual with the Church as the bride of Christ. **87** Bede's word-play on 'desert' does not readily transfer to English. See Martin 1986, 36–37. **88** cf. Jer., *Nom.* (*CCSL* 72, 143, 28–29).

immediately on learning of his safety, ordered it to be filled up with earth again. ²Cock-crow is the voice of preachers, and though they sang of the true dawn and day of faith that was to come after the darkness of error, ³there were some among the people of the Gentiles who doubted whether the Lord had really vanquished the ancient enemy and therefore thought it better to cover up and carefully conceal their belief in his name. ⁴Later, however, when they acknowledged the light of truth, with the dawn breaking, so to speak, and the crowing of the cock becoming more frequent, ⁵(i.e. the voice of the teachers, who by the eager flight of their heart were accustomed to soar to heavenly desires), ⁶they dispelled from their mind every cloud of doubt, and overthrowing the enemy, sincerely acknowledged Christ to be the bridegroom of the holy Church.

23

32⇐   *8.22* ¹Delighted at Tobias' survival, his marriage ties (with the family) and his wedding to his daughter, Raguel **had two fat cattle and four rams slaughtered and a banquet prepared for all his neighbours and all his friends.** ²Delighted at the faith in Christ and the calling of the Gentile world to God, the Gentile people made so much progress in the Lord that some from among their number also became teachers and
27⇐   these same ones later even became martyrs. ³These are indeed the cattle because they bear the light yoke of the gospel,[89] for by preaching they beget and nurture those also who would advance further towards bearing the same yoke. ⁴They are the rams too because (they are) the fathers and leaders of the peoples who follow them, of whom it is said: *Bring to the Lord the offspring of rams.*[90] ⁵They are moreover fat cattle because they are teachers filled to overflowing with the grace of heavenly love, of which (grace) the psalmist prays: *Let my soul be filled as with marrow and fat.*[91] ⁶They are the two slaughtered cattle because all who for Christ either voluntarily mortify their body themselves, that they may become a

---

89 cf. Mt 11.30.   **90** Ps 28.1; the offspring of rams *(Douay)*: *filios arietum*: lit. 'the sons of rams'. Note that these words, which are in the Greek and the Vulgate, are not in the Hebrew of the corresponding Psalm, i.e. Ps 29, and consequently not in the *RSV*.   **91** (a) as with marrow and fat: Ps 62.6(63.5): *Sicut adipe pinguedinis*: lit. 'as with the suet *(adeps)* of fatness', a metaphorical expression for 'richness, abundance' common in biblical writings. *Adeps*, and *pinguedo* are both synonymous in this sense with the normal word for 'marrow', *medulla*, the word which is used in the Vulgate at Gen 45.18 to translate Pharaoh's words to Joseph: 'that you may eat the *fat* of the land'. (b) Gregory identifies the fatlings of Mt 22.4 with the fathers of the New Testament: 'When they receive the gift of inner fatness, they flee their earthly desires and are raised to the heights on the wings of their contemplation. What else is having your thoughts on low things but a kind of mental leanness? But there are those who, through their understanding of heavenly things, are now being nourished by their holy desire for the things of heaven. Receiving the food of inner delight, they are being fattened, so to speak, with a more abundant sustenance. The psalmist was longing to be well fed with this fatness when he said: *May my soul be filled with marrow and fat'* *(Homilies on the Gospels*, 38).

living victim, or hand it over to the enemy to be killed, [7]these assuredly, have learnt to withstand the enemy *with the weapons of uprightness to the right and to the left,*[92] i.e. in prosperity and adversity. [8]They are the four slaughtered rams because holy teachers and martyrs preserve the four books of the holy gospel by faith and action, because they are supported by the four cardinal[93] virtues of prudence, fortitude, temperance and justice, [9]for they instruct the flock of Christ throughout the whole world which is divided up into four quarters.[94] [10]Raguel had cattle and rams slaughtered because the Gentile people taught that those who had come to the faith from their own stock were like | those whom, because of their outstanding virtue, the enemy desired to tempt and succeeded not in conquering after they were tempted but rather in making victorious as martyrs. [11]Or at all events he had those killed whom he taught to crucify their flesh for Christ with its vices and passions.[95] [12]And by their death he prepared a banquet for all his neighbours and friends because the progress, life, suffering and crown of the saints give joy to many, and they receive, as it were, a banquet from those by whose examples they are refreshed.

32⇐

[13]

24

8.23 [1]**And Raguel implored Tobias to stay with him two weeks.** [2]We too implore our Lord, praying that he stay with us till we attain the perfection of holy rest through the grace of the Holy Spirit whereby we may rest both from servile actions, i.e. sins in the body, and from wicked thoughts in the mind, [3]and that he may rest in our heart and body who says: *On whom shall my spirit rest but on the one who is humble and calm and trembles at my words?*[96]

25

24⇐ **9.3** [1]Tobias asks the angel to take **the animals and the servants**[97] and go **to Gabael in Rages of the Medes** and give him back his **promissory note** and take **the money from him** and ask **him to come to** his **wedding**; and he agrees. [2]The faithful, i.e. his members, ask the Lord to take some of the believers and entrust them with the task of preaching the word and to come himself among them to gather to his faith the Gentiles who have not yet accepted the mysteries of the faith but have merely heard tell of them, [3]and graciously grant that, through obedience to the faith, they may give back the talent of the word which they have learnt of by hearsay, [4]and that they themselves too, by believing and by upright

---

92 2 Cor 6.7. **93** cardinal: *primis*: lit. 'first, primary'. **94** *infra* §26.4 (Tob 9.6). **95** cf. Gal 5.24. **96** Is 66.2. **97** and the servants: *siue* lit. 'or the servants...', but the sense requires 'and', which is how the *Douay* translates it. *Siue (seu)* is often used copulatively in Late Latin; cf. Hofmann-Szantyr §272, p.504.

living, may be numbered ⟨among the company⟩ at the wedding-feast[98] of the holy Church at which the bridegroom is Christ, ⟨and⟩ at which from water he has made new wine[99] i.e. gives a spiritual understanding of the law. [5]And the Lord does not refuse but, gives a favourable hearing to the prayers of the petitioners,[100] and incorporates new peoples into the Church every day. [6]As we have said above,[101] this can be understood as applying in a special way to the nations which received the letter of the law through the seventy translators, and therefore were able to embrace the faith more quickly inasmuch as they possessed it in well-known books.

35⇐

24⇐

26

9.6 [1]So **taking four of Raguel's servants and two camels, Raphael went to Rages of the Medes** and telling him (i.e. Gabael) all about Tobias, received the money and made him come with him to the wedding. [2]The preachers chosen from the Gentiles through whom the Lord gathers in others too are Raguel's servants and camels: [3]servants because they serve the needs of those | they evangelize; camels because with the deference of brotherly love they also carry the burdens of their infirmity. [4]But the reason why there were four servants and two camels has been shown above where two cows and four rams were slaughtered.[102] [5]These with Raphael's help bring Gabael to Tobias' wedding when holy preachers bring new peoples together into the unity of the Church of Christ with his assistance.

24⇐

[14]

27

10.1–3 [1]**As** Tobias **was delaying on account of the wedding** his parents were worried **because he had not come back to them on the day agreed.** [2]And now as Christ through faith delays in the Church assembled from the Gentiles, all who are converted to faith in him individually from among the Jews are deeply distressed in spirit that the Lord, detained as he is among the Gentiles, is slow in coming to save them.[103] [3]And it is very appropriate to their circumstances that the mother who was poor and, as it were, bereft of husband and son, kept saying with great sorrow:

---

98 that they... may be numbered ⟨among the company⟩ at the wedding-feast: *ut... ad nuptias... aggregentur.* The verb *aggrego* primarily means 'add to the flock'. Our translation is an adaptation to the present context. **99** cf. Jn 2.1–10. **100** gives a favourable hearing to the prayers of the petitioners: *bene rogantium uota suscipiens*: I have taken *bene* with *suscipiens* and treated the participle as a finite verb. One might arguably take *bene* with *rogantium* and render the clause: 'gives a hearing to/acknowledges/accepts the prayers of those who ask properly'. But theologically the balance of probability favours our translation since the object of the prayers and the petitioners' intention are good in themselves. **101** *supra* §3.9 (Tob 1.10). **102** *supra* §23.6–9 (Tob 8.22). **103** cf. Tob 10.4.

10.4–6 *¹*Alas, alas, my son, why did we let you go abroad, ⟨you who are⟩ **the light of our eyes, the staff of our old age, the consolation of our life, the hope of our posterity? Considering that we had everything together in you alone, we ought not to have let you go away from us;** *²*and the answer Tobit gives to console her:**¹⁰⁴Hush! Don't be upset; our son is safe; the man we let him go with is very trusty**, is appropriate to the circumstances of these very people
30⇐ from among the Jews who now believe, *³*who console themselves and their own folk with the thought that there will really come a time when the Lord will come back to them, *⁴*and that then all Israel will be saved,¹⁰⁵ knowing that the Lord who made this promise is very trusty.¹⁰⁶ *⁵*For, as we pointed out above,¹⁰⁷ this Tobit, in the manner customary in the scriptures, denotes both the unbelievers through his blindness and the believers through his faith.

10.9 *¹*Raguel requests Tobias to stay on with him for a longer time but is not heeded, as Tobias says: *²***I know that my father and mother are at this very moment counting the days, and their soul within them is in anguish.** *³*So when all the Gentiles come in, no one will be able to prevent God from granting salvation to Israel as well, and
30⇐ enlightening its blindness which came upon a part of it.¹⁰⁸*⁴*For the divine mercy remembers that the believers among the Jews experience great sadness and continual grief of heart at the blindness of the unbelievers, their relatives according to the flesh, who are Israelites.

   *⁵*So Raguel let Tobias go off to his parents, giving him Sarah together with a great deal of property.¹⁰⁹ *⁶*The Church's teachers eventually send Christ | back, together with the Church itself full of the riches of the virtues,   [15] to enlighten by faith and enrich with the property of good works the Jewish people from whom he had taken flesh. *⁷*The angel and Tobias went on ahead to his parents; *⁸*then his wife followed with his property and
36⇐ household after his father had been given back his sight.¹¹⁰ *⁹*Divine grace goes ahead to enlighten the blindness of the Jewish people, and in their writings they recognize that Christ is true God and man. *¹⁰*And so at last, after acknowledging the true faith, as if rejoicing at seeing the angel and

---

104 the answer Tobit gives to console her: *quodque Tobias consolans eam respondet* (lit. 'and what Tobit, consoling her, answers'). **105** cf. Rom 11.26. **106** very trusty: *satis fidelis*: lit. 'trusty enough'. 'Very' translates *satis* which does, indeed, mean 'enough', but here (in parallel with Tobit's words of reassurance) in the positive sense of 'enough to fulfil all one's needs', or 'as much as one could possibly require', not just 'adequately', in the often minimal English use. **107** *supra* §5.2–6 (Tob 2.3–11). **108** cf. Rom 11.25–26; cf. *supra* §5.5 (Tob 2.10), n. **109** cf. Tob 10.10. **110** cf. Tob 11.3–8.

their son whom they have not seen for a long time, [11]they join the holy Church which has been assembled from among the Gentiles by sharing in the heavenly mysteries.

30

11.9 [1]As they were nearing the house **the dog which had been with them on the way ran ahead and, arriving as if bringing the news, showed his joy by wagging his tail.** [2]One must not dismiss with scorn the figure of this dog which is a traveller and the companion of an angel. [3]So, as we have also pointed out above,[111] he represents the Church's teachers who by combating heretics often drive off troublesome wolves from the supreme pastor's fold. [4]To them fittingly applies the fact that it is natural to dogs to repay a favour to those who are kind to them and patrol in restless vigil for their masters' safety.[112] [5]The reason why the dog ran ahead is that the teacher first preaches salvation,[113] then the Lord, the enlightener, cleanses hearts. [6]And he (the writer) made the charming observation: *arriving as if bringing the news*, because, of course, every sincerely believing teacher is a messenger of truth; [7]charmingly *did he show his joy by wagging his tail*, for the tail which is the end of the body suggests the end of a good work, i.e. its perfection, or at any rate the reward which is granted without end. [8]The dog then showed his joy by wagging his tail when he saw once more his masters' homestead from which he was absent for a long time; [9]teachers rejoice at the results of their work when they realize that by means of their ministry Judea is to be brought together again by the Lord; [10]they rejoice at receiving an eternal reward and with this same reward common to all the elect they cheer the hearts of those they preach to when they promise them that Christ's grace will come without delay.

36⇐

---

111 *supra* §11.4 (Tob 6.5–8).   112 (a) patrol in restless vigil for their masters' safety: *sollicitas excubias pro dominorum salute praetendere*: lit. 'extend anxious night-watchings for...' I owe this suggestion to Tom McIntyre. Here we see Bede's rhetorical powers at their best. Note the hypallage in the phrase *sollicitas excubias*, where the adjective *sollicitas*, which in meaning belongs to 'dogs', is transferred to the *excubias* ('night-watchings'). One cannot capture all the semantic nuances of either *sollicitas* ('restless, on the move, agitated') or *excubias* ('lying out on guard') or *praetendere* ('spread, deploy or stretch out before (another) as a protection'). Dogs stretch a cordon of security around their masters and so act as 'sentries'. Hence the choice of 'patrol'. 'Some might prefer "prowl" as being more appropriate with reference to dogs but "patrol" gives the underlying feel of "sentry-go". The challenge at the gate when the visitor is still out of human sight and earshot.' (TMcI). (b) Bede believes that animals and birds can teach important lessons. In his prose *Life of Cuthbert* he includes a story about the ravens on Cuthbert's island-hermitage of Farne 'in which human pride and contumacy are openly condemned by the obedience and humility of birds.... Let it not seem absurd to anyone to learn a lesson of virtue from birds, since Solomon says: *Go to the ant, thou sluggard, and consider her ways and learn wisdom.* (Prov 6.6)'. (*VCP* 20).   113 Note the word-play here on the various meanings, secular and sacred, of the Latin word *(salus) salute, salutem*: 'health/safety/welfare' and 'salvation'.

11.10 *¹Accordingly when the dog signalled the arrival of Tobias **his blind
father got up and began to run, stumbling on his feet.*** ²On hearing
the word of salvation from the teachers, the Hebrew people get up from the
long deep sleep of their unbelief ⟨and⟩ run with love to the Lord, ³albeit
stumbling in the steps of their actions until they receive the light of full
faith and good works when they have been reborn in Christ and been given
instruction.

*⁴**And giving a servant his hand he ran to meet his son.***[114]   [16]
⁵The blind man gives his hand to the servant that he may run to meet
his Lord without the foot of his action stumbling, ⁶who, even if he himself
does not yet fully see the road of faith, nevertheless strives to give to the
one who knows the light of truth well the assent by which he may reach
the Lord.[115]

32

11.11 *¹**And welcoming him he kissed him as did his wife also, and
they began to weep for joy.*** ²Judea, on welcoming at last the embrace
of Christ with joy, joins weeping ⟨to it⟩ also, rejoicing that it believes,
grieving that it has been so late in reaching the Lord.

33

11.13 *¹**Then Tobias taking some of the fish's gall anointed his
father's eyes.*** ²And the Lord reveals more openly to believers how great
is the malice of the ancient dragon who once eagerly longed to devour him
in the passion, but instead was himself killed because of this and lost his
members, i.e. those whom he was hitherto holding in thrall.

34

11.13–15 *¹**A white film like the skin of an egg began to come out
of** Tobit's **eyes** after they had been anointed **with the fish's gall, and
he recovered his sight.*** ²And the Jewish people on realizing the very
bitter malice of the most wicked enemy will recover the light they have
28⇐ lost. ³The white film which had obstructed his eyes denotes the folly of
self-indulgence. ⁴For *they have a zeal for God but ⟨it is⟩ not based on
knowledge,*[116] ⁵and as he (Paul) says again, *seeking to establish their own*

---

114 Tob 11.10.   **115** for...he nevertheless: *qui ... tamen*: lit. 'who...nevertheless'.
116 not based on knowledge *(NIV)*: *non secundum scientiam*: lit. 'not according
to knowledge' *(Douay; RCR)*. The phrase is variously rendered: 'not enlightened'
(RSV), 'misguided' *(NJB)*; '(but it is) with imperfect understanding' *(Knox)*.

righteousness they did not submit to the righteousness of God.[117] [6]The black pupil ⟨of the eye⟩ sees, the white one grows dark; [7]and people who in their own estimation are wise, saying: *Are we also blind?*[118] in such people there is no truth. [8]On the other hand, those who are aware of their frailty and ignorance and know how to say: *My God, enlighten my darkness,*[119] are destined to enjoy the light of life in the Lord. [9]Moreover the white film was well compared to the skin of an egg. [10]By the egg hope is surely indicated, because it is obviously not alive, not an animate creature, but it is hoped by the bird that laid it that sometime it may live, walk, run and fly. [11]And the Apostle says: *But if we hope for what we do not see, we wait ⟨for it⟩ with patience*[120] [12]Hence in the gospel parable by the term⟨s⟩ bread, fish and an egg[121] the three supreme virtues, namely faith, hope and love are symbolized. [13]The reason why the Jewish people still have a veil in front of their heart is so that they may not understand the grace of Christ; [122] [14]they have a white film because they are, in their opinion, white and upright compared to everyone ⟨else⟩, [15]but they have this white film like the skin of an egg because they suffer from mental blindness in the very fond and futile hope of a Christ who is to be born in the flesh and set them free and give them a great |kingdom throughout the world. [16]But any of them from whom the black darkness of error is removed will recognize that Christ has already come and redeemed the world with his blood. [17]To these what follows fittingly applies because

30⇐

30⇐

[17]

35

11.16–18 [1]on getting back his sight, Tobit, **together with his wife and all his acquaintances, began to glorify God,** saying: **I bless you, Lord God of Israel, for having chastised me and saved me, and, look, I see my son Tobias. And after seven days Sara his son's wife arrived.** [2]The seven days suggest the light of the grace of the Spirit which is received in sevenfold form.[123] [3]The reason why his son's wife arrives seven days after Tobit is given the light ⟨of vision⟩, is that after Judea is given the light through faith, after it receives the grace of the Holy

---

117 Rom 10.2–3.   **118** Jn 9.40.   **119** Ps 17.29(18.28).   **120** Rom 8.25; cf. Aug., *Quaest. Eu.* II, XXII. (*CCSL* 44B 66, 11–12); *Serm.* 105 (*PL* 38, 620–621). Compare Bede's statement in *Hom* 2.14: 'The certainty of our hope is prefigured by the egg. No offspring is yet discernible in the egg, but the birth of the bird to come is hoped for. The faithful do not yet look upon the glory of the fatherland on high, in which they believe at the present ⟨time⟩, but they await its coming in hope. Hence the Apostle says: *But if we hope for what we do not see, we await it through patience.* (Rom 8.25).'   **121** cf. Lk 11.11–12.   **122** cf. 2 Cor 3.15.   **123** cf. Is 11.2–3.

37⇐ Spirit, *⁴the Church will come in to it so that there may be *one fold and one shepherd*¹²⁴ and one house of Christ supported upon one cornerstone.*¹²⁵

⁵And the cattle and camels and his wife's property in abundance also arrived.¹²⁶ ⁶The many individuals from among the faithful, the many virtues of the Church are then incorporated with the Hebrew people.

36⇐ **⁷But also the money he had received from Gabael:**¹²⁷⁸The knowledge of the scriptures too which they once used to lend to the Gentiles is then returned to them.

36

11.20–21 ¹**Tobit's kinsmen came to congratulate him on all the good things the Lord had done for him, and for seven days they** feasted with him. ²This is what Moses said in his canticle: *Nations, rejoice together with his people.*¹²⁸ ³They feast for seven days together because they rejoice in the gifts and virtues of the Spirit. ⁴As he is about to return to heaven the angel more clearly explains to them who he is and why he has come, and that he is to return to God.¹²⁹ ⁵And for this people who are then making progress ⟨in the faith⟩, the Lord lays open wider the gifts of his knowledge, revealing and showing to all of them that he is in the Father and the Father in him.¹³⁰ ⁶Accordingly the angel returns to God, ⟨and⟩ Tobias remains with his father. ⁷And the Lord is understood by the elect as equal to the Father in his divinity, ⟨and⟩ of one nature with us in his humanity.

37

13.1 ¹Then **Tobit the elder opening his mouth blessed God** confessing his sternness and mercy as well as reminding the faithful always to preach about his acts of kindness, ⟨and⟩ have a deep fear of his punishments; ²and, |imbued with the spirit of prophecy from the heavenly [18]

36⇐ Jerusalem our mother,¹³¹ he sings many hymns of praise.¹³² ³And the Jewish people when converted to the faith at the end of the world will have many teachers and prophetic men to set the minds of their neighbours on fire with heavenly desires when by frequent proclamation they make the everlasting joys of their heavenly homeland resound in their ears.¹³³

---

124 Jn 10.16.   125 cf. Eph 2.20; 1 Pet 2.5–6; Bede attaches great significance to the scriptural image of the cornerstone. Commenting on the *Seven Catholic Epistles*, (1 Pet 2.7), he again sees the cornerstone as a symbol of Jewish and Gentile unity in Christ. On Bede's use of architectural imagery from scripture, see Holder 1989 ("Allegory and History"); O'Reilly 1995, xxxix–li; see also Deshman 1986, 273–78. 126 Tob 11.18.   127 ibid.   128 cf. Deut 32.43; Rom 15.10.   129 cf. Tob 12.6–20. 130 cf. Jn 14.10.   131 cf. Gal 4.26.   132 cf. Tob 13.2–22.   133 in their ears: *eis*: lit. 'for them'.

14.5 *¹*The elder Tobit **at the hour of his death summoned to him his son Tobias and the latter's seven sons, (his grandsons), and told them** that the destruction of Nineveh was near and the restoration of Jerusalem and of the land of Israel.[134] *²*And at that time in Judea the teachers and those who were believers and upright, whether living on in this world or on the point of leaving it, admonish their neighbours that the world is already approaching its end and the good things of the future life are very soon to come. *³*They give this warning to those especially whom they see to have been born again through the Lord's grace and to be filled with the gift of the sevenfold Spirit. *⁴*This is the significance of the fact that the sons of Tobias the younger, were seven in number, and that these were young men, i.e. strong in faith[135] and getting the upper hand of the malicious one.

14.12–13 *¹***Direct your steps away from**[136] Nineveh, **for I see that its iniquity will be the end of it.** *²*The meaning of this too is to say to his hearers among the faithful: *³*'Direct the intention of your heart in such a way as to turn your back on the desires of this world and of an earthly lifestyle and seek after heavenly things with your whole mind'; *⁴*for it is well known that the multitude of the perverse is so great, and so great the violation of God's commandments throughout the world, that it cannot be put an end to except by the destruction of the world itself, *⁵*just as ⟨happened⟩ long ago in the deluge, and the wiping out of the whole human race.

14.14–15 *¹*So Tobias **departed from Nineveh with his wife and children and his children's children and returned to his parents-in-law and found them in a good old age.** *²*This the Lord does every day; *³*this he is going to do till the end of the world, when having abandoned those whom he knows not to be his own, he turns to visit and enlighten the hearts of those whom he has predestined to eternal life.[137] *⁴*For these he finds in a good old age when he rejoices that they have by his bounty long been zealous for good works; *⁵*but[138] he sees in a bad

33⇐

---

134 cf. Tob 14.6–8. **135** cf. +1 Pet 5.9. **136** away from: *ut exeatis de*: lit. 'that you may go away from'. **137** cf. Rom 8.29; Eph 1.5. **138** but: *alioquin*: note this use of *alioquin* as a simple adversative conjunction found in the Vulgate and Ecclesiastical Latin generally; cf. Job 2.5: *alioquin mitte manum tuam et tange os eius et carnem*: 'but put out your hand and touch his bone and his flesh.'

old age, and therefore passes by, those who, ⟨though⟩ living longer, are immature in judgement, and not venerable for purity of good deeds as ⟨they would be⟩ for their white hairs, but are stooped from the burden of their vices.**139** *6*Of such Isaiah says: *The child shall die a hundred years old and the sinner a hundred years old shall be accursed.***140** *7*Deservedly shall the person lie under a curse for his sins, who, though having lived for many years, yet has never troubled to give up his frivolity of mind.

*8***He found them**, he says, **in health in a good old age and took** care of them, | **and he himself closed their eyes and acquired all the** [19] **inheritance of Raguel's house.141** *9*And our Lord and saviour takes care of those whom he knows to continue in the health of good works. *10*He closes the gaze of their heart to the enjoyment of the present life and raises it to the contemplation of perpetual light; *11*he brings them after this life's end to heavenly things; *12*his is the inheritance of which the prophet sings to him: *Arise, O God, judge the earth, for you will have inheritance among all the nations.***142**

41

14.16–17 *1***And after he had lived** a great many **years in the fear of the Lord, all his kinsmen buried him with joy.** *2*The burial of Tobias denotes the end of the whole world, when our Lord with his whole body *which is the Church***143** he has redeemed, enters into eternal rest, *3*while the angels felicitate him on the community of redeemed mankind and assign to each one of them i.e. the members of their founder, a place in the various mansions of their heavenly homeland according to the diversity of their merits.

*4***And all his generation continued in good life and a holy manner of living.144** *5This means* the one *generation* throughout the entire universe and the whole duration of the world *of those that seek the Lord, of those that seek the face of the God of Jacob.***145** *6*Of it likewise he says: *The generation of the upright shall be blessed.***146** *7*Now what life is better, what manner of living holier, than to dwell forever in the glory of one's founder?

*8***So that they were acceptable both to God and to all the inhabitants of the land:147** *9*When they have been brought to their heavenly homeland, men will be acceptable to God by whose grace they have been redeemed; *10*they will be acceptable also to the angels whose number they will complement, ⟨and⟩ with whom they are to be joined

---

139 purity of good deeds: *candore bonae actionis*: lit. 'for the dazzling whiteness of. . . .'; no doubt Bede, (possibly influenced by the popular etymology of his day which erroneously linked the two words), is playing on the similarity in meaning and form between *canitie* ('whiteness of hair') and *candore*. **140** Is 65.20. **141** Tob 14.15. **142** Ps 81(82).8. **143** Col 1.24. **144** Tob 14.17. **145** Ps 23(24).6. **146** Ps 111(112).2. **147** Tob 14.17.

forever in a fraternal fellowship. *11*For these are the inhabitants of the land of which the Lord says: *Blessed are the meek for they shall possess the land,*[148] of which the psalmist in his desire to see it said: *12I believe that I shall see the goodness of the Lord in the land of the living.*[149]

---

148 Mt 5.4.   **149** Ps 26(27).13.

COMMENTARY OF BEDE THE PRIEST
ON THE CANTICLE OF HABAKKUK

1

21⇐ *¹*The canticle of the prophet Habakkuk**¹**, which you requested to have
expounded to you, my dearly beloved sister in Christ, is mainly a procla-
18⇐ mation of the mysteries of the Lord's passion. *²*Hence too according to
the usage of the holy universal and apostolic Church, on the sixth day
of the week, ⟨the day⟩ on which this passion was accomplished, it is the
custom to recite it**²** solemnly at the morning praises every week.**³** *³*But it
also gives a mystical account of his incarnation, resurrection and ascension into heaven, as well as of the faith of the Gentiles and the unbelief of
the Jews.**⁴** *⁴*For on contemplating the condition of the present world, the
prophet had seen the peace enjoyed by sinners and the afflictions of the
upright; *⁵*he had seen the wicked rolling in riches and the innocent subjected to daily beatings; *⁶*instead of justice he had seen wickedness, and
instead of uprightness iniquity; *⁷*he had seen the tears of the innocent and

---

1 The text of Habakkuk which Bede uses varies widely from that of the Vulgate. The
author is, in fact, using an Old Latin *(VL)* text which in turn is an almost verbatim
version of the Septuagint *(LXX)*. For a better understanding of the lemmata and
commentary, readers reasonably familiar with biblical Greek would do well to consult
the *LXX* in Rahlfs' critical edition. Those less familiar with Greek might like to consult
Brenton's English version. For details see Bibliography under Septuagint.   **2** it is the
custom to recite it: *solet... repeti:* lit. 'it is wont to be repeated'.   **3** at the morning
praises: *in laudibus matutinis;* cf *RB* 116: 'Benedict calls *Lauds* the "morning praise"
(*matutinae* (i.e. *laudes*)) or the "morning celebration" (*matutinorum solemnitas*)'.
However, Fr MacGinty considers this use of the term 'morning praises' in Bede 'an
extremely interesting one because the experts when discussing "Lauds" as the name
given to what was "morning prayer", all attribute the development to the *RB*'s use of
"Lauds" for the three final psalms (148–150). Further it is said that the term *Laudes*
as *the name of the Hour* does not appear until several centuries after even Bede's
day. This could mean that the usage, in fact, was appearing (or dawning) at the
time of Bede. I have not seen it noted in any of the liturgical studies, but then most
such studies concentrate on liturgical or paraliturgical texts.' In *CCM* I, which gives
texts from the seventh to the eighth century, we find the following expressions used
(references are to page and line): *Ordo Romanus XVI* 18.8,11,20: *Matutini Laudibus;*
XVII 29.1,13: *Matutinis, Mattutine;* 44.8: *Matutinis et Vespertinis Laudibus* (sic);
XVIII 48.8: *Matutinis;* 50.1: *Matutinis Laudibus* 50.4: *Matutinorum Laudibus; Ordo
Casinensis,* I (c.750) 101.4: *post Matutinas horas;* (*Memoriale qualiter,* c.800) 233.8
and 269.12: *Matutinas Laudes;* 273.3: *Matutinos* 14: *Matutinis.* In *CCM* VII (edited
1983–86) in four parts presenting the older forms of the Cluniac customaries, which
basically represent 10th- and 11th-century use, we find in Part 2, in three Mss at 34.20:
Matutinas Laudibus (sic); at 84.23 simply *Matutinas,* but in the fourth Ms, (siglum
C), 47.12 and 50.9, we read *Laudes* only, whereas the other three have *Matutinis
Laudibus.* Note the fluctuation in terminology and the preponderance of joint forms.
4 On Bede's understanding and use of the terms 'unbelief' (*perfidia*) and 'unbelievers'
(*perfidi*) see Plummer 1896, ii, 18–19. On the medieval understanding of *perfidi*
generally see de Lubac 1961, 2.I, 153–181.

none to offer consolation, and those bereft of help unable to withstand the ferocity of all their calumniators. *8*And knowing that these and countless things of the kind could not possibly come about without God's prevision, he was greatly troubled in spirit, and, sighing deeply in his inmost heart, cried out to the Lord: *9How long more shall I call without your hearing me? Shall I, suffering violence, shout aloud to you without your saving me?*5 And again: *Your eyes are too pure to see evil*6 *and you cannot look upon iniquity.* *10Why do you not turn your attention to those who do evil things,*7 *and remain silent while the wicked person devours the one who is more upright than he, and make men like the fish of the sea and the reptile that has no ruler?*8

*11*But all at once in the midst of these musings he recalled to mind the providential design*9* of the Lord's incarnation and passion which he knew of through the spirit of prophecy, *12*and he realized that he had complained much more bitterly than he ought of the afflictions of the saints in this life, who had been promised eternal rest in the life to come, *13*(since even God's very Son who appeared in the flesh, who was to be born of the Holy Spirit and the virgin mother and live in the world without any sin, was not to leave the world without the suffering of the cross); *14*and making his prayer to the Lord for his own wrongdoings he began as follows:

[382]

2

3.2 *1***Lord, I heard your tidings and was afraid.** *2*Now, the tidings are those of the Lord our saviour which he heard from his Father to the effect that he would become incarnate,**10** be born into the world, *3*spend his life as the almighty one among the weak, as the upright one among sinners, as God among human beings, *4*perform heavenly deeds, teach heavenly precepts, promise heavenly gifts, *5*be tempted, scourged, mocked, put to death,**11** ascend into heaven *6*and, sending down the Spirit from above, enlighten the world by the grace of truth. *7*These tidings he himself quite frequently mentions in the gospel when he says: *8but he who sent me is truthful and what I hear from him I speak in the world.*12 And again: *9but I have called you friends, because all that I have heard from my Father I have made known to you.*13 And of him John the Baptist too ⟨says⟩: *10He*

---

5 Hab 1.2; . . . without your hearing ⟨me⟩: *et non exaudies*: lit. 'and you will not hear'; . . . without your saving me: *et non saluabis*: lit. 'and you will not save'. **6** Your eyes are too pure to see evil: *Mundi sunt oculi tui, ne uideas mala:* lit. 'Your eyes are pure that you may not see evil'. **7** Why do you not turn your attention. . .?: *Quare non respicis super iniqua agentes. . . ?* The negative here is not found in either the Hebrew or the Greek *(LXX)*; it is found in the Vulgate, though at least one codex omits it; cf. *Biblia Sacra*, app. crit. ad loc. **8** Hab 1.13–14. **9** providential design: Bede's word *dispensatio* combines the ideas of plan, benefaction, and balance implicit in his further comments. **10** that he would become incarnate: *ut ueniret in carnem*: lit. 'that he would come into the flesh'. **11** cf. + Lk 18.32 **12** Jn 8.26. **13** Jn 15.15.

who comes from heaven is above all; and he bears witness to what he has seen and heard.[14] [11]These tidings of the Lord, then, the prophet heard and he was afraid because he had been complaining of the afflictions of the upright in the world, [12]since departure | from the world in death was also the portion of the Lord himself who prospers our journey of salvation and life;[15] [13]he was afraid because he had voiced a complaint about the tribulations of the saints, who were not only to be rescued by the Lord from the tribulations of the saints, but were even to be crowned eternally with the Lord.

3

3.2 [1] **I contemplated your works and grew fearful.** [2]These, doubtless, are the works by which he redeemed the world, becoming obedient to the Father even to the point of accepting death, death on a cross;[16] [3]so that, as the same Apostle says again, *through death he might destroy him who had the power of death, i.e. the devil.*[17] [4]And clearly the more intently one reflects upon these works, the more one trembles over the actions of one's frailty.

---

14 Jn 3.31+32. **15** cf. Ps 67.21(68.20); cf. also *infra* §35.6–9; since departure from the world in death was also the portion of the Lord himself: *cum et ipsius domini,... exitus essent mortis de mundo.* Here Bede builds in a reference to *Vg* Ps 67.21(68.20): *Deus noster Deus saluos faciendi et Domini Domini exitus mortis:* 'Our God is a God who saves, and to the Lord, Yahweh, belongs escape (lit. 'escapes') from death'. But he quotes it in the 'accommodated sense', playing on two of the several meanings of *exitus,* and adapting the meaning of the genitive *Domini* to his context. Note that *exitus,* like its counterpart in the original Hebrew, is plural in form but singular in sense; cf. Davidson: 19, §17, Remark 2: 'In (Hebrew) poetry plural comes to be used for singular without difference of meaning.' e.g. Jn 1.13: *qui non ex sanguinibus... nati sunt* 'who are born not of blood....' Bede's adaptation also accounts for the uncomfortable use of *mortis* as a genitive of definition, which I translate 'in death'. Some scholars consider the whole phrase corrupt and the apparatus reflects the doubts of a number of the scribes. One suspects that Bede may have been influenced by Augustine's commentary on the text of the psalm where he writes: *'Prosperum iter faciet nobis Deus sanitatum nostrarum, Deus noster, Deus saluos faciendi.' Multum gratia commendatur. Quis enim saluus esset, nisi ipse sanaret? Sed ne occurreret cogitationi: Cur ergo morimur, si per eius gratiam salui facti sumus? continuo subiecit: 'Et Domini exitus mortis:' tanquam diceret: Quid indignaris humana conditio habere te exitum mortis? Et Domini tui exitus non alius quam mortis fuit. Potius ergo consolare quam indignare: nam 'Et Domini exitus mortis. Spe enim salui facti sumus: si autem quod non uidemus speramus, per patientiam expectamus.' Patienter e⟨r⟩go etiam ipsam mortem feramus, illius exemplo, qui licet nullo peccato esset debitor mortis, et Dominus esset, a quo nemo animam tolleret, sed ipse eam a semetipso poneret, etiam ipsius fuit exitus mortis.* Aug. *Enarr. in Ps.* 67, 21, *CCSL* 39, 890, 29, 2–15. I owe this reference to Fr MacGinty. **16** cf. Phil 2.8. **17** Heb 2.14.

4

3.2 ¹**Between two living beings you will become known.**[18] ²*Between two living beings* may be taken to mean 'between Moses and Elijah'; ³for it was there on the holy mountain[19] it became known to the three disciples that he was to die, when he told them what he was to suffer in Jerusalem. ⁴It was there it became known that he was to be raised up again and be immortal, when his countenance became bright like the sun and his garments shining white like snow. ⁵It was there it became known that he was the Son of God, when the voice of his Father from the heavens said to him: ⁶*This is my beloved Son, in whom I am well pleased; listen to him.*[20]

⁷It may also quite appropriately[21] be taken to mean 'between two thieves'[22] (in the sense that) by dying crucified between them[23] it became known that he was a man. ⁸From the darkening of the sun, the quaking of the earth and the rest of the miraculous happenings around the cross which the evangelist relates, it became known that he was God. ⁹From his own appeal to his Father for his executioners[24] it became known how merciful he was. ¹⁰It was by this example too that the prophet, who in the Spirit foresaw these events, was reminded not only to bear patiently | the   [384]

---

18 (a) Between two living beings: *in medio duorum animalium:* ἐν μέσῳ δύο ζῴων *LXX.* Like the Greek word ζῷον in its widest sense, the Latin word *animal* which renders it, means 'a living being' and is here so translated. It is sometimes taken in the narrower sense of 'animal', and accordingly some have translated the text as 'between two animals'; (b) you will become known: in the Vulgate for this portion of the verse Jerome has *in medio annorum notum facies:* 'in the midst of the years thou shalt make it known.' *(Douay).* However, in his *Habakkuk* commentary he discusses the Old Latin version which Bede uses here and which also features in the liturgy, both at Lauds and in the Good Friday readings. He says that, according to the simple interpretation and the common opinion, the verse refers to the crucifixion of Christ between two thieves — the explanation that Bede gives in our text. Jerome suggests that the verse may signify the saviour known in the primitive Church between the Jewish and Gentile peoples, or the Lord made known between the two testaments, or the Father proclaimed through the Son and Holy Spirit, just as he once spoke from the midst of the two golden cherubim on the Ark of the Covenant (Ex. 25.22), *Commentarium in Abacuc Prophetam CCSL* 76A, 620–21, 94–114. Bede, commenting on the tabernacle, discusses the meaning of the cherubim and suggests that 'the Lord speaks from the midst of the two cherubim because through the two testaments he instructs us in the true faith with one harmonious voice; or perhaps he speaks from the midst of the cherubim because God the Father deigned to manifest his will to the human race through his Only-begotten who appeared in the flesh between the two testaments. What Habakkuk said can also be taken in this sense: *In the midst of two living beings you will be known.'* *DTab* 1.5. A propos of the liturgical importance of Hab 2.3, Ó Carragáin argues that the verse and its exegesis lie behind panels on the Ruthwell and Bewcastle crosses in Northumbria (1986 and 1987), Irish and Pictish sculpture (1988) and the "Arrest of Christ" page in the Book of Kells (1994). **19** cf. Mt 17.1ff.; Mk 9.2–13; Lk 9.28–36; cf. *infra* §10.5. **20** Mt 17.5. **21** quite appropriately: *non inconuenienter:* lit. 'not inappropriately' **22** cf. Lk 23.39–45. **23** (in the sense that) by dying...: *inter quos crucifixus moriendo innotescebat, quia homo erat:* lit. 'by dying crucified between whom, it became known that he was a man.' In the use of relative pronouns, as in so many other respects, English lacks the flexibility of Latin. **24** cf. Lk 23.34.

pressure of his woes,[25] but also bestow the favour of his kindness upon those persecuting him.

5

3.2 [1] **When the years draw nigh you will become known; when the time comes you will be revealed.** [2]⟨This⟩ denotes the years and time of which the Apostle says: *when the fulness of time had come, God sent his son born of a woman, born under the law, that he might redeem those who were under the law.*[26] [3]That is, the prophet saw that these times and these years were still a long way off, and he greeted them from a distance when he said that when the years drew near and the time came, the Lord would be revealed and become known. [4]For in an earlier passage also he heard when the Lord said to him: *As yet the vision is a distant one but it will eventually appear and will not prove false.*[27] *If it makes some delay wait for it, because it will certainly come and will not be late.*[28]

[5]Hearing the tidings of him and pondering upon the events of his passion, he was in fear and very alarmed because he was deeply affected by the fleeting happiness of the wicked and the temporal affliction of the good. [6]But afterwards when he had done appropriate penance for his transgressions he was confident that he could obtain pardon for what he had done wrong.[29] [7]That is why he adds appropriately:

6

3.2 [1] **When my soul is deeply troubled, in your wrath you will remember mercy.** [2]*When my soul,* he says, *is deeply troubled,* shaken to its depths by the due grieving of satisfaction and repentance for fear of your anger and punishment, (which in my heedlessness I greatly fear I have incurred), [3]I believe I shall all the more speedily obtain the clemency

---

25 the pressure of his woes: or, less probably, 'the oppression of the wicked'. 26 Gal 4.4–5. 27 will not prove false: *non mentietur:* lit. 'will not lie'; cf. *infra* §37.1 Hab 3.17 where the same idiom is used of the olive-tree: *mentietur opus oliuae,* 'the labour of the olive-tree will prove false to its promise' lit. 'will lie' i.e. 'will disappoint', in other words, 'will fail'. 28 Hab 2.3. If it makes some delay wait for it, because it will certainly come: *si moram fecerit expecta illum, quia ueniens ueniet et non tardabit: illum* refers to the 'vision' *uisus* and has been translated accordingly as 'it'. However, in the *LXX* the pronoun corresponding to *illum* is likewise masculine αὐτόν, whereas if it referred to the word for 'vision' ὄρασις in the first sentence it should be feminine. Thus Brenton correctly translates it as 'him' and accordingly makes the subject of each of the verbs 'he'. The question here, of course, is, how did Bede understand the text or was he adapting the scripture text to his context and playing on two possible acceptations of *uisus,* i.e. as a participle 'the one seen' or as a noun, 'vision'? cf. the *JB* note on the passage: 'The vision has an energy of its own, since it is the expression of a divine word, moving to fulfilment; cf. Is 55:10–11. The Advent liturgy uses this verse to express expectation of the Messiah. See also Heb 10:37.' 29 pardon for what he had done wrong: *ueniam erratus:* lit. 'the pardon of his aberration'.

of the act of pardon I desire from you. *4*And here one must seriously meditate upon the wonderful swiftness of God's mercy. *5*He said he was so deeply troubled in spirit at the thought of the Lord's anger, and shortly afterwards added that he (the Lord) had turned from anger to mercy. *6*Similar to this is the saying of the psalmist: *I will confess against myself my transgressions to the Lord and you forgave the infidelity of my heart.*³⁰ *7*But indulgence of this kind there may be for the very smallest sins. *8*However, the graver our guilty actions are, | the greater and longer the [385] penance and tears and alms they call for. *9*Thus far the prophet has given a brief summary of the apprehension of mind he was stricken with on hearing of and soberly pondering the issue of the Lord's incarnation and passion. *10*He immediately goes on to describe at greater length what the tidings were, and what were the works of the Lord he was so deeply affected by when he focused on them. There follows ⟨the verse⟩:

7

3.3 *¹* **God will come from Lebanon and the holy one from the shady and thickly-wooded mountain.** *²*Lebanon is the highest mountain in Phoenicia, noted for its tall, incorruptible, aromatic trees, of which, moreover, the Lord's temple in Jerusalem was made, as scripture testifies.³¹ *³*Which is why it is customary in the scriptures occasionally to designate even the temple itself by the name Lebanon. *4*Hence the saying of Zechariah concerning the Chaldaean army which was about to come against him: *Open your gates, Lebanon, and let fire consume your cedars.*³²

22⇐ *5*The reason why God comes from Lebanon is that the Lord when he appeared in the flesh scattered the first seeds of the gospel in the temple itself and from there filled the whole world with the shoots of his faith and truth. *6*Which is why Isaiah says: *out of Zion shall go forth the law, and the word of the Lord from Jerusalem.*³³ *7*Now he scattered the first seeds of the faith there not only through the agency of the apostles who, filled with the Holy Spirit after his resurrection, laid the first foundation

32⇐ of the Church by preaching in the same place, *8*and whose *voice went out through all the earth, and their words to the end of the world,*³⁴ but even of his own accord he first bore witness in that temple to the faith that one must have in him, *9*when, sitting among the teachers at the age of twelve, he questioned them as a young man, but answered as the God of eternal majesty those who were teaching; *10*when after having been sought and found by his parents, | he actually said out of his own mouth, intimating [386] that he was God and the Son of God, *11 Why is it that you have been*

---

30 Ps 31(32).5. In case the reader is puzzled by the odd sequence of tenses in this quotation: 'I will confess... and you forgave', the verse as found in the psalm is phrased thus: 'I *said*, "I will confess...; " *then* you forgave....' **31** cf. 2 Chron 2.16; cf. + 3 Kings 5.6ff.; cf. + *DTemp* 2.4. **32** Zech 11.1. **33** Is 2.3. **34** Ps 18.5(19.4); Rom 10.18.

looking for me? Did you not know that I must be in my Father's house?[35]
*12*But it is to be noted that in the Hebrew scriptures this verse runs: *God* ⟨*is*⟩ *from Teman*,[36] i.e. will come from the south. *13*Taken literally this is readily understandable because Bethlehem where the Lord was born is situated to the south of Jerusalem.[37] *14*And when on the fortieth day after his birth he was brought by his parents to Jerusalem in order that a victim might be offered on his account according to the law,[38] God did indeed come from the south. *15And the holy one*, he says, ⟨*comes*⟩ *from a shady, thickly-wooded mountain.* *16*This is the same holy mediator between God and men,[39] who above is plainly called God; of him Gabriel when announcing the good news to the virgin mother said: *17Therefore the holy child which is to be born will be called the Son of God.*[40] *18*On the other hand, the mountain from which it is foretold this holy one is to come can be taken to mean the kingdom of the Jews, from which he took human origin. *19*From it too Daniel saw the stone hewn without ⟨the use of human⟩ hands,[41] i.e. Christ procreated without male intervention, who crushed the kingdoms of the world, and filled the whole universe with the glory of his name.*20*Manifestly this mountain is called shady and densely-wooded with good reason, for it has many fruit-bearing trees, *21*i.e. many people who are holy and loaded down with the fruits of virtues, and who both satisfy our hunger with the very delicious flavour of their teaching, *22*and by the protection of their intercession afford shade to our frailty lest it become baked dry of the inner fresh growth of love by the heat of tribulation. *23*And with this figure what the apostle Peter ⟨did⟩[42] agrees; *24*that is to say, this mountain's towering tree not only gives refreshment to those hungering and thirsting for holiness,[43] but also heals the ailing by the shadow of his body. *25*And clearly these holy and lofty-minded people can also be denoted by the term 'south' from which God was said to come, *26*in view, that is, of the love with which they are habitually aflame in the Lord and the teaching by which they act as a shining light[44]

---

35 Lk 2.49; in my Father's house: the phrase used in both the Greek and the (Vulgate) Latin is 'in the things which are my Father's', which is sometimes translated: 'about my Father's business'. **36** Hab 3.3. **37** cf. Jer., *In Abacuc* (*CCSL* 76A, 623, 195–98). **38** that a victim might be offered... according to the law: *ut daretur hostia secundum legem pro eo*. The problem here concerns the phrase, *pro eo*. The translation, 'in exchange for him'/'as a redemption price for him', would fit perfectly in the light of Exodus 13.2,12: 'The Lord said to Moses, "Consecrate to me all the first-born; whatever is the first to open the womb among the people of Israel, both of man and beast, is mine.... Every first-born of man among your sons you shall redeem"'. The *hostia*, then, would be the redemption price which according to Numbers 18.15 was five shekels of silver. But Bede is manifestly referring to the gospel of Luke 2.22–24. There, however, the *hostia* in question was 'a pair of turtle-doves or two young pigeons' which, as we know from Leviticus, was not the redemption price but Mary's purification offering. In view of the ambiguity of the original, I have chosen to translate *pro eo* as 'on his account', leaving it open to the reader to interpret the sentence as seems fit; cf. Bede *In Lucam* I (*CCSL* 120, 61, 1664–1673; 63, 1731–1742) **39** cf. 1 Tim 2.5. **40** Lk 1.35. **41** cf. Dan 2.34. **42** cf. Acts 5.15. **43** cf. + Mt 5.6. **44** cf. + Mt 5.16.

to people. [27]It is, of course, from this | 'south' that God came because he [387]
condescended to become incarnate through these people. [28]It is from this 'south' that God comes every day when, as we read or heed their words or examples, the love or knowledge of the truth is more perfectly engendered in our heart. There follows ⟨the verse⟩:

8

3.3 [1] **His majesty has covered the heavens and the earth is full of his praise.** [2]After outlining the providential design of the Lord's incarnation, he then went on to speak of[45] the mystery of the ascension in accordance with the saying of the psalmist: [3]*Its rising is from the end of the heavens, and its circuit to the end of them*;[46] [4]for his majesty covered the heavens because he, who through his incarnation was made a little lower than the angels, was crowned with glory and honour[47] through his resurrection, [5]and all things were placed beneath his feet,[48] and at the preaching of the apostles the whole earth was filled with his praise. [6]This very fact is briefly but quite explicitly summed up at both the beginning and the end of the same psalm, when it is said: [7]*O Lord, our Lord, how majestic is your name in all the earth, for your greatness is exalted above the heavens*[49] [8]But even before his passion and resurrection, when the word made flesh was dwelling amongst us,[50] his majesty covered the heavens, because even the humanity he had assumed, mortal as it was, still excelled the heavenly powers. [9]*And the earth is full of his praise*, as these same powers of heaven truly knew, because he who, by virtue of his humanity, was then dwelling on earth, was the creator of the earth, as also of the entire creation, by virtue of his divinity. [10]Which is why even at his birth they sang in chorus: *Glory to God in the highest and on earth peace to people of good will.*[51]

9

3.4 [1] **His brightness will be like the light.** [2]The brightness of the Lord our saviour's miracles and teaching will enlighten believers. [3]Which is also why he is called 'the sun of justice'[52] in the scriptures; [4]but because
| this same brightness could not shine perfectly on the world until[53] he [388]
demolished death's dominion by temporarily tasting death, [5]and by rising

---

45 went on to speak of: ***subiunxit:*** lit. 'added'. **46** Ps 18.7(19.6). **47** cf. Heb 2.7–9. **48** cf. Ps 8.8(6); Heb 2.8 **49** Ps 8.2,10(1,9). **50** cf. Jn 1.14. **51** Lk 2.14. **52** cf. Mal 4.2. In keeping with his admiration for Jewish faithfulness under the law and his use of light/darkness and sight/blindness imagery to represent good and evil or knowledge and ignorance, Bede, commenting on the temple, refers to 'the Jews who in ancient times used to make use of the ***sun of justice*** on account of the teaching of the law', in contrast with 'us ⟨Gentiles⟩ who for a long time clung blind-heartedly to the slavery ⟨of Satan⟩.' *DTemp* 20.14. **53** until: ***nisi:*** lit. 'unless', 'except'.

from the dead had bestowed on the world the gift of the hope and faith of the resurrection, it is rightly added ⟨that⟩

10

3.4 [1] **Horns are in his hands and there the strength of his glory is confirmed,**[54] [2]for he designates as horns the crossbeam of the cross which, while fastened to it, he held with his hands, [3]so that, conquering all death by this kind of death, he might confirm the power of his glory in the hearts of the elect, in case they should be held back from his love by any terrors or enticements; [4]and also there was promised to them the glory of future immortality through which *the last enemy, death, will be destroyed.*[55] [5]Finally on the holy mountain,[56] in the presence of Peter, James and John, his brightness shone like the light; [6]and they were, it is true, enchanted with a glimpse of this brightness, yet how frail and weak they still were was proved at the time of his passion; [7]but it was after he had taken the horns of the cross in his hands that the power of his glory was confirmed, [8]so much so that it could not be driven from the hearts of the faithful either by terrors or scourging or even death itself.[57] [9]In the horns may be suggested, after the manner of the prophets, the kingdoms of this world. [10]The lofty powers of the human mind, whether for good or evil, may be denoted by the term horns. [11]And the horns are in Christ's hands because he is king of kings and Lord of lords.[58] [12]The horns are in his hands so that, as he humbles one person and raises up another, *he may smash all the horns of sinners* by which they are vainly raised to prominence, [13]and that *the horns of the upright may be exalted,*[59] i.e. their desires centred on God whereby they strive to surmount every obstacle in their struggle with wickedness and vice.

---

54 Bede further discusses the mystical significance of horns in his commentary on the tabernacle, when he considers the horns projecting from the altar of incense (Ex 30.2–3). He again says that horns can have both a good and a bad significance, indicating 'the eminence of faith and of the virtues with which we ought to strike out against and overcome the hostile advances of our ancient enemy,' but also 'the armies of the vices that endeavour to fight against us.' (*DTab* 3.11). Bede goes on to connect horns, in the good sense, with scripture's clean animals which are horned and represent good people, 'so that it is mystically disclosed that the only people who can be incorporated into a spiritual union with the Church of God are those who by the strength of their faith prove that they are unconquered in their battle with the vices.' These are the good people/clean animals to whom Bede refers at §37.12, (Old Testament Jewish oxen bearing the yoke of the law), and at T23.3 (Gentile cattle bearing the light yoke of the gospel). On clean animals see *Intro.*, 9–10. **55** +1 Cor 15.26; (direct quotation). **56** cf. Mt 17.1ff; Mk 9.2–13; Lk 9.28–36; cf. *supra* §4.3. **57** cf. Jer., *In Abacuc* (*CCSL* 76A, 625–26, 277–304). **58** cf. Deut 10.17. **59** Ps 74.11(75.10).

11

3.4 *¹* **And he produced a steadfast love of his fortitude.** ²Even before his passion the saints did indeed love Christ's fortitude with a most intimate love; ³but even this love was not steadfast until, | after his passion [389] and resurrection had been accomplished, he gave them more fully the grace of the Holy Spirit. ⁴But then it became so firm that it could not be broken even by the power of the horns of kings, i.e. of the arrogant.

12

3.5 *¹* **His word will go before him and will go out⁶⁰ into the fields.** ²Before the Lord came in the flesh the words of the prophets went before him to bear witness to him who was to come; ³and these same words went out into the fields when by the preaching of the apostles they were proclaimed throughout the whole world. ⁴On the other hand, it was not merely in the writings of the prophets that the Lord preceded the word of preaching, but also in the apostles when they announced to the world that the good news of the coming of Christ had already been realized; ⁵the word had gone before him because, of course, the true doctrine had first reached the ears of those who were to be taught, ⁶and then faith and the understanding of the word enlightens hearts and renders them worthy to have God dwell within them.⁶¹ ⁷And this is indicated typologically in the gospel when the Lord himself sent his disciples to preach *in every town and place he himself was to come to.*⁶² ⁸And this we observe happening to this day in the same order, for the Lord follows his preachers, because it is first necessary that the word of the teacher be heard, and that the light of truth be thus firmly fixed in the heart of the hearer. Hence it is aptly added:

13

3.6 *¹* **His feet stood and the earth moved.** ²For when at the teacher's preaching the footprints of the truth are firmly fixed in the hearer's mind, the mind itself is later agitated in the course of its reflection and deeply

---

60 will go out: here our Latin text has the aorist (or simple past) form *exiuit*. In my opinion the form should be *exibit* and I have translated accordingly. Phonetically the letters *b* and (consonantal) *u (v)* were commonly confused in Latin, as indeed they still are in some Romance languages, notably Spanish. Hence their frequent confusion by scribes. The future form *exibit* is what one would expect at this point since (a) the sense requires it and (b) the *LXX*, on which the Latin version of Habakkuk used by Bede is based, here has the future form: πορεύσεται. Besides, even though the Vulgate version differs here, the future tense is used in both members of the corresponding parallelistic verse: *ante faciem eius ibit mors/et egredietur diabolus ante pedes eius.* **61** cf. + Rom 8.11; renders them worthy to have God dwell within them: *deo inhabitatore dignos efficit:* lit. 'renders them worthy of God as an indweller'. **62** Lk 10.1 (+direct quotation).

affected. *3*On the other hand, the Lord's feet may quite fittingly be taken to mean the actual teachers through whom the word is ministered, *4*since he who is of his own accord present everywhere is carried to the whole world by them as if by his own feet.[63] *5*Now these feet stand and the earth moves, because the more resolutely the holy teachers persist in preaching and safeguarding the truth, the sooner the hearts of the earthly-minded are jolted[64] into doing | penance for their deviations; *6*and since this same act of repentance is not by any means to be credited to the human preacher but to the grace which enlightens, it is properly added:

14

3.6 *1* **He gave a look and the nations melted,** which is to state openly: 'The Lord took pity and the nations repented.' *2*And this, of course, was the look he gave Peter too when he had denied him; *3*and moved to compunction at the memory of his sin, the latter soon afterwards dissolved in tears.

15

3.6 *1***The mountains were violently shattered.** *2*He gives the name mountains to the proud and those giving themselves airs because of the power, wisdom or wealth of this world.[65] *3*These, when the Lord turned his gaze on them, were not just shattered but violently shattered;[66] *4*whereas when he showed compassion, some of these people not only renounced their vain and proud haughtiness but even impugned it by their lifestyle as well as by their preaching. *5*Finally Saul and Matthew were mountains, the former raised up from the wisdom of the human word, the latter from the mammon of iniquity; *6*but when each of them had been converted to the tutorship of humility, and became a disciple of Christ, the mountains were indeed violently shattered.[67]

---

63 cf. *infra* §14.12. **64** are jolted: *se... incutiunt:* 'jolt themselves'; lit. 'shake themselves; cause themselves to tremble'. Note the use of the reflexive, which came to replace the passive in later Latin, as it largely does in Romance. **65** Commenting on the temple, Bede writes that 'all of us human beings were born on the mountain of pride because we take our carnal origin from the first human being's prevarication which pride was the cause of; but those of us *preordained to life* (Acts 13.48) by God's grace, who were hewn by being catechized and by receiving the mysteries of the faith, were transferred from the mountain of pride to the mountain of the house of the Lord (cf. Is 2.2), and, rescued from the power of darkness (cf. Col 1.13), we reached the citadel of the virtues, which is in the unity of the holy Church.' *D Temp* 3.3; cf. also *D Temp* 2.3: 'Hiram sent Solomon cedar and pine-wood hewn in Lebanon to put in the house of the Lord because the converted Gentiles sent to the Lord men once famous in the eyes of the world but now cast down and humbled from the mountain of their pride by the axe of the Lord's reproof.' **66** cf. Mt 26.69–75; Mk 14.66–72; Lk 22.55–62. **67** cf. Mt 9.9; Acts 9.3,22.

16

3.6 *¹* **The eternal hills vanished.** *²*Proud people are designated by the term 'hills' as well as 'mountains', except perhaps that they are puffed up with a lesser degree of arrogance, yet without being innocent of the charge of vanity, and consequently ⟨are⟩ of sufficiently sound disposition to deserve to be raised up by the Lord. *³*And they are rightly called 'eternal hills' because when, after being temporally humbled, they climb down from their haughty eminence of pride, they are glorified eternally and raised up by him who says: *⁴And everyone who humbles himself will be exalted.*⁶⁸ *⁵*Another translation of 'the eternal hills' puts it more simply as *the hills of the world* which is used in contradistinction to 'the hills of the Lord', *⁶*i.e. holy men, who, by spurning all that is temporal and basest through loftiness of spirit, are worthy of such a name; *⁷*and it is of them that the psalmist says to the Lord: | *Let the mountains receive peace for the* [391] *people, and the hills uprightness.* ⁶⁹

17

3.6–7 *¹* **I saw the journeys of his eternity compared with his labours.**⁷⁰ *²*The journeys are those of the Lord's temporal existence whereby he came into the world that he might appear for a time to men. *³*They are, on the other hand, the journeys of his eternity whereby, after his bodily departure from the world, he returned to the Father with whom he dwelt eternally, even while he was temporally spending his life in the world. *⁴*These journeys, of course, he himself desired when, as he was approaching his passion, he said to his Father: *⁵I have glorified you on earth, I have accomplished the work which you gave me to do.*⁷¹ *⁶*This referred to the journeys of the temporal existence he had assumed, and he immediately added with reference to his eternal journeys: *⁷And now Father, do you glorify me in your own presence with the glory which I had in your presence before the world existed.*⁷² *⁸*These journeys of eternity, on the other hand, the prophet saw compared with his (the Lord's) labours, i.e. those of his incarnation and passion, of which it has been said earlier: *⁹God will come from Lebanon,* or from the south, and *there are horns in his hands,*⁷³ and other words of this kind, which are found in abundance in this same canticle. *¹⁰*Of these labours the Apostle says: *He humbled himself having become obedient unto death, even death on a cross;*⁷⁴ *¹¹*and he directly added concerning the journeys of his eternity and those things which he the mediator between God and men⁷⁵ merited: *¹²Therefore, God also has exalted him and bestowed on him a name which is above every*

---

68 Lk 14.11.   **69** Ps 71(72).3.   **70** compared with his labours: *prae laboribus.* **71** Jn 17.4.   **72** Jn 17.5.   **73** Hab 3.3–4.   **74** Phil 2.8.   **75** cf. 1 Tim 2.5.

name, that in the name of Jesus every knee should bow, in heaven and on earth and under the earth, and every tongue confess that Jesus Christ is Lord, to the glory of God the Father.[76] [13]And (it was) through these same labours of his and through these same journeys of his eternity, when he returned to the Father after completing the labours of his passion, that not only the Jewish but the Gentile people too were to attain eternal rest. [14]For this reason it is fittingly added:[77]

18

3.7 [1]The tents of Ethiopia will be terror-stricken, and the tents of the land of Midian. [2]For as everyone knows,[78] the Ethiopians and
33⇐ Midianites are Gentile peoples. [3]By their names are intimated all the nations of the Gentiles, which, on hearing the gospel preaching, were stricken with a wholesome fear. [4]Just as the prophet, when he heard and feared the still future tidings of the Lord, meditated upon the future works of his incarnation and was stricken with fear, [5]so the nations, when the same tidings were proclaimed to them through the ministry of the apostles, and when these same works had already been accomplished, [6]began to serve the Lord in fear and rejoice with trembling be-
34⇐ fore him.[79] [7]And he does well to mention first the Ethiopians who are at the ends of the earth, so as to intimate in mystical terms that the voice of preachers would go forth over the entire world and their words to the ends of the earth.[80] [8]In this mystery too the minister of Candace queen of the Ethiopians, the first-fruits of the Gentiles, (as we read in the Acts of the Apostles,[81] when Philip preached the gospel), received the faith and the mysteries of Christ.[82] [9]The Midianite people, on the other hand, took its origin by Keturah from one of Abraham's sons who was called Midian[83] and (its territory) is in the desert of the Saracens to the east of the Red Sea in Arabia.[84] [10]Let the Ethiopians, then, be

---

76 Phil 2.9–11. **77** In the Latin the last two sentences form one long sentence which, literally translated, would have read: 'and because through these same labours...it is fittingly added.' **78** For as everyone knows...Gentile peoples: *Aethiopes namque et Madianitas gentium esse populos quis nesciat?* lit. 'For who does not know that the Ethiopians and Midianites are peoples of the Gentiles?' **79** cf. Ps 2.11. **80** cf. Ps 18.5(19.4); Rom 10.18. **81** cf. Acts 8.27. **82** On this Ethiopian's conversion see Bede's *Comm. on Acts* 8.27a–8.27c. See also Henderson 1980, 9–12. **83** cf. Gen 25.1–2. **84** All peoples are descended from Abraham by faith (Gal 3.29), but here Bede reminds us that the Midianites are also his physical children by his wife Keturah. Bede shares the belief that the Saracens among whom they live are physically descended from Abraham too. They are the children of Ishmael, Abraham's son by Hagar, the servant of his wife Sarah (Gen 16.15). Sarah herself, as Bede says, 'bore Isaac the son of the promise, i.e. all the free people of the Church (*DTob* 16.11; cf. Gal 4.22–31). The location of the Midianites among the Saracens, and their blood connection with them dramatizes the effect of their conversion to a wholesome fear of God, for Bede regards the Saracens as a fierce race, like Ishmael himself, whose hand was against every man and all men's hands against him (Gen 16.12). In his exegesis Bede depicts the Saracens as violent and anti-Christian, and in the *HE* describes them as a 'terrible plague' (*HE* 5.23). See Plummer, 1896, ii , 339.

awestruck at the name of Christ, so that faith in him[85] which is to
reach the ends of the earth may be sealed. *11*Let the Midianites also
be awestruck at the intimation that the Mediterranean peoples too are
to be saved through this ⟨faith⟩. *12*On the other hand, the fact that he
does not say, 'the Ethiopians and Midianites will be terror-stricken', but
says, *13the tents of the Ethiopians will be terror-stricken and the tents
of the land of Midian,* is to be understood according to the manner of
speaking employed, when in the gospel it was said: *14And the whole town
went out to meet Jesus;* [86] and in the psalm: *15and your inebriating
cup,*[87] whereas it was not the actual town but those who were in the
town that went out; *16*nor is it the actual cup but what is in the cup
that usually inebriates. *17*And this figure|of speech is called in Greek
metonymia, i.e. transference, ⟨as⟩ when by the container the contents are
indicated.[88]

[393]

19

**3.8 *1*Was your wrath against the rivers, Lord, or was your fury
against the rivers or your indignation against the sea?** [89] *2*The term
'rivers' and 'sea' represents the hearts of unbelievers, which are rightly
called rivers because by the whole force of their tendency they flow down
towards lower ⟨levels⟩; *3*⟨they are called⟩ the sea because they are inwardly
darkened by disordered and bitter thoughts and exalt themselves above
the rest by the swollen waters of boasting.[90] *4*Have these people then, he
says, who, from heavenly desires, immerse their minds in the craving for
the basest things, and who, inconstant as they are through their disdainful
arrogance of attitude, set themselves up against their neighbours, *5*have
they sinned so gravely that the wrath they deserve endures against them
never to be assuaged? *6*Or will you, when you appear in the world, bestow
the favour of your mercy on all those throughout the world who sin either
venially or seriously? *7*For I do indeed observe that you are going to
send your apostles to preach your glory to the nations; *8*but who the

---

85 faith in him: *fides eius*: lit. 'his faith'; the genitive *eius* is here used in the
objective not the subjective sense. **86** Mt 8.34. **87** Ps 22(23).5. **88** Bede discusses
metonymia at greater length in his rhetorical textbook, *De Schematibus et Tropis* (*On
Figures and Tropes*). 'Metonymy is a kind of substitution of names. There are many
types of this trope. For example when the name of a container is used to designate
its contents (Gen 24.20): "Pouring out the pitcher into the troughs" *(Douay).* Or
Lk 16.7: *Take thy letter* (Tannenhaus tr.). The pitcher is not poured, but rather that
which it contains; and it is not the letter which is taken, but the paper upon which
it is written. Again (1 Sam 6.8): "And send it away, that it may go." Not the ark
but only the cart in which the ark is contained, and the cattle which were leading the
cart were able to move. Metonymy often reveals the effect of an action through its
cause and, conversely, the cause of an action through its effect' (Tannenhaus tr. 1973,
109). **89** or was your fury against the rivers: this puzzling repetition is explained by
a dittography in the Hebrew text, where the phrase 'against the rivers' is repeated;
cf. *NJB* which omits it in the translation **90** Bede frequently uses the restless sea
as an image of evil. See Intro., 18.

believers are to be is for you, not human beings, to know. For this is what follows:

20

3.8 [1] **Since you will surely mount your horses, and your riding ⟨thereon⟩ is salvation.** [91] [2]That is, through the enlightenment of your grace, you will mount the hearts of your elect, through whom, under your guidance, ⟨people⟩ may walk the path of the virtues, [3]and proclaim you throughout the whole world, bringing the life of eternal salvation to the world by preaching the gospel. [4]And the figure of his 'riding' was illustrated even literally in the Lord, when, on his way to Jerusalem he was seated on a donkey, while the crowds which preceded and followed him and came to meet him sang together:[5]*Hosanna, blessed is he who comes in the name of the Lord.*[92] | [6]In this riding there were echoes of salvation[93] because, of course, what was meant was the spiritual journey of those who under the Lord's leadership are brought by the apostles to see the realms of the Jerusalem that is above, which is the mother of us all.[94]

[394]

21

3.9 [1]**You will surely bend your bow at sceptres, says the Lord.**[95] [2]He calls the coming of the divine visitation an unexpected bow and he foresaw that by it even sceptres, i.e. the kingdoms of the world, were to be put to the test. [3]Therefore hinting at what the Lord, by mounting his horses, i.e. his apostles and their successors, does among them, filling and guiding them with his grace, the prophet says: [4]*you will surely bend your bow at sceptres,* i.e. through ⟨your⟩ teachers you will surely threaten that your judgement is suddenly to come, [5]so that whoever is frightened at the threat of wrath as at a bent bow, and takes care to crave your mercy, may not experience the shooting of arrows, i.e. the threat of everlasting punishments. [6]On the other hand, when after first stating, *you will surely bend your bow at sceptres,* he added: 'says the Lord', he means God the Father, of whom the Son himself says: [7]*the Father does not judge anyone, but has given all judgement to the Son.*[96]

---

91 your riding ⟨thereon⟩ is salvation: *equitatus tuus sanitas* lit. 'your riding is health'. The word *equitatus* in classical Latin very frequently means 'cavalry'. Note that the Vulgate here has *quadrigae,* lit. 'four-horse teams', then 'chariots (drawn by four horse teams)', then simply 'chariots', which is how the *Douay* translates it, as indeed does Brenton in his version of the *LXX,* although that text reads: ἡ ἱππασία σου σωτηρία of which the Bede's *VL* text, *equitatus tuus sanitas,* is a literal rendering. 92 Jn 12.13. 93 there were echoes of salvation: *sanitas resonabat:* lit. 'healing resounded'. 94 cf. Gal 4.26. 95 Here Bede's text is much closer to that of the *LXX* which reads: Ἐντείνων ἐνέτεινας τόξον σου ἐπὶ σκῆπτρα. The only difference is that the Greek uses the past tense of the verb instead of the future. 96 Jn 5.22.

79

22

3.9 [1] **The earth shall be cleft by rivers.** [2]The rivers in this context are not the ones concerning which in an earlier passage[97] he feared the Lord's anger and wrath; rather he means those of which he himself says in the gospel: [3]*The one who believes in me, as the scripture says, out of his belly shall flow rivers of living water.*[98] And the evangelist commenting says:[4]*Now this he said about the Spirit which those who believed in him were to receive.*[99] [5]So the earth is cleft by these rivers when the hearts of the earthly-minded, watered by the words of saving doctrine, wear down, by humbling themselves, the hardness of their unbelief, [6]and open up the bay of inward reflection which had been ruinously closed, to |welcome the words of healing reproof or exhortation. [7]This is explained at greater length immediately after when it is said:

[395]

3.10 [1] **The waters will see you and the peoples will be in pain.** [2]For when the hearts of sinners are torn to the point of acknowledgement and confession of the truth by the frequent addresses of teachers, as by the washing of frequent waters, [3]they see the Lord in the meantime through faith, and grieve at having withdrawn from him through sin; [4]but when the grief of repentance is over they see him more fully in the life to come in clear view and rejoice in his blessed vision forever. [5]The saying, *the earth shall be cleft by rivers*[100] can also be understood as meaning that the earth was to be cleft in order that rivers should spring from it afresh,[6]which ancient tales recount as having often happened, so that, for instance, when there was an earthquake, rivers which did not exist appeared. [7]That this can happen no one doubts who intelligently observes that the earth is full of innumerable veins of water just as the human body is full of veins of blood. [8]Viewed in this way the earth is split up by rivers when, after the earthly-minded conscience is torn to repentance, [9]it immediately makes such progress by the gift of God's grace that it can even of itself produce streams of doctrine for others, [10]and water their parched hearts either by its example or its word so as to bring forth the fruits of virtues.

---

97 cf. Hab 3.8 *supra* §19.1.   98 Jn 7.38.   99 Jn 7.39.   100 Hab 3.9.

3.10 [1] **Sprinkling waters on its ways, the deep gave forth its voice from the full extent of its envisioning.**[101] [2]The same teachers are symbolized by the term 'the deep' as by that of 'rivers' above; [3]but they are rivers by reason of the force of the stronger invective by which they break down the hardness of the worldly spirit so as to do penance for its transgressions. [4]But they are rightly called 'the deep' on account of the depth of knowledge with which they themselves are inwardly filled, [5]as Solomon attests who says: *words from a man's mouth are deep water.*[102]

20⇐ [6]Sprinkling waters on its ways, then, the deep gives forth | its voice when [396] holy preachers, [7]inwardly filled in their heart with a deep knowledge of the truth, outwardly exercise the ministry of the word for their hearers, [8]revealing gradually and partially, according to the capacity of the weak, the insights, both many and rich, that they themselves inwardly possess. [9]'On its ways', on the other hand, means in their works, i.e. those of the teachers themselves or of their audience. [10]For they sprinkle waters on their ways when, wherever they go, as well as preaching orally, they show examples of upright living to those whose eyes are always upon them.

---

101 from the full extent of its envisioning: *ab altitudine fantasiae suae.* (a) As his application of this text at 24.15–18 indicates, Bede takes these words in senses familiar to his readers from biblical Latin (cf. *L&S s.vv.*). He used his texts critically (cf. 37.29) and certainly knew that his interpretation was not always consistent with the literal sense, whether (as here) of the *LXX* behind his own text: ἔδωκεν ἡ ἄβυσσος ... ὕψος φαντασίας αὐτῆς 'the deep raised the height of its form' (cf. Brenton: 'raised its form on high'), or of the Vulgate reading: ('*altitudo manus suas leuauit*' 'the deep raised its hands', a literal translation of the Hebrew text). But Bede's datum is the language-understanding of his educated readers, and his criterion is the value of the sense for instruction. Fr Hurst suggests: 'from the depth of its being'. Whereas the Greek ὕψος means 'height', the corresponding Latin word, *altitudo*, also has the meaning 'depth' as well as several others, notably 'extent' (cf. Rom 11.33); (b) in the *LXX* all examples of φαντασία (transliterated here as *fantasia*) show it to mean 'a form, image, apparition, appearance'. Thus Wis 18.17 'Then at once apparitions in dreadful dreams greatly troubled them'. At Hab 2.18 it is used with reference to an idol which the writer calls φαντασίαν ψευδῆ. At Hab 3.10 the *LXX* translator would seem to be making a rhetorical point, viz., since idols (images, false appearances) show what is not there, those who worship the false appearances of man's handiwork are envisaged as being punished by being shown the true appearance of God as manifested in a series of natural disasters, e.g. the deep rises up from unseen depths to its true height, 'the height of its form'. φαντασία derives from the same root as the verb φαίνω 'I show'. What may interest those preoccupied with the level of Bede's knowledge of Greek or even Hebrew is the question as to what Hebrew word underlies φαντασία here in the *LXX*. Owing to the similarity in sound, the Hebrew word for 'appearance, form', תֹּאַר, תֹּאר is sometimes confused with the word תּוֹר which means 'mode, manner'. This word (cf. its feminine תּוֹרָה [Tōrāh] 'instruction, direction, precept, law,' the 'Torah') comes from the root יָרָה which among other things means 'show' and then 'teach' — to the ancient Hebrews a teacher was a 'show-er'. Now, for what the observation is worth, in Bede's commentary here he is stressing the 'showing' or revelatory role of teachers. However, even granting his fondness for paronomasia, the likelihood of this linkage is extremely remote, and, unless one had evidence that he constantly referred to the Greek, one could hardly avoid the apparent sense of the Latin, perhaps with as much feeling of 'extent' as 'depth' in the rendering of *altitudo*. **102** Prov 18.4.

*11*They sprinkle waters on the ways of the spectators too when they show them in advance, both by precept and lifestyle, what pathways of conduct they follow. *12*If, on the other hand, one follows the reading which some codices have: *13You will scatter waters on the ways,* it is obvious that God is being told that he himself will dispense waters from the springs of Israel far and wide among the nations of the whole world, when he says to his disciples: *14Go and teach all the nations, baptizing them in the name of the Father and of the Son and of the Holy Spirit.*[103] *15*On the other hand, when he said that the deep gave forth its voice, he did well to add: *from the full extent of its envisioning,* *16*because the wonderful thing the holy preachers proclaim to us outwardly proceeds, of course, from that fount of wisdom whereby they themselves are inwardly more wonderfully enlightened by the contemplation of heavenly joys. *17*Did not the great deep give forth its voice from the full extent of its envisioning when the apostle Paul said: *18Our mouth is open to you, Corinthians; our heart is wide. You are not restricted by us; you are restricted rather in your own affections. I speak as to children: Widen your hearts also?*[104] *19*Now where he was to come from or in what sequence, that the world might be sprinkled with waters and the abyss of heavenly wisdom thunder upon the lands, is shown immediately after when it is said:

22⇐

25

3.11 *1* The sun rose and the moon took its place in due sequence.[105] *2*For the Lord, i.e. the sun of justice,[106] after his passion and resurrection, rose into heaven, and when the Spirit was sent by the Father, he enlightened the Church and spread it throughout the whole world so that in due sequence, *3*i.e. after the mystery of the Lord's incarnation was accomplished, it might rise from the illness of its unbelief and be steadfast in the faith, act manfully and be strengthened[107] in his love. *4*And because he had compared Christ to the sun and the Church to the moon, he fittingly turned to this same sun and directly added:

[397]

---

103 Mt 28.19.   104 2 Cor 6.11–13.   105 Compare Abbot Ceolfrith of Wearmouth-Jarrow's letter to King Nechtan of the Picts on the spiritual significance of the correct calculation of the date of Easter. Citing Hab 3.11 in its Old Latin form, as Bede does here, Ceolfrith writes: 'The sun of righteousness with healing in his wings (Mal 2.4), that is, the Lord Jesus, overcame all the darkness of death by the triumph of his resurrection. So, ascending into heaven, he made his Church, which is often typified as the moon, full of the light of inward grace, by sending his Spirit down upon her. This plan of our salvation is what the prophet had in mind when he said, *The sun was exalted and the moon stood in her order.*' HE 5.21; cf. Plummer 1896, ii, 334. 106 cf. Mal 4.2.   107 cf. + Deut. 31.6; +Josh 1.18; +1 Chron 22.13;+Jud 15.11 (*Vg*); +Ps 26(27).14; +30.25(31.24); +1 Mac 2.64; +1 Cor 16.13.

3.11 ¹ **In the light your darts will go, because of the brilliance of the flash of your arms.** ²Now Christ's darts are his words by which the hearts of men are pierced so that, when the saving wound is inflicted, the faithful soul can say: *I have been wounded by love.*[108] ³That is to say, these darts go in the light, because by the ministry of teachers the words of truth became publicly known to the world, according to what Truth itself commanded them, saying: ⁴*What I say to you in the dark, tell in the light; and what you hear in private preach upon the rooftops.*[109] ⁵And since the glory of miracles too followed the words of light, ⟨he adds⟩ *because of the brilliance of the flash of your arms.*[110] ⁶For fighters in battle shoot their enemies with darts ⟨and⟩ protect themselves from wounding by arming themselves with weapons; ⁷for which reason darts properly suggest the words of preachers by which they overcome the perversity of unbelievers, and arms[111] the miracles by which they authenticate the truth of their preaching.[112] ⁸Christ's darts go in the light, they go because of the brilliance of his arms, ⁹for this reason that the great deeds he did, the mysteries he revealed, the precepts he laid down, the rewards he promised, ¹⁰have already, through the writings of the gospel, become known to the entire world more clearly than the sun. ¹¹But, of course, holy teachers too, because they are children of light,[113] and the things they do or say by virtue of his gift, shine brightly by their light and brilliance.

27

3.12 ¹ **You will bring low the land with your threatening, and in your rage you will pull down the nations.**[114] ²By threatening the severity of judgement with which the wicked are sentenced you will wholesomely humble those who are in the habit of preferring earthly to heavenly things, ³that by gradually retrenching their earthly appetites they may begin to have a taste for and seek the things that are above;[115] ⁴and, by venting your anger upon them, you will condemn eternally those

[398]

---

108 Song 5.8.   **109** Mt 10.27; what you hear in private: *quod in aure auditis:* lit. 'what you hear in the ear', an idiomatic expression directly translated into Latin from the Greek; cf. English 'to have a word in someone's ear'.   **110** And since...the flash of your arms: *Et quoniam eloquia lucis secuta est etiam claritas miraculorum, in splendore fulgoris armorum tuorum.* As it stands this sentence is incomplete. Something like 'he adds' is required before the text, *because of the brilliance of the flash of your arms.*   **111** darts properly suggest...and arms: *in iaculis merito...in armis...insinuantur:* lit. 'by darts are properly suggested...and by arms ....'   **112** Compare the conversion of King Aethelberht of Kent by Augustine: 'At last, the king, as well as others, believed and was baptized, being attracted by the pure life of the saints and by their most precious promises, whose truth they confirmed by performing many miracles.' (*HE* 1.26).   **113** cf. + Lk 16.8.   **114** pull down: *detrahes:* the Greek here has κατάξεις 'break down'; cf. *LXX:* Ἐν ἀπείλῃ ὀλιγώσεις γῆν, καὶ ἐν θυμῷ κατάξεις ἔθνη.... **115** cf. Col 3.1–2.

who thought it beneath them to be brought low for the moment for the sake of being raised on high for ever; *5*and it is to avert this happening to them that the psalmist prays when he says: *6Lord, rebuke me not in your anger, nor chasten me in your wrath.*[116]

28

3.13 *1***Lord, you went forth for the salvation of your people to save your anointed ones.**[117] *2*The mediator between God and men[118] went forth from the Father and came into the world *not to judge the world but that the world might be saved through him.*[119] *3*He terms 'anointed' all the elect who are quite rightly called by this name in virtue of the anointing of the grace of the Spirit. *4*Hence the saying of the psalmist about those wishing to harm the saints being restrained by the prohibition of God: *5And he rebuked kings on their account: 'Touch not my anointed ones.'*[120] *6*Now he saved his 'anointed ones', not those whom he found to be 'anointed', but whom, by going forth from the Father and appearing in the flesh, he made 'anointed', i.e. his own anointed, through the spirit of adoption.[121] *7*Reminding his audience of this anointing, the apostle John says: *8And let the anointing which you received from him remain in you.*[122] *9*In some editions this verse is found as follows: *10You went forth to save your people through Jesus your anointed one* which is taken as addressed to the Father, because he went forth to save his people through Jesus Christ his own Son. *11*For *God was in Christ reconciling the world to himself;*[123] *12*and because this going forth, i.e. his coming into the world, was to be not merely for the resurrection of the faithful, but also for the perdition of unbelievers, it is fittingly added:

29

3.13 *1***You sent death upon the heads of your enemies, you have raised the bonds up to their neck.** *2*For he who offered the joy of salvation to his chosen ones whom the prophet had called 'anointed ones' is the one who sent eternal death to those who did not take the trouble to be anointed with his grace. *3*And it is well known that this came to pass

[399]

30⇐

---

116 Ps 6.2.   117 to save your anointed ones: *ut saluos facias christos tuos.* For readers unfamiliar with Greek or Latin the term 'christ' is an anglicization of the Greek verbal adjective (nominative singular masculine) χριστός = 'anointed' (transliterated 'christos' and Latinized as 'christus'); it was used by the Greek translators of the Hebrew Bible to render the Hebrew word מָשִׁיחַ (transliterated 'messiah' = 'anointed'). Both these words, Hebrew and Greek, came to be used as proper nouns 'Messiah' and 'Christos', and as such are more familiar to us. The Latin translation of χριστός (as opposed to its transliteration *christus*) is *unctus* = 'anointed'. Lawrence T. Martin in the translation of Bede's *Hom* 1.16, based on Hurst's edition *CCSL* 122, 114, retains the Greek form, writing 'christs'.   118 cf. 1 Tim 2.5.   119 cf. + Jn 3.17.   120 Ps 104(105).14–15.   121 cf. + Rom 8.15.   122 I Jn 2.27 .   123 +2 Cor 5.19, (direct quotation).

84

even bodily in the very Jewish people who persecuted to the death the
Lord who appeared in the flesh. *4*Not many years had elapsed after they
had crucified him when the Roman army attacked them; *5*and, with the
sole exception of those who had seceded to the faith of the grace of the
gospel, they suffered an overwhelming defeat and were moreover deprived
of their very kingdom and fatherland;*124**6*and this is the reason why he
says: *You have raised the bonds up to their neck,* the neck, that is, of their
kingdom, whereby they had risen up against the Lord. *7*Of this ⟨neck⟩*125*
the blessed protomartyr Stephen said to these people as they raged against
him too: *8You stiff-necked people, uncircumcised in heart and ears, you
have always resisted the Holy Spirit.*126* *9*But the Lord raised the bonds up
to this neck when he sent an enemy force to overthrow the proud people
not merely of the Jews but also of all who refused to accept the humility
of the Christian faith. *10*The Lord lays pride low according to what the
psalmist sings of the saints: *11And two-edged swords in their hands to
wreak vengeance on the nations, and chastisement on the peoples to bind
their kings with chains and their nobles with fetters of iron;*127* *12*'of iron',
i.e. because eternal, from which, once secured, they could never be freed.
*13*But should anyone say it is to be read in the plural number as: *14You
have raised the bonds up to their necks,* the meaning is the same: *15For the
Lord is just: he has cut asunder the necks of sinners.*128*

30

3.14 *1*You have cut off in a frenzy*129*the heads of the mighty;
the nations will be shaken by it. *2*For *alienatio* the Greek has*130*
in exstasi, which some have translated *in stupore,*131* others *in excessu
mentis. *3*But whether it is called *stupor* or *alienatio* or *excessus mentis,*132*
one and the same thing is meant when, agitated and rendered speechless
by a sudden astonishing occurrence, one is left cut off from one's mental

[400]

30⇐

---

124 and...deprived of their very kingdom and fatherland: here I follow the text of
Migne which reads: *et ipso...regno ac patria priuata* instead of the reading of our
CCSL edition which has: ...regno ac patri....   125 Of this ⟨neck⟩: *de quo:* lit. 'of
which'.   126 Acts 7.51.   127 Ps 149.78.   128 Ps 128(129).4.   129 in a frenzy: *in
alienatione* (our text following *VL*); ἐν ἐκστάσει *LXX* which Brenton inadequately
translates 'with amazement'. The Hebrew and Vulgate bear scant resemblance to
either the *LXX* or Bede's *VL* text.   130 the Greek has: *in graeco scriptum est:* lit.
'in (the) Greek is written'.   131 *in stupore:* 'in a state of stupefaction'; 'speechless'.
132 *excessus mentis:* 'a frenzy, trance, transport' (depending on the emotion in
question, whether of joy, anger, awe or whatever); lit. 'a going out of (one's) mind';
cf. our expression: 'taking leave of one's senses'. In Acts 11.5 the same Greek phrase,
ἐν ἐκστάσει, occurs as the *LXX* Habakkuk has here. There the Vulgate uses the
same Latin, *in excessu mentis,* to translate it. The Latin is in turn rendered 'in an
ecstasy' in the *Douay*; the *Knox* version of the New Testament entitled 'A translation
from the Latin Vulgate *in the light of the Greek originals',* renders it 'in a trance', as
do the *RSV* and *NJB* working from the Greek originals.

faculties.[133] [4]That this happened to the Jews the gospel story often relates when it says that they were stunned and astounded at the teaching and miracles of Jesus: [5]*Where did this man whose father and mother we know come by all this?*[134] [6]And in the Acts of the Apostles when the cripple was healed by Peter and John at the Temple gate ⟨the author⟩ says: [7]*They were filled with wonder and amazement,*[135] and, of course, in this amazement, i.e. astonishment or delirious rapture, many of the people were inspired[136] to believe in the Lord; [8]but the heads of the mighty i.e. the chief priests and elders were cut off by their unbelief[137] from the destiny of the faithful. [9]The nations too were shaken by it when, having heard or seen the miracles of the Lord and his apostles, they were so dumbfounded and astonished that they cursed and disavowed the gods they had worshipped, and devoutly embraced the new faith of Christ.[138] [10]And of these it is fittingly added:

31

3.14 [1]**They will open their mouths like a poor person eating in secret**. [2]For just as a poor person who has remained fasting for some time, should he find food somewhere, is immediately at pains to refresh himself with it in secret [3]and is reluctant to take it out in public in case by any chance it be snatched by someone else and he die of hunger, [4]so, no doubt, so ⟨did⟩ the Gentile peoples ⟨act⟩[139] when, through the apostles, they were offered the bread of the word from which they had remained

---

133 is left cut off from one's mental faculties: *a sensu suae mentis redditur alienus.* The words *redditur alienus a* literally mean 'is rendered estranged from'. **134** Jn 6.42; note that Bede's text here is not in agreement with either the Vulgate or the Greek Testament where the words *Vnde huic haec omnia* are not attested. **135** Acts 3.10. See Bede, *Comm. on Acts* 3.10 and *Retractatio* (*CCSL* 121, 118, 6–9); cf. Aug. *Enarr.,* in Ps 30,1 (*CCSL* 38, 186, 1, 315). **136** inspired: *prouocatus:* 'roused, excited'. The *OLD,* s.v. *prouocatus,* suggests that the sense of 'roused, excited' comes from the basic sense of 'challenged': *provocat me in aleam:* 'challenged me to a game' (Plautus, *Curculio,* 2,3,75); *provoco aliquem ad pugnam* 'I challenge someone to fight' (common in Cicero and Livy). **137** by their unbelief: *non credendo:* lit. 'by not believing'. **138** Miracles play an important role in the conversion process. The Whitby *Life of Gregory,* echoing Gregory's own position, states: 'Miracles are granted for the destruction of the idols of unbelieving pagans, or sometimes to confirm the weak faith of believers; most of all they are granted to those who instruct the pagans, and so, the more gloriously and frequently they are manifested in those lands, the more convincing they become as teachers.' (Colgrave (ed. and tr.) 1968, 79). Gregory himself, says Bede commenting on the *Moralia,* 'declares that St Augustine and his companions led the English race to the knowledge of the truth, not only by preaching the word but also by showing heavenly signs.' (*HE* 2.1). In a letter to Eulogius of Alexandria, not included in the *HE,* Gregory compares Augustine's miracles to those of the apostles (*Registrum Epistularum Libri* viii — xiv, *CCSL* 140A, 551, 25–31). He also instructs Augustine on miracles, using the New Testament miracles of Christ's disciples as his model (*HE* 1.31). **139** so... ⟨did⟩... ⟨act⟩: The sentence *Sicut enim* (line 544)... *doctrinis* (line 553) is awkwardly long in English. So I have divided it at 'for some considerable time' (§31.4), introducing the words 'did... act' here, and 'They' at §31.5 to repair the break in sense.

fasting for some considerable time. ⁵⟨They⟩ straight away opened the mouths of their heart and began to relish it with the keenest possible appetite, ⁶taking all the more trouble to listen to the scriptures and read them, the longer was their memory of having, in the most abject kind of poverty, subjected their ⟨ears⟩ and mind to the bondage of worthless, indeed even harmful | teachings. ⁷On the other hand, it is intimated how [401] the poverty of the nations came to partake of the banquet of the word, when it is immediately added:

32

3.15 ¹**You sent your horses into the sea, churning up many waters.**¹⁴⁰ ²For by 'the sea' ⟨the writer⟩ means the world, by 'God's horses' holy preachers, and by 'many waters' the peoples of the nations. ³When God's horses were sent into the sea many waters were churned up ⁴because, when heralds of the word scattered in all directions throughout the world, the hearts of the Gentiles were agitated, some to believe and accept the mystery, but others to argue against or even persecute the heralds of this faith; ⁵hence the psalmist well says: *All that saw them were disquieted, and everyone was afraid, and they proclaimed the works of God and understood his doings.*¹⁴¹ ⁶For all were indeed disquieted but not all were afraid and declared the works of God; ⁷but those who were human beings and yet really were bereft of human reason were compared to dumb beasts of burden and became like them. ⁸Such people, even though disquieted and deeply affected by the miracles of the saints, nevertheless refused to fear God or proclaim or understand his deeds. ⁹Now, of these horses, i.e. holy preachers, it is also well said above:¹⁴² *For you will assuredly mount your horses,* ¹⁰and now of these same ones it is added: *You sent your horses*

---

140 Gregory writes: 'Anyone who is alive in humility, in chastity, in sound teaching and in charity has become a horse of our Creator, harnessed to the chariot of God, with God as the charioteer...and these horses are referred to thus: *Thou dost trample the sea with thy horses, the surging of mighty waters.* (Hab 3.15) And so God has his chariots, for he is the master of the souls of the saints and he drives where he will with those holy souls.' *On the Canticle of Canticles,* 246. In his commentary on the Temple Bede sees preachers as God's chariots. There, he describes preachers sent out across the earth as 'chariots of God, and fast ones too, because as they sped about from one place to the next, they brought God into the hearts of believers.' These chariots of God included Paul and Barnabas in the earliest days of the Church and later Augustine, Paulinus and the other missionaries sent by Gregory to convert the English (*DTemp* 20.7). Columbanus, writing to Pope Boniface IV, employs the image of horses, chariots and the sea when referring to the conversion of Ireland. He speaks of 'that time when the Son of God deigned to be man, and on those two most fiery steeds of God's spirit, I mean the apostles Peter and Paul, whose dear relics have made you blessed, riding over the sea of nations, troubled many waters and increased his chariots with countless thousands of peoples, the Most Highest Pilot of that carriage Who is Christ, the true Father, the Charioteer of Israel, over the channels' surge, over the dolphins' backs, over the swelling flood, reached even unto us.' Walker (ed. and tr.) 1957,49. **141** Ps 63(64).9. **142** Hab 3.8; *supra* §20.1.

into the sea, ¹¹so that it may be inferred from each of the two sentences that the Lord has sent preachers into the world in such a way as to ensure that he may never be absent from these same people as they preach; ¹²but that as a charioteer is in charge of his horses, he may ever be in charge of¹⁴³ their minds for their guidance.

33

3.16 ¹**I kept watch and my belly trembled with terror at the sound of the prayer of my lips.** ²By his belly he means his mind in the manner customary with the prophets, because just as food is taken into the belly to reinvigorate the body's strength and vitality, ³devout considerations are taken into the mind | for the sustenance and maintenance of one's interior life lest it grow weak. ⁴It is for this reason the prophet says *I kept watch,* focusing intently on the future sufferings of Christ and his subsequent glories, the reprobation of my people, the faith of the Gentiles, ⁵when these Gentiles were disturbed at the new preaching, ⟨and⟩ the persecution that was to be instigated against believers by unbelievers; ⁶*and my heart*¹⁴⁴ *trembled with terror* at the things that I myself foresaw and said would come to pass. ⁷Or at all events he said *I kept watch* after contemplating the very different condition of the human race, in trepidation of spirit exercising greater caution, lest I should happen to sin in deed, or word or heart, or lest, while preaching to others, I myself should become a castaway;¹⁴⁵ ⁸and it is to be noted that he says he became greatly alarmed at the sound of the prayer of his lips, since he seems not to have prayed at all in the whole of this prophecy, ⁹but merely to be setting down in writing the future mysteries of Christ and the Church; ¹⁰and yet he is not wrong in calling his prophecy a prayer seeing that he also prefaced it with the title, ¹¹*The prayer of the prophet Habakkuk for his transgressions,*¹⁴⁶ because whatever a holy man utters is wholly and entirely a prayer to God; ¹²everything a person does whose honest intention is to please the Lord intercedes for him before the Lord and commends him to the Lord.

[402]

34

3.16 ¹**And there came a trembling throughout my bones.** ²Just as scripture is accustomed occasionally to characterize our frail human

---

143 be in charge of: *praesit.* Alternatively, to reflect the contrast with 'be absent from' *(absit)* in the earlier clause, one might prefer to render *praesit* here as 'be present to'. I have chosen the regular classical sense 'be in charge of' since the 'charioteer' simile requires it. This is a good example of word-play in Bede's Latin. **144** my heart: here as later (at §34.4) the Latin text Bede is quoting has *cor,* not *uenter* as in the lemma. **145** cf. + 1 Cor 9.27. **146** Hab 3.1

actions[147] by the name 'flesh', [3]so by the term 'bones' it is accustomed to characterize courageous and spiritual deeds. [4]That is why he says: *My heart trembled with terror*[148] at the things which I foresaw were to come into the world; [5]and whatever spiritual strength I thought was in me, it all shook violently as if it were weak, when I considered both the greater powers and the sufferings of Christ's blessed apostles; | [6]and this is more clearly explained by the following expression when it is said: [403]

35

3.16 [1]**And beneath me my strength was shaken.**[149] [2]Now, he properly says that his strength was shaken not 'in' him but 'beneath' him; [3]because, when rapt in contemplation of the heavenly mysteries, the prophet saw himself raised[150] somehow or other above himself; [4]and the higher he rose in the light of contemplation, the more imperfect he saw himself in merit of action. [5]For when raised aloft to gaze on heavenly things, he was with good reason deeply perturbed about the things he had done in this life.[151] [6]But the prophet's strength was troubled and his bones shook violently, his belly trembled with terror, [7]not only because he knows he was less perfect in conduct, but also because he says that all who devoutly wished to live in Christ would suffer persecutions; [8]but he saw too that Christ who entered the world, would not leave the world without the punishment of sin, in accordance with what he had pointed out even at the very beginning of his canticle. [9]Yet this fear and trembling did not remain without consolation for the one for whom hope of future rewards reduced present adversities, and rendered them lighter. [10]For this is the import of what follows:

36

3.16 [1]**I shall rest in the day of my tribulation that I may go up to the people of my deportation.** [2]For he who does not doubt that through his temporal afflictions he will gain eternal joys, rests not only on the day of recompense but also on the day of tribulation, according to the saying of the Apostle: [3]*For it is by hope that we have been saved.*[152] [4]And again: *Rejoicing in hope, patient in tribulation.*[153] [5]However, the rest of

---

147 our frail human actions: *carnales nostras actiones.* Our translation reflects the sense of the epithet *carnalis* which Bede has in mind throughout this commentary. This in turn reflects biblical usage especially that of St Paul for whom the term 'flesh' (Latin caro, Greek σάρξ) signifies natural, human finitude, weak, mortal, liable and even prone to be ensnared by sin: the human creature left to itself as opposed to being under the influence of the God's Spirit. **148** Hab 3.16. **149** shaken: *turbata:* lit. 'troubled'. **150** saw himself raised: *se… esse uidit eleuatum:* lit. 'saw that he was raised'. **151** in this life: *in infimis:* lit. 'in the lowest' (*sc.* level or condition of human existence as opposed to the highest, viz. the beatific vision). **152** Rom 8.24. **153** Rom 12.12.

the elect in this life consists in this, to renounce the craving for trifling things, and strive with total concentration of mind and by daily progress in good works to go up and change their abode for the fellowship of those who went before them | in Christ, [6] and who, when the struggles against [404] their passions were over, received the crown of life, [154] [7] after the example of those who, under the leadership of Zorobabel and Joshua, were once deported from Judea to Babylon but returned once more to their homeland. [155] [8] These scripture calls the children of the deportation, [156] [9] and tells how they restored by the enthusiasm of their great dedication the sacred things which the enemy had destroyed. [157] [10] This is the clearest figure of our own condition. [11] For in our first parent we were removed from our heavenly homeland and brought into the Babylon, i.e. the confusion, [158] of this world; [12] but by the bounty of the Lord Jesus Christ, our king and high priest of whom Zorobabel and Joshua were a type, [13] we were recalled once more to the homeland and vision of supreme peace, which is what the name 'Jerusalem' means; [159] [14] (but) only in such a way that, meanwhile by practising works of mercy in the Jerusalem of the present Church, [15] we may get ready according to circumstances for entry into the heavenly Jerusalem which is the mother of us all. [16] If, on the other hand, one reads ⟨the text⟩ without specific reference, as it is found in certain codices: [17] *I shall rest in the day of tribulation*, and *my* is not added, [18] it can be understood in accordance with what is sung of the just man in the psalm: [19] *The Lord will deliver him in the day of trouble*, [160] because, of course, on the day of judgement when eternal tribulation overtakes [161] the reprobate, eternal rest conversely welcomes in [162] the just; [20] but even before that final and general judgement the saints rest in the day of tribulation, going up to the people of their deportation, [21] when, transferred from the world after good works, they are given a share in heaven of the joys of the just who have gone before them, [22] while their persecutors, | likewise taken from [405] this life, undergo the torments of Gehenna to be afflicted for ever. [23] On the other hand, the day of tribulation can also be understood of this life; [24] for then as the shortage of temporal goods gets more acute, those who had set inordinate store by such things suffer pain, surrounded, as it were, by woes; [25] but each of the elect, though bodily undergoing the same hardships, have rest in the Lord because of their spirit's firm hope, [26] knowing

31⟸

---

154 cf. Jas 1.12.   **155** cf. 1 Ezra 1–2.   **156** cf. 1 Ezra 6.16 and passim.   **157** cf. 1 Ezra 3.7–13; 1 Chron 22.4; 2 Chron 2.9,14.   **158** cf. Jer., *Nom.*, (*CCSL* 72, 62, 18).   **159** cf. Jer., *Nom.*, (*CCSL* 72, 121, 9–10).   **160** Ps 40.2(41.1); in the day of trouble: *in die malo:* lit. 'in the evil day'.   **161** overtakes: *conprehendit:* lit. 'seizes'.   **162** welcomes in: *suscipiat:* I have chosen this rendering because the verb *suscipere* in Roman society had, among other things, the meaning 'to take up' a new-born child from the ground; the father recognized the infant as his own by placing his arms under it and lifting it up; from this action we see the force of the *sub-* in the compound of *capere* (*suscipere* ← *sub+capere*). The next stage in the semantic development of this verb is 'adopt', and then (as in our text) 'welcome in' as a member of one's household.

that the heavier the burden that weighs upon them in this life,[163] the higher up they will go, after their afflictions, to the eternal fellowship of their heavenly compatriots. [27]And what follows is in fitting accord with this interpretation:

37

27← *3.17–18* [1]For the fig-tree will bear no fruit and there will be no spring in the vines; the labour of the olive-tree will be false to its promise[164] and the fields will yield no food. The sheep have pined away from the pasture,[165] and there will be no cattle in the stall: But I shall glory in the Lord, I shall rejoice in God my saviour. [2]Because whereas all worldly people and lovers of this life are dismayed when abundance of this world's possessions runs short, the just are not saddened by the loss of creature comforts. [3]Rather they have the joy of possessing the heavenly kingdom promised to Christ's poor, bearing in mind his promise of consolation in which he said: [4]*Fear not little flock, because it has pleased your Father to give you a kingdom.*[166] [5]And how wonderful ⟨is⟩ the faith, hope and love of the prophet! [6]The Son of God has not yet appeared as a man or received the name of Jesus from his parents, [7]and ⟨yet⟩ he (the prophet) foreseeing this name in the Spirit, bears witness that amid adversities he rejoices in him who was to be born long afterwards in the flesh and open to his faithful the gate of

35← their heavenly homeland. [8]On the other hand, should one desire that these verses also be expounded figurally, the fig-tree, the vine, and the olive-tree were the Synagogue of the Jews, [9]when in its dedication to God it preserved the sweetness of good works and the ardour of love ⟨and⟩ produced the rich abundance of a compassionate disposition. [10]Sheep and

26← |oxen had a typological significance among that people; [11]that is to say,   [406] sheep ⟨were reflected⟩ in those who humbly listened to the voice of the supreme pastor; [12]oxen, on the other hand, in those who, by assiduously bearing the yoke of the law, were preparing to produce the fruits of good works by zealously teaching and chastening the hearts of their hearers, as

27← if ploughing the land of the Lord; [13]and while these lived spiritual lives, the very extensive fields of the divine scriptures were producing spiritual food for them, [14]fields whose nourishment was the delight of the one who became like a beast of burden before the Lord and stayed ever close to him saying: [15]*The Lord guides me and I shall want for nothing; in his*

---

163 in this life: *in infimis;* cf. above §35.4.   164 will be false to its promise: *mentietur:* cf. *supra* §5.4, Hab 2.3.   165 have pined away from the pasture: ... *ab esca:* lit. '...from the food'. This elliptical and ambivalent expression is purposely left in its literal form here rather than translated according to its real meaning since it is elucidated by Bede a little further on.   166 Lk 12.32.

place of pasture he has laid me down to rest.[167] [16]But when its owner came to it for the third time, i.e. in the making of the law by Moses, in zealous rebuke and exhortation through the prophets, in the offer of grace through himself, this fig-tree failed to bear the fruit of virtue; [17]this is why it was doomed to his execration by its perpetual sterility. [18]The produce on the Lord's vines failed long ago, i.e. the fruits of love among the general masses of the Jews. [19]This is why, when he was thirsty, they offered him vinegar instead of wine, [20]i.e. when he desired the sweetness of virtues to be shown him[168] they proffered him bitterness; when he longed for their virtues they proffered him vices. [21]The yield of the olive-tree was false to its promise when this people anointed the heads of the worthless with the unction of adulation, [22]and echoed with its untruthful mouth the prophet's truthful utterances when he said: [23]*As a fruitful olive-tree in the house of God, I have hoped in the mercy of God.*[169] [24]This is why at the hour of final retribution it is going to bring extinguished lamps[170] and, together with its darkness, is to be precluded from entry into its heavenly homeland. [25]The fields do not produce food when this people, on opening the pages of the divine scriptures, is unable, for lack of proper understanding, to find the pastures of truth. [26]The sheep pine away from the pasture because, for those who lack the refreshment of inner sweetness, there is no source from which the innocence of a simple life can come. [27]Now what was said was this: *The sheep have pined away*

27⇐

27⇐

---

167 Ps 22(23).1; (a) guides: *regit (Vg)*; the familiar translation, 'is my shepherd', found, e.g., in the *RSV*, is a direct rendering of the Hebrew. (b) Compare Bede's comment on the text: *Where there are no oxen the manger is empty; but where there is plenty of corn, the strength of the ox is evident.* (Prov 14.4): 'These ⟨words⟩ are applicable on a higher level, for oxen mean Catholic teachers, the manger the congregation of listeners, the grain the fruits of good works. Therefore it is idle for the proud person to get conceited and for ill-informed eloquence to sound upon the ears of those who are beneath them because where the preachers are not learned, it is futile for a crowd of people to flock to them. On the other hand, where acts of virtue are much in evidence it is perfectly clear that it is no heretic that is prattling emptily, but that the one who has learnt both to ruminate with pure mouth upon the very word of truth and to walk the path of truth with the proper foot of discretion, has laboured for the harvest (grain) of the word. Nor is it surprising that we have said that by the manger are meant the listeners, since the ox is fed from the manger whereas the teacher is wont to nourish his audience with the word. But it is to be observed that it is by the labour of the ox that the manger is filled and the ox itself is fed from the crib by its own produce because, of course, the faithful preacher both refreshes his audience with the word and himself benefits before the Lord from the same nourishment. This is prefigured by the work of Elijah who is fed by the widow of Zarephath whom he himself feeds.' (1 Kings(3 Kings) 17.8–16)' Tr. Seán Connolly from *In Prouerbia Salomonis CCSL* 119B, 83, 17–33. **168** the sweetness...to be shown him: *uirtutum suauitatem in se:* lit. 'the sweetness of virtues towards him'. **169** Ps 51.10(52.8). **170** cf. + Mt 25.1–10.

from the| pasture i.e. because pasture was lacking,[171] just as the prophet   [407]
in the psalm says:[28]*And my flesh is changed because of oil,*[172] i.e. because
there was no oil to refresh or anoint me.[173] [29]*They finally pined away*
(as some codices have it) by reason of the fact that the sheep did not eat;
27⇐ *there are no cattle in the stall,*[174] [30]for the stalls of heavenly scriptures do
indeed abound[175] among the Jews [31]but because the latter do not taste
the food of heavenly meaning in them, those who bear the sweet yoke
of the gospel[176] are not there. [32]And the prophet reflecting on all these
29⇐ things that were to befall the unbelieving section of his people, [33]at once
showed what he himself would do, together with the faithful ones of this
same people, [34]indeed with the brotherhood of the entire Church which
was to be or had been assembled in Christ all over the globe, when he
said: [35]*I on the other hand shall rejoice not in my own uprightness but,*
in my belief in God's protection, I shall rejoice in the Lord my Jesus, i.e.
saviour,[177] [36]because it is not in myself but in him that I reckon salvation
to be; [37]and as if we were to ask him why he gloried in the Lord and
rejoiced in God the Saviour whom he called his own by the grace of his
great love, [38]he forthwith, as if intimating the really just grounds of his
joy, ended his canticle thus:

---

171 To appreciate the choice of 'from' (*ab*) here, one needs to look at the Septuagint
Greek which underlies the *VL* text that Bede is using. The Greek has the preposition
ἀπό which is not only a cognate of *ab* but has the same basic meaning 'from'. Moreover
like our 'from' it can in a given context also mean 'because of/as a result of/on account
of'. Translated in full, i.e. unelliptically, the preposition would here mean 'for/because
of the/ lack of', as Bede rightly observes. As has been remarked in regard to the text
of Romans 11.25 in the Tobit Commentary, (cf. *InTob* 5.5 n.), translators in antiquity
and even until relatively recent times felt obliged out of reverence for the sacred text to
give a slavishly literal rendering. Little if any account was taken of the idiom or genius
of the target language. As a consequence exegetes often found it necessary to elucidate
the translation, as our author does here.   **172** Ps 108(109).24.   **173** i.e. because there
was no oil to refresh or anoint me: in the Latin edited text this clause is printed
in italics as if it were part of the quotation from Psalm 108(109); it is, in fact, the
author's explanatory remark, not part of the psalm.   **174** Hab 3.17.   **175** The text
here reads as follows: *Quoniam quidem abundant apud Iudaeos praesepia caelestium*
litterarum, sed quia pabulum caelesti⟨s⟩ intellectus in his non sapiunt, quae suaue
iugum euangelii baiulant absunt.   The punctuation retained in our *CCSL* edition
(most probably following the codices), i.e. a full stop before *Quoniam*, makes the
sentence as it stands incomplete, consisting as it does of a succession of subordinate
clauses. This is probably why the phrase *Quoniam quidem abundant* is found in only
five (the five earliest) of the twelve codices on which the edition is based, whereas
the remaining seven read: *Quondam quidem (h)abundabant:* 'True (the stalls of
heavenly scriptures) did at one time abound (among the Jews).' I have emended the
punctuation, changing the full stop to a comma, to reflect what I believe to be the
only way of taking the phrase *quoniam quidem abundant,* namely, as an explanatory
continuation of what has been said: *They finally pined away... there are no cattle in*
the stalls.   **176** cf. Mt 11.30.   **177** Hab 3.18. In the *CCSL* here at line 723 the
word *meo* should be italicized since it is part of the verse quoted, as is clear from the
Hebrew, *LXX* and Vulgate texts.

38

3.19 [1]The Lord God, my strength, will both perfectly strengthen my feet and will mount me upon high places that I may be victorious by his glory; [2]as if to say openly: 'Beneath me indeed my strength is shaken, i.e. when I contemplate the condition of human frailty which is found ⟨here⟩ below; [3]but when I raise the eyes of my mind to the favour of God's assistance, I trust in him to be able to perform acts of virtue. [4]He can lead the steps of my actions to the summit of a firm end; [5]he can set me upon the heights, namely, that through the contemplation of everlasting goods, I may scorn as of no account all the eminence of worldly power. | [6]All the temptations that beset me, whether from adversities or the allurements of the world, I shall overcome by his glory, [7]i.e. when in everything I do I seek not my own glory[178] but that of him from whom I recall having received whatever good I do.' [8]For those who refer to his glory the whole credit for their success are deservedly helped by the Lord, [9]so that, having been proved by the temptations they have overcome, they may win the palm of their heavenly calling. [10]Some codices have the reading: *That I may be victorious in his canticle*[179] which has in view one and the same meaning. [11]For in the Lord's canticle everyone is victorious who knows how to give him thanks from the heart in all the tribulations one suffers, [12]knowing that *with those who love God everything works for good,*[180] [13]and is accustomed to chant with blessed Job: *May the name of the Lord be blessed.*[181] [14]Finally the apostles Paul and Silas amid scourging, darkness, and prison chains were singing a hymn to God;[182] [15]and so with God's assistance they suddenly emerged victorious, because, of course, even though their feet seemed bound with straps, they had nevertheless crowned the advance of their deeds with miracles.[183] [16]On the other hand, the end of this canticle of the prophet is in admirable accord with the beginning. [17]For it comes about that the one who, in a spirit of faith, fears and becomes alarmed on hearing and reflecting upon the works of the Lord when he appeared in the flesh, [18]despises things which in this life are driven about by the varying conditions like the heaving ocean, and glories and rejoices in him alone whose bliss he can fully enjoy forever; [19]he is helped by him so as to be neither broken by the adversities of the present world nor corrupted by its allurements; [20]he both sings the praises of his grace in the present life in order that he may deserve to be victorious, and never leaves off singing in the life to come because he has been victorious. [21]It also comes about that such a person overcomes the

[408]

---

178 cf. + Jn 8.50. **179** Hab 3.19. **180** Rom 8.28. **181** Job 1.21. **182** cf. Acts 16.25. **183** with miracles: *uirtutibus:* the basic meaning of the word *uirtus* (nom. plural *uirtutes*), from *uir*, 'man', is 'manliness', 'manhood'; from this it came to mean man's excellent qualities of body or spirit: 'strength, courage, excellence, worth, merit, virtue'; in Christian literature it acquired the sense in which I have taken it here, i.e. 'miracle', 'a work of power', 'a mighty work'.

world by the glory of the Lord, [22]i.e. the same glory of his, both frequently recalled to mind in the time of struggle,[184]and eternally contemplated in the time of reward, [23]according to what he himself promised: *Blessed are the clean of heart for they shall see God.*[185] [24]It is to be noted, on the other hand, now that Habakkuk's prayer or | canticle has been expounded, that his name too, which means 'embracing',[186] is in keeping with the meaning of this prayer. [25]For it is manifest that he, who bears witness that he gloried and rejoiced in him alone, embraced the Lord with the inward love of his heart and clung close to him.[26]Now, dearly beloved sister and virgin of Christ, would that we too, by loving him, might become worthy of such a name. [27]For if we strive to embrace him with our whole heart, our whole soul and our whole strength,[187] he too will deign to clasp us in the arms of his love, mindful of his promise in which he says: [28]*The one who loves me will be loved by my Father and I will love him and will reveal myself to him;* [188] [29]and so we shall merit to be reckoned among the members of that bride who, full of joy, is accustomed to sing to her creator, i.e. her heavenly bridegroom:[30]*His left hand is under my head, and his right hand shall embrace me.*[189] Amen.

[409]

19⇐

---

184 in the time of struggle, and... in the time of reward: *in tempore certaminum et... in tempore praemiorum*: lit. 'in the time of struggles and... in the time of rewards'. **185** Mt 5.8. **186** cf. Jer., *Nom.*, (*CCSL* 72, 124, 15–16). **187** cf. Mt 22.37; Mk 12.30; Lk 10.27. **188** Jn 14.21. **189** Song 2.6. In his commentary *On The Canticle of Canticles*, Bede says: 'For by the left hand he denotes the mysteries of his incarnation and the gifts of his presence; but by his right hand are symbolized the rewards which the elect will share in the future which include not only the vision of God's majesty but the splendour of his glorified humanity and of this one mediator of God and men (cf. 1 Tim 2.5). Hence the bridegroom aptly longed for his left hand to be placed under her head but his right hand to embrace her that she might, both now through his temporal assistance, rest from the bustle of the world, and then enjoy the clear vision of him forever. And indeed no whirlwind ever disturbs the eternal rest of the saints. Hence it is rightly said, *And his right hand will embrace me*, because, of course, the presence of God's majesty will surround his own on all sides in his heavenly kingdom, lest any thought of unhappiness should spoil the bliss worthy of God, or fear of its ending cause anxiety' (Tr. Seán Connolly, from *In Cantica Canticorum*, (*CCSL* 119B, 342, 175–187). Cf. *DTab* 1.8, where Bede writes: 'Surely the left hand of the bridegroom is placed under the head of the bride because the Lord raises up the minds of the faithful with temporal benefits, separating them from earthly pleasures and longings so that they may desire and hope for eternal blessings. And he shall embrace her with his right hand because by revealing the vision of his majesty he glorifies her without end.'

95

SELECT BIBLIOGRAPHY

PRIMARY SOURCES

Alcuin, *The Bishops, Kings and Saints of York*, ed. and tr. P. Godman (Oxford, 1982).

Aldhelm, *De Virginitate*, ed. R. Ehwald, *MGH AA* 15 (Berlin, 1919) 211–323; tr. M. Lapidge and M. Herren, in *Aldhelm: The Prose Works* (Ipswich, 1979), 51–132.

Ambrose, *De Tobia*, ed. C. Shenkl, *CSEL* 32.2, 519–573; ed. with Italian tr. M. Giacchero *Ambrosii De Tobia* (Genoa, 1965); English tr., L. M. Zucker, *S. Ambrosii De Tobia: A Commentary with an Introduction and Translation.* (Washington D. C., 1933).

Augustine, *De Civitate Dei*, ed. B. Dombart and A. Kalb, *CCSL* 47–8 (Turnhout, 1955); ed. and tr. by G. E. McCracken, W. M. Green, D. S. Wiesen, P. Levine, E. M. Sanford, and W. C. Greene, *LCL*, 7 vols. (London and Cambridge, Mass., 1957–72).

————, *Enarrationes in Psalmos 51–100*, ed. D. Eligius Dekkers and Johannes Fraipont *CCSL* 39 (Turnhout, 1956).

Bede, *Chronica Maiora*, ed. C. W. Jones, *CCSL* 123B (Turnhout, 1977) 495–535; sixth age translated in J. McClure and R. Collins (ed. and tr.), Bede: *The Ecclesiastical History of the English People. Cuthbert's Letter on the death of Bede. The Greater Chronicle. Bede's Letter to Egbert* (Oxford, 1994) 307–340.

————, *De Schematibus et Tropis*, ed. C. B. Kendall, *CCSL*, 123A, 142–171 (Turnhout, 1975); tr. G. H. Tannenhaus *On Schemes and Tropes* in *Readings in Medieval Rhetoric*, ed. J. M. Miller, M. H. Frosser, T. W. Benson (Bloomington and London, 1973) 96–122.

————, *De Tabernaculo*, ed. D. Hurst, *CCSL*, 119A, 1–139 (Turnhout, 1969). tr. A. G. Holder, *On the Tabernacle* in *Translated Texts for Historians Series* (Liverpool University Press, 1994).

————, *De Templo*, ed. D. Hurst, *CCSL*, 119A, 142–234 (Turnhout, 1969). tr. S. Connolly, *On the Temple* in *Translated Texts for Historians Series* (Liverpool University Press, 1995).

————, *Epistola ad Ecgberctum*, ed. C. Plummer, *Venerabilis Baedae Opera Historica*, 2 vols. (Oxford, 1896) I, 405–23. tr. J. McClure and R. Collins, 1994, 343–357.

————, *Expositio Actuum Apostolorum*, ed. M. L.W. Laistner, *CCSL* 121 (Turnhout, 1983), 3–99; tr. L. T. Martin, *Commentary on the Acts of the Apostles*, Cistercian Studies Series 117 (Kalamazoo, 1989).

————, *Historia Abbatum*, ed. C. Plummer, *Venerabilis Baedae Opera Historica, I*, 364–87. Tr. D. H. Farmer in *The Age of Bede* (Harmondsworth, 1983), 185–211.

————, *Historia Ecclesiastica Gentis Anglorum*, ed. C. Plummer, *Venerabilis Baedae Opera Historica*; ed. and tr. B. Colgrave and R. A. B. Mynors (Oxford, 1969), with the English tr. reprinted in McClure and Collins (ed. and tr.) 1994, 3–298.

————, *Homiliae Euangelii*, ed. D. Hurst, *CCSL*, 122 (Turnhout, 1965); tr. L. T. Martin, and D. Hurst, *Homilies on the Gospels* 2 vols. *Cistercian Studies Series*, 110–11 (Kalamazoo, 1991).

————, *In Cantica Canticorum Allegorica Expositio*, ed. D. Hurst *CCSL* 119B (Turnhout, 1983) 166–375.

————, *In Epistolas VII Catholicas*, ed. M. L.W. Laistner *CCSL* 121 (Turnhout, 1983) 181–342; tr. D. Hurst, *Commentary on the Seven Catholic Epistles* Cistercian Studies, Series 82 (Kalamazoo, 1985).

————, *In Ezram et Neemiam Prophetas Allegorica Expositio*, ed. D. Hurst *CCSL*, 119A (Turnhout, 1969) 235–392.

————, *In Habacuc*, ed. J. E. Hudson *CCSL*, 119B (Turnhout, 1983) 377–409.

————, *In Lucae Euangelium Expositio*, ed. D. Hurst *CCSL*, 120 (Turnhout, 1960) 1–425.

————, *In Primam Partem Samuhelis Libri IIII*, ed. D. Hurst *CCSL* 119 (Turnhout, 1962) 1–287.

————, *In Prouerbia Salomonis*, ed. D. Hurst, *CCSL* 119B (Turnhout, 1983) 23–163.

————, *In Tobiam*, ed. D. Hurst, *CCSL* 119B (Turnhout, 1983) 1–19.

————, *Libri Quattuor in Principium Genesim*, ed. C. W. Jones *CCSL* 118A (Turnhout, 1967).

————, *Retractatio in Actuum Apostolorum*, ed. M. L.W. Laistner *CCSL* 121 (Turnhout, 1983) 103–163.

————, *Vita Sancti Cuthberti* (prose), ed. and tr. B. Colgrave, *Two Lives of St Cuthbert* (Cambridge, 1940) 142–307.

Biblia Sacra iuxta uulgatam uersionem, ed. R. Weber, 2 vols. (Stuttgart, 1969; 3rd ed., 1984).

Bunyan, J., *The Pilgrim's Progress*, ed. H. H. Keeble (Oxford, 1984).

————, *Grace Abounding to the Chief of Sinners*, ed. W. R. Owen (Harmondsworth, 1987).

Cassiodorus, *Institutiones*, ed. R. A. B. Mynors (Oxford, 1937); tr. L. W. Jones, *An Introduction to Divine and Human Readings* (New York, 1946).

Columbanus, *Sancti Columbani Opera*, ed. and tr. G. S.M. Walker (Dublin, 1970).

Corpus Consuetudinum Monasticarum vol. I ed. Kassius Hallinger, OSB vol. I (Schmitt, Siegburg, 1963ff.); vol. VII (ibid., 1983–86).

Cuthbert, *Epistola De Obitu Bedae*, ed. and tr. Colgrave and Mynors (1969) 580–587. English translation reprinted in McClure and Collins (ed. and tr.) 1994, 343–357.

Earliest Life of Gregory the Great, ed. and tr. B. Colgrave (Kansas, 1968; repr. Cambridge, 1985).

English Historical Documents c.550–1042, vol. 1 ed. D. Whitelock (London, 2nd ed. 1979).

Gildas, *The Ruin of Britain and Other Works*, ed. and tr. M. Winterbottom (London and Chichester, 1978).

Gregory, *Expositio in Canticum Canticorum*, ed. P. Verbracken, *CCSL* 144 (Turnhout, 1963); tr. D. Turner in *Eros and Allegory. Medieval Exegesis of the Song of Songs* (Kalamazoo, 1995), 217–47.

————, *Homiliae in Euangelia*, ed. in *PL* 76; tr. D. Hurst, *Homilies on the Gospels Cistercian Studies Series* 123 (Kalamazoo, 1990).

————, *Moralia in Iob*, ed. M. Adriaen, *CCSL* 143, 143A, 143B (Turnhout, 1979–85).

————, *Registrum Epistularum* Libri VIII–XIV, ed. D. Norberg, *CCSL* 140A (Turnhout, 1982).

Holy Bible, Douay version (Catholic Truth Society, London, 1956).

————, tr., R. Knox: *Holy Bible: Old Testament* (London, 1949) in 2 vols.; *New Testament*, (London, 1945).

————, *Jerusalem Bible*, ed. A. Jones (London, 1966).

————, *New Jerusalem Bible*, ed. H. Wansbrough (London, 1985).

————, *New Testament*, Revised Challoner-Rheims Version, ed. Catholic Scholars under patronage of Episcopal Committee of the Confraternity of Christian Doctrine (Brooklyn, 1986).

Jerome, *Commentariorum in Abacuc Prophetam ad Chromatium*, ed. M. Adriaen, *CCSL* 76A (Turnhout, 1970) 618–54.

————, *Commentariorum in Zachariam Prophetam*, ibid., 747–900.

————, *de Nominibus Hebraicis*, ed. P. de Lagarde, *CCSL*, 72 (Turnhout, 1959).

————, *de Situ Locorum*, ed. in *PL* 23.

Liber Pontificalis, ed. L. Duchesne and C. Vogel, 3 vols. (Paris, 1886–1956); tr. R. Davis, *Book of Pontiffs* (Liverpool, 1989).

Marvell, A., *Andrew Marvell. The Complete Poems*, ed. E. S. Donna (London, 1972).

Rule of Benedict: A Guide to Christian Living with commentary by George Holzherr (tr. Monks of Glenstal Abbey) (Four Courts Press, Dublin, 1994).

Septuaginta (2 vols.) ed. A. Rahlfs; 3rd edition (Stuttgart, 1949).

The Septuagint with Apocrypha: Greek and English (tr. Sir Lancelot C. L. Brenton) (London, Bagster, 1851; reprinted by Zondervan Publishing House, Grand Rapids, Michigan, n. d.).

Verecundus Iuncensis, *Commentarii super Cantica Ecclesiastica*, ed. R. Demeulenaere, *CCSL* 93 (Turnhout, 1976).

Vita Sancti Cuthberti Auctore Anonymo, ed. and tr. B. Colgrave, *Two Lives of St Cuthbert*, (Cambridge, 1940), 60–139.

Walahfrid Strabo, *Vita Galli*, ed. B. Krusch, *MGH Scr. Mer.* IV (Hannover and Leipzig, 1902) 280–337.

SECONDARY SOURCES

Ackroyd, P. R., *The Cambridge History of the Bible* vol. 1 (Cambridge, 1970).

Blair, J. and Sharpe R., eds., *Pastoral Care Before the Parish (Studies in the Early History of Britain)* (Leicester, 1992).

Bolton, W. F., 'An Aspect of Bede's Later Knowledge of Greek', in *Classical Review*, 13 (1963), 17–18.

Bonner, G., *Saint Bede in the Tradition of Western Apocalyptic Commentary* (Jarrow Lecture, 1966). Reprinted in *Bede and his World. The Jarrow Lectures*. vol. 1.

————, ed. *Famulus Christi: Essays in Commemoration of the Thirteenth Centenary of the Birth of the Venerable Bede* (London, 1976).

Brown, G. H., *Bede the Venerable* (Twayne's English Authors Series) 443 (Boston, 1987).

Campbell, J., 'Bede' in *Latin Historians*, ed. T. A. Dorey (London, 1966), 159–90. Reprinted in his *Essays in Anglo-Saxon History* (London, 1986). 1–27; cf. also 29–49.

————, 'The First Century of Christianity in England', in *Ampleforth Journal*, 76 (1971), 12–29. Reprinted in his *Essays in Anglo-Saxon History*, 47–67.

————, 'Observations on the Conversion of England: A Brief Commemorative Review Article', *Ampleforth Journal*, 78 (1973), 2, 12–26. Reprinted in his *Essays in Anglo-Saxon History*, 69–84.

Capelle, P., 'Le rôle théologique de Bède le Vénérable', in *Studia Anselmiana*, 6 (1936), 1–40.

Carroll, Sr. M. T. A., *The Venerable Bede: His Spiritual Teachings (Catholic University of America Studies in Mediaeval History* n. s. 9; Washington, D. C., 1946).

Charles-Edwards, T. M., 'Bede, the Irish and the Britons', in *Celtica*, 15 (1983), 41–52.

Cohen, J., 'The Jews as the Killers of Christ in the Latin Tradition, from Augustine to the Friars', *Traditio* 39 (1983) 1–27.

Colgrave, B., *The Venerable Bede and his Times* (Jarrow Lecture, 1958). Reprinted in *Bede and his World. The Jarrow Lectures*, vol. 1.

Cowdrey, H. E. ., 'Bede and the "English People" ', in *Journal of Religious History*, 11 (1981), 501–23. Reprinted in his *Popes, Monks and Crusaders* (London, 1984), No. 3.

Crépin, A., 'Bede and the Vernacular', in *Famulus Christi*, ed. G. Bonner, 170–193.

Davidse, J., 'The Sense of History in the works of the Venerable Bede', in *Studi Medievali*, 23 (1983) 647–95.

Davidson, A. B. *Hebrew Syntax*, 3rd edn. (T & T Clark, Edinburgh, 1901).

de Lubac, H., *Exégèse médiévale: Les quatre sens de l'Écriture*, 2 vols. in 4 parts (Paris, 1959–1964).

Deshman, R., 'The imagery of the living *Ecclesia* of the English monastic reform', in P. Szarmach ed., *Sources of Anglo-Saxon Culture* (Kalamazoo, 1986), 261–82.

Fell, C. E., 'Hild, Abbess of Streonaeshalch', in *Hagiography and Medieval Literature: A Symposium.*, ed. H. Bekker-Nielsen et al. (Odense, 1978), 1–13.

Foot, S., 'The Parochial Ministry in Early Anglo-Saxon England: The Role of Monastic Communities', in *The Ministry: Clerical and Lay*, ed. W. J. Sheils and D. Wood (*Studies in Church History* 26; Oxford and Cambridge, Mass., 1989), 43–54.

Fry, D. K., 'The Art of Bede: Edwin's Council', in *Saints, Scholars, and Heroes*, ed. M. H. King and W. M. Stevens (Collegeville MN, 1979), 191–207.

Goffart, W., *The Narrators of Barbarian History, AD 550–800*, (Princeton, 1988).

Hamilton-Thompson, A., ed. *Bede, his Life, Times, and Writings: Essays in Commemoration of the Twelfth Centenary of his Death* (Oxford, 1935).

Hanning, R. W., *The Vision of History in Early Britain*, (New York, 1966).

Henderson, G., *Bede and the Visual Arts* (Jarrow Lecture, 1980). Reprinted in *Bede and His World. The Jarrow Lectures*, vol. 2.

Higham, N. J., *An English Empire. Bede and the early Anglo-Saxon Kings* (Manchester, 1995).

Hofmann, J. B. und Anton Szantyr, *Lateinische Syntax und Stilistik*, zweiter Band (Munich, 1965).

Holder, A. G., 'Allegory and history in Bede's interpretation of sacred architecture', in *American Benedictine Review* 40, (1989), 115–31.

————, 'New Treasures and Old in Bede's *De tabernaculo* and *De templo*, in *Revue Bénédictine*, 99 (1989), 237–249.

Hollis, S., *Anglo-Saxon Women and the Church. Sharing a Common Fate* (Woodbridge, 1992).

Hunter Blair, P., *'Bede's Ecclesiastical History of the English Nation and its Importance Today'* (Jarrow Lecture, 1959). Reprinted in his *Anglo-Saxon Northumbria*, No. 7 and in *Bede and his World. The Jarrow Lectures.*

————, *The World of Bede* (Cambridge, 1970).

————, 'The Historical Writings of Bede', in *Spoleto*, 17 (1970), 197–221. Reprinted in his *Anglo-Saxon Northumbria*, No. 10.

Jenkins, C., 'Bede as Exegete and Theologian', in *Bede: His Life, Times and Writings*, ed. A. Hamilton Thompson, 152–200.

Jerome Biblical Commentary, R. E. Brown, J. A. Fitzmyer, R. E. Murphy (eds.), (Prentice Hall, New Jersey, 1968).

Jones, C. W., 'Some Introductory Remarks on Bede's Commentary on Genesis', in *Sacris Erudiri* 19 (1969–70), 113–198. Reprinted in W. M. Stevens (ed.), *Bede, the Schools and the Computus* (Aldershot, 1994), No.4.

Jones, P. F., *A Concordance to the Historia Ecclesiastica of Bede* (Medieval Academy of American Publication, 2; Cambridge, Mass., 1929).

Kendall, C. B., 'Bede's *Historia Ecclesiastica:* the Rhetoric of faith', in *Medieval Eloquence: Studies in the Theory and Practice of Medieval Rhetoric*, ed. J. J. Murphy (Berkeley, 1978), 145–72.

————, 'Imitation and the Venerable Bede's *Historia Ecclesiastica'*, in *Saints, Scholars, and Heroes*, ed. M. H. King and W. M. Stevens, 161–190.

King, M. H. and W. M. Stevens, *Saints, Scholars and Heroes: Studies in Medieval Culture in Honour of Charles W. Jones* (Collegeville, 1979).

Ladner, G. B. C., 'The symbolism of the biblical cornerstone in the medieval west', in *Medieval Studies*, 4, (1942) 43–60. Repr. G. Ladner, *Images and Ideas in the Middle Ages. Selected Studies in History and Art* (Rome 1983) I, 171–96.

Laistner, M. L. W., 'The Library of the Venerable Bede', in *Bede, His Life, Times, and Writings*, ed. A. H. Thompson, 237–266.

Lapidge, M. ed., *Bede and his World. The Jarrow Lectures*, 2 vols. (London, 1995).

Leclercq, J., *The Love of Learning and the Desire for God* (New York, 1961).

Lewis, C. T. and C. Short, *A Latin Dictionary* (Oxford, 1879, reprinted Oxford, 1966).

Levison, W., 'Bede as Historian', in *Bede: His Life, Times and Writings*, ed. A. H. Thompson 111–151.

McClure, J., 'Bede's Old Testament Kings', in *Ideal and Reality*, ed. P. Wormald, D. Bullough and R. Collins, 76–98.

————, 'Bede's *Notes on Genesis* and the training of the Anglo-Saxon clergy' in *The Bible in the Medieval World: Essays in Memory of*

Beryl Smalley (Studies in Church History, Subsidia 4, Oxford, 1985) eds. K. Walsh and D. Wood, 17–30.

Mackay, T. W., 'Bede's Biblical Criticism: the Venerable Bede's Summary of Tyconius' *Liber regularum'*, in *Saints, Scholars, and Heroes: Studies in Medieval Culture in Honour of Charles W. Jones*, ed. M. H. King and W. M. Stevens, 209–31.

Mann, J., 'Allegorical buildings in medieval literature', *Medium Aevum* 63, (1994) 191–209.

Markus, R. A., 'Gregory the Great and a Papal Missionary Strategy', in *The mission of the Church and the Propagation of the Faith*, ed. G. J. Cuming, *Studies in Church History*, 6 (1970), 29–38. Reprinted in his *From Augustine to Gregory the Great*, No. 2.

————, *Bede and the Tradition of Ecclesiastical Historiography*, (Jarrow Lecture 1975). Reprinted in his *From Augustine to Gregory the Great*, No. 2. Reprinted in *Bede and His World. The Jarrow Lectures*, vol. 1.

Marsden, R., *The Text of the Old Testament in Anglo-Saxon England* (Cambridge, 1995).

————, 'The survival of Ceolfrith's *Tobit* in a Tenth-Century Insular Manuscript', *Journal of Theological Studies* 45 (1994) 160–170.

Martin, L. T., 'Bede's Structural use of Word-play as a Way to Teach' in *From Cloister to Classroom*, ed. E. R. Elder (Kalamazoo, 1986) 27–46.

Mayr-Harting, H. M. R. E., *The Coming of Christianity to Anglo-Saxon England* (London, 1972; 3rd ed. 1991).

————, *The Venerable Bede, the Rule of St. Benedict, and Social Class*, (Jarrow Lecture, 1976). Reprinted in *Bede and His World. The Jarrow Lectures*, vol. 1.

Meyvaert, P., *Bede and Gregory the Great* (Jarrow Lecture, 1964). Reprinted in *Benedict, Gregory, Bede and Others* (London, 1977), No. 8, and in *Bede and His World. The Jarrow Lectures*, vol. 1.

————, 'Bede the Scholar', in *Famulus Christi: Essays in Commemoration of the Thirteenth Centenary of the Birth of the Venerable Bede*, ed. Gerald Bonner (London, 1976), 40–69. Reprinted in *Benedict, Gregory, Bede and Others* (London, 1977), No. 16.

————, 'Bede and the Church Paintings at Wearmouth-Jarrow', in *Anglo-Saxon England* 8 (1979), 63–77.

Michael, R., 'Antisemitism and the Church Fathers' in M. Perry and F. M. Schweitzer (eds.), *Jewish-Christian Encounters over the Centuries* (New York, 1994) 101–130.

New Jerome Biblical Commentary, R. E. Brown, J. A. Fitzmyer, R. E. Murphy (eds.), (Prentice Hall, New Jersey, 1990).

Ó Carragáin, E., 'Christ over the Beasts and the Agnus Dei: Two multivalent panels on the Ruthwell and Bewcastle crosses' in *Sources of Anglo-Saxon Culture*, ed. P. E. Szarmach (Kalamazoo, MI, 1986) 377–403.

—————, 'The Ruthwell Cross and some Irish High Crosses: some points of comparison and contrast' in M. Ryan (ed.), *Ireland and Insular Art* (Dublin, 1987), 118–28.

—————, 'The meeting of St Paul and St Anthony: visual and literary uses of a eucharistic motif', in *Keimeila*, ed. G. MacNiocaill and P. F. Wallace (Galway, 1988), 1–58.

—————, " *'Traditio Evangeliorum'* and *'Sustentatio'*: the relevance of liturgical ceremonies to the Book of Kells", in *The Book of Kells. Proceedings of a conference at Trinity College Dublin, 6–9 September 1992* ed. F. O'Mahoney (Aldershot, 1994), 398–436.

Olsen, G. W., 'Bede as Historian: The Evidence from his Observations on the Life of the First Christian Community at Jerusalem', in *Journal of Ecclesiastical History*, 33 (1982) 519–30.

Orchard, Dom B., ed. *A Catholic Commentary on Holy Scripture* (London, 1952).

O'Reilly, J., Introduction to *Bede: On the Temple*, tr. S. Connolly (Liverpool, 1995) xvii–lv.

—————, 'The Trees of Eden in Medieval Iconography' in *A Walk in the Garden. Biblical, Iconographical and Literary Images of Eden*, ed. P. Morris and D. Sawyer (Sheffield, 1992) 167–204.

Oxford Latin Dictionary (OLD), ed. P. G. Glare (Oxford, 1983).

Parkes, M., *The Scriptorium of Wearmouth-Jarrow* (Jarrow Lecture, 1982). Reprinted in *Bede and His World. The Jarrow Lectures*, vol. 2.

Ray, R. D., 'Bede, the Exegete, as Historian', in *Famulus Christi* (1976) 125–140.

—————, 'Bede's *vera lex historiae*', in *Speculum*, 55 (1980) 1–21.

—————, 'What do we know about Bede's Commentaries?', in *Recherches de Théologie ancienne et médiévale*, 49 (1982), 5–20.

—————, *De Consensu Evangelistarum* and the historical education of the Venerable Bede', in *Studia Patristica*, 16 (1985) 557–63.

—————, 'The triumph of Greco-Roman rhetorical assumptions in pre-Carolingian historiography', in *The Inheritance of Historiography 350–900*, ed. C. Holdsworth and T. P. Wiseman (Exeter, 1986) 67–84.

Santoro, V., 'Sul concetto di *Brittannia* tra Antichità e Medioevo', in *Romanobarbarica* 11 (1992) 321–34.

Scully, D., *'Gens innoxia.* The Irish in Bede's *Ecclesiastical History'*. (Forthcoming article.)

Smalley, B., *The Study of the Bible in the Middle Ages* (Oxford, 1952).

Spicq, C., *Esquisse d'une histoire de l'exégèse latine au moyen âge* (Paris, 1944).

Stancliffe, C., 'Kings who opted out', in *Ideal and Reality*, ed. P. Wormald, D. Bullough and R. Collins, 59–94.

Sutcliffe, E. J., 'The Venerable Bede's Knowledge of Hebrew', in *Biblica*, 16 (1935) 301–306.

Thacker, A., 'Bede's Ideal of Reform', in *Ideal and Reality in Frankish and Anglo-Saxon Society*: ed. P. Wormald, D. Bullough and R. Collins, 130–53.

————, 'Monks, preaching and pastoral care in early Anglo-Saxon England', in J. Blair and R. Sharpe ed. (1992) 137–70.

————, 'Bede and the Irish', in *Beda Venerabilis. Historian, Monk and Northumbrian*, ed. L. A. J. R. Houwen and A. A. MacDonald (Groningen, 1996) 31–59.

Tugène, G., 'L'Histoire "ecclésiastique" du peuple anglais: réflexions sur le particularisme et l'universalisme chez Bède,' in *Recherches Augustiniennes*, 17 (1982) 129–72.

Wallace-Hadrill, J. M., *Bede's Ecclesiastical History of the English People: A Historical Commentary* (Oxford, 1988).

Walsh, K. and D. Wood eds., *The Bible in the Medieval World: Essays in Memory of Beryl Smalley* (Studies in Church History, Subsidia 4, Oxford, 1985).

Ward, B., 'Miracles and History: a reconsideration of the Miracle Stories used by Bede' in Bonner ed. (1976) 70–76. Reprinted in B. Ward, *Signs and wonders. Saints, Miracles and Prayers from the 4th century to the 14th* (Aldershot, 1994), no. 9.

————, *The Venerable Bede, (Outstanding Christian Thinkers series)*, (London,1990).

West, P. J., 'Rumination in Bede's account of Caedmon', *Monastic Studies* 12 (1976) 217–26.

Whitelock, D., 'Bede and His Teachers and Friends', in *Famulus Christi*, ed. G. Bonner (London, 1976), 19–39.

Wieland, G., 'Caedmon, the clean animal', *American Benedictine Review* 35 (1984) 194–203.

Wilken, R. L., *The Land Called Holy. Palestine in Christian History and Thought* (New Haven and London, 1992).

Wormald, P., 'Bede, the *Bretwaldas*, and the Origins of the *Gens Anglorum*', in *Ideal and Reality* (Oxford, 1983), 99–129.

————, D. Bullough and R. Collins eds. *Ideal and Reality in Frankish and Anglo-Saxon Society: studies presented to J. M. Wallace-Hadrill* (Oxford, 1983).

INDEX OF BIBLICAL QUOTATIONS AND ALLUSIONS

The asterisk indicates a reminiscence or allusion.

Matthew *continued*
11.30 .... *H37.31;*T23.3
17.1ff. *H4.3;*H10.5
17.5 .... H4.6
22.37 .... *H38.27
25.1–10 .... *H37.24
26.69–75 .... *H15.3
28.19 .... H24.14;T11.2

Mark
9.2–13 .... *H4.3;*H10.5
12.30 .... *H38.27
14.33 .... T13.2
14.35–36 .... T13.3
14.66–72 .... *H15.3

Luke
1.35 .... H7.17
2.14 .... H8.10
2.49 .... H7.11
9.22.44 .... *H2.5
9.28–36 .... *H4.3;*H10.5
10.1 .... H12.7
10.27 .... *H38.27
11.11–12 .... *T34.12
12.32 .... H37.4
14.11 .... H16.4
16.8 .... *H26.11;*T14.9
18.32 .... *H2.5
22.55–62 .... *H15.3
23.34 .... *H4.9
23.39–45 .... *H4.7

John
1.14 .... *H8.8; T9.4
2.1–10 .... *T25.4
3.17 .... *H28.2
3.31+32 .... H2.10
5.22 .... H21.7
6.42 .... H30.5
7.38 .... H22.3
7.39 .... H22.4
8.12 .... T8.5
8.26 .... H2.8
8.50 .... *H38.7
9.40 .... T34.7
10.16 .... T8.9;T35.4
12.13 .... H20.5
14.10 .... *T36.5
14.21 .... H38.28
15.15 .... H2.9;T16.14
17.4 .... H17.5
17.5 .... H17.7

Acts
2.3 .... *T16.5
3.10 .... H30.7
3.22 .... T3.4
5.15 .... *H7.23
7.51 .... H29.8
8.27 .... *H18.8
9,3,22 .... *H15.6
10.44–48 .... *T11.3

Romans
8.11 .... *H12.6
8.15 .... *H28.6
8.24 .... H36.3
8.25 .... T34.11
8.28 .... H38.12
8.29 .... *T14.9;*T40.3
10.2–3 .... T34.4–5
10.18 .... H7.8;*H18.7
11.25 .... T5.3
11.25–26 .. *T3.15;T8.10;*T29.3
11.26 .... *T28.4
12.12 .... H36.4
15.10 .... T36.2

1 Corinthians
9.27 .... *H33.7
15.26 .... H10.4
16.13 .... *H25.3;*T5.7

2 Corinthians
2.11 .... T15.5
3.15 .... *T34.13
5.19 .... H28.11
6.7 .... T23.7
6.11–13 .... H24.18

Galatians
4.4–5 .... H5.2
4.26 .... *H20.6
4.26 .... *T37.2
4.28 .... *T16.11
5.24 .... *T23.11

Ephesians
1.5 .... *T40.3
1.22–23 .... *T14.7
2.20 .... *T35.4
5.8 .... *T14.9
5.14 .... T5.8
5.23 .... *T14.7

Philippians
2.8 .... *H3.2;H17.10
2.9–11 .... H17.12

109

INDEX OF PATRISTIC SOURCES

INDEX OF NAMES AND SELECTED THEMES

Bk=Book; Tb=Tobit; Tbs=Tobias; n.=footnote; ‖=parallels etc. (*see* Preface)

Abraham: Sarah's name befits Church because of Sarah, wife of —, who bore Isaac son of the promise, i.e. free people of Church, T16.11; Midianite people took origin by Keturah from one of —'s sons Midian, H18.9

Acts of Apostles testify to Gentiles' welcome for Lord's word, T18.2: minister of Candace, queen of Ethiopians, first-fruits of Gentiles, as we read in —, H18.8

adoption: those whom Christ made his anointed through spirit of —, H28.6

adversities: hope of future rewards reduces & lightens —, H35.9; H36.3; (the prophet) bears witness that amid — he rejoices in him (Jesus) who was to be born long afterwards, H37.7; all temptations, whether from — or allurements of the world, I shall overcome by his glory, H38.6; — of present world, H38.19

affliction(s) (*see* suffering(s)): — of saints/the upright/ in this life, H1.4,12; H2.11; the heavier the burden that weighs upon them in this life the higher up they will go (in heaven) after —, H36.26; temporal — of the good, H5.5; eternal tribulation overtakes reprobate, H36.19; intercession of virtuous affords shade from heat of tribulation, H7.21–22; day of tribulation, H36.1,17; he who does not doubt that through his temporal — he will gain eternal joys, rests not only on day of recompense but also on day of tribulation, H36.2; tribulations of saints, H2.13; patient in tribulation, H36.3; day of tribulation can mean this life, for those who set inordinate store by temporal things suffer pain, surrounded by woes, H36.23–24; pressure of (prophet's) woes, H4.10

allurements of present world, H38.6,19

alms: graver guilty actions call for greater penance tears & —, H6.8

Ananias: Azarias son of —, T9.1; — = 'favour of Lord', T9.2

angel(s), (*see* archangel, Gabriel, Raphael): — bound demon ‖ restrained him from harming faithful, T21.1–2; — ‖ (Christ's) divinity, T6.9; dog that is traveller & companion of —, T30.2; — greets Tb, T8.1; Jacob while wrestling with — was both lamed & blessed, T5.17; Lord's miracles showed he was — i.e. messenger, of Father's will, T8.3; — & man ‖ the one person of mediator between God & men, T6.6; — more clearly explains who he is, why he has come & that he is to return to God, T36.4; — Raphael (which means 'healing of God'), T7.1; — assign each of redeemed a place in heaven, T41.3; coming of — to Tbs ‖ Christ's coming on earth, T7.4; — felicitate (Lord) on community of redeemed mankind, T41.3; redeemed mankind in heaven will complement number of —, T41.10; — with whom (elect) are to be joined forever in fraternal fellowship, T41.10

anger (it see fury, rage, wrath): Lord, rebuke me not in your —, H27.6; cf. was your indignation against the sea? H19.1; due repentance for fear of your — & punishment, H6.2; (prophet) deeply troubled at thought of Lord's —, H6.5; (prophet) feared Lord's — & wrath, H22.2; Lord had turned from — to mercy, H6.5; Lord venting — upon those refusing to humble themselves, H27.4

animals (*see* living beings)

Annunciation: Gabriel announcing good news to virgin mother, H7.16

anoint: –ing, H28.7–8; –ing of Tb's eyes with fish's gall ‖ Lord reveals devil's malice, T33.1–2; –ing heads of worthless with unction of adulation, H37.21; all elect −ed with grace of Holy Spirit, H28.3; by appearing in flesh Christ made (believers) his −ed through spirit of adoption, H28.6; Christ saved his −ed, H28.6; Lord's chosen ones called −ed, H29.2; eternal death for those refusing to be −ed with Christ's grace, H29.2

apostles: Lord's horses ‖ — & their successors, H21.3; first seeds of faith sown in temple through −' preaching, H7.7; — ‖ horses mounted by Lord, H20.2–6;, H21.3; −' preaching, H12.3,7; *effects of:* −' preaching, H8.5

Arabia: desert of Saracens to east of Red Sea in —, H18.9

archangel (*see* angel, Gabriel, Raphael): Tbs married Sarah after tying up devil on instructions & with aid of — (Raphael), T6.4; divinity of our saviour ‖ —, T6.5

arms: (i.e. weapons) ‖ miracles to authenticate truth of preaching, H26.7

arrogant (*see* pride)

ascension: Christ's —, T10.3; mystery of —, H8.2–3

Assyrians: captivity of Jews by —, T2.1–2; Shalmaneser king of —, T2.1

Azarias son of Ananias, T9.1: — = 'Lord is my helper', T9.2

Babylon, H36.7: — = 'confusion of this world', H36.11

bad: men's good deeds have — meaning & their — deeds a good meaning, T5.2

banquet: Raguel had — prepared for neighbours & friends, T23.1; Raguel had — prepared ‖ progress, life, suffering & crown of saints give joy to many, T23.12

baptism: demon driven out by means of water of — ‖ demon bound by angel, T21.1

Baptist: John the —, H2.9

baptize: Peter −d (Cornelius' household) with water, T11.3

beasts: thieves & — ‖ unclean spirits & heretical men, T11.4

beatific vision H23.4

beatings: innocent subjected to daily —, H1.5

belief: (*see* faith)

believe: Tb −ing & confessing what the Father says..., T3.6; Tb −ing & confessing that he would commit no sin, T3.10; Jews who — at end of world, T3.15

believer(s): faith of —, T10.3; Tb ‖ unbelievers through blindness & — through faith, T28.5; Jacob ‖ — by his blessing, T5.17; Lord's promises to — among Jewish people, T8.7–8; Lord bids Church at first betrothal (in person of each individual —) to renounce Satan..., T20.2; faithful ask Lord to entrust some of — with preaching the word, T25.2; — among Jews sad at blindness of Israelite unbelievers, T29.4; Lord reveals to — malice of ancient dragon, T33.2; in Judea — admonish neighbours of approaching end of world & good things of future life soon to come, T38.2; our saviour's miracles & teaching will enlighten —, H9.2; faith of —, persecution by unbelievers, T10.3; persecution to be instigated against — by unbelievers, H33.5

belly H33.1: — = mind, H33.2; prophet's — trembled with terror, H35.6–7

Bethlehem where Lord was born, H7.13: — situated south of Jerusalem, H7.13

betrothal: Lord bade Church at its — to renounce Satan & confess faith in trinity for remission of sins, T20.2–3

bind: angel bound demon in desert of upper Egypt ‖ restrained him from harming faithful, T21.2–3

black: that God is light written in — ink, T5.3

blessing: Jacob by his — ‖ believers, T5.17

blind: Tb became —, T5.1; Tb wearied with burying & –ed, T5.6

blindness: Tb's — ‖ — has come upon part of Israel, T5.5; — overcame people of Israel especially before incarnation, T5.11; Raphael sent to rid Tb of — & Sarah of demon, T7.1; Tb ‖ unbelievers through — & believers through faith, T28.5; believers among Jews sad at — of unbelievers, T29.4

bliss: everlasting — of heaven, H38.18

body: our Lord is head of his Church & Church is his —, T14.7; Lord with his whole — the Church he has redeemed, T41.2

bondage: (Gentiles') — of idolatry, T7.2

bones ‖ courageous & spiritual deeds, H34.3: (*see* flesh)

born again: those — through Lord's grace & filled with sevenfold Spirit, T38.3

bow: bend — at sceptres, H21.1–5; bending — at sceptres ‖ teachers' threat of God's sudden judgement, H21.4

bridegroom: true — our Lord, T6.3; Gentiles acknowledged Christ to be — of holy Church, T22.6; wedding-feast of Church at which — is Christ, T25.4; heavenly —, H38.29

bride: we shall merit to be reckoned among members of that — (i.e. Church), H38.29

burial of Tbs denotes end of whole world, T41.2

bury: Tb wearied with –ing falls asleep & is blinded, T5.1ff.

calumniator: the helpless unable to withstand ferocity of –s, H1.7

camels: cattle & — & Sarah's property in abundance ‖ the many virtues of Church incorporated with Hebrew people, T35.6; Raguel's — & servants = preachers chosen from Gentiles, T26.2; servants & — with Raphael's help bring Gabael to Tbs' wedding ‖ preachers bring new peoples into Church of Christ with his help, T26.5

Candace: minister of — queen of Ethiopians, H18.8

Canticle of Habakkuk a proclamation of mysteries of Lord's passion, H1.1

captivity: Tb in —, T2.1; Tb taken captive by king of Assyrians, T2.2; Assyrian — ‖ — of human race, T2.2

carnal: Christ broiled flesh of fish in those whom he found —, T16.4; Christ rendered the — spiritual & strong by fire of his love, T16.4

cattle & camels & Sarah's property in abundance ‖ the many virtues of Church incorporated with Hebrew people, T35.6: martyrs whether by death or mortification ‖ two slaughtered —, T23.6; Raguel had two fat — & four rams slaughtered, T23.1; *explanation as to* why Raguel had — & rams slaughtered, T23.10–11

Chaldaean army: saying of Zechariah concerning —, H7.4

chalk: name of devil written even in pure white — still means deep darkness, T5.4

Christ: (Note: In both of our texts the titles 'Christ' and 'the Lord' are used interchangeably of the same person. It may be worth noting, however, that compared with 'Christ', the title 'the Lord' is used much more frequently, particularly in *InHab*, occurring some 120 times in all as against 50 occurrences of 'Christ': almost two and a half times as often.); Bk of Tb contains greatest mysteries of — & Church, T1.3; — broiled flesh of fish in those he found

115

carnal, T16.4; dearly beloved sister in —, H1.1; divinity of — intimated in Lk 2.49, H7.10–11; Father saves through —, H28.10–11; Gentile people delighted at faith in —, T23.2; Gentiles acknowledged — as bridegroom of holy Church, T22.6; Gentiles entrusting to Jews mysteries of — for their salvation, T3.16; Habakkuk writes of future mysteries of —, H33.9; Jesus — king & high priest typified by Zorobabel & Joshua, H36.12; — king of kings & Lord of lords, H10.11; — = anointed, H28.1; — saved his anointed, H28.6; — made believers his anointed by incarnation, H28.6; — made believers his anointed through spirit of adoption, H28.6; procreation of — without male intervention, H7.19; (prophet) focusing on future sufferings of —, H33.4; –'s promise of consolation, H37.3; — (stone from mountain) crushed kingdoms of world, H7.19; virgin of —, H38.26; — was to be born of Tb's own kin, T3.3; wedding-feast of Church at which bridegroom is —, T25.4; with –'s assistance preachers bring new peoples into Church, T26.5; Church will come in to it (Judea) that there may be one house of — supported upon one cornerstone, T35.4

Christian: Lord overthrows those who reject humility of — faith, H29.9

Church: after Judea is given light through faith, after it receives grace of Holy Spirit, — will come in to it, T35.3–4; — will come in to it (Judea) that there may be one house of Christ supported upon one cornerstone, T35.4; — after Lord's incarnation tossed to & fro like waves, T4.6; Bk of Tb contains greatest mysteries of Christ & —, T1.3; — bride of Lord, T16.10; brotherhood of entire — assembled in Christ worldwide, H37.34; cattle & camels & Sarah's property in abundance ‖ the many virtues of — incorporated with Hebrew people, T35.6; enemies of — ‖ thieves & beasts, i.e. unclean spirits & heretical men, T11.4; — enlightened so as to rise from illness of its unbelief, H25.3; — = founder's spiritual home, property & sheep, T11.4; Gentiles acknowledged Christ as bridegroom of holy —, T22.6; Gentiles receive Jews who believe into unity of —, T3.15; Habakkuk writes of future mysteries of —, H33.9; Lord incorporates new peoples into — every day, T25.5; Sarah's name befits — because of Sarah, Abraham's wife, who bore Isaac son of promise, i.e. free people of —, T16.11; Lord bade — at betrothal to renounce Satan & confess faith in trinity for remission of sins, T20.2–3; Lord with his whole body — enters into eternal rest, T41.2; preachers bring new peoples together into unity of — with Christ's assistance, T26.5; Tbs delaying at wedding ‖ Christ delays in — of Gentiles, T27.1–2; teachers ‖ dogs defending —, founder's spiritual home, property & sheep, T11.4; usage of holy universal & apostolic —, H1.2; wedding-feast of — at which bridegroom is Christ, T25.4; that by practising works of mercy in Jerusalem of present — we may prepare for entry into heavenly Jerusalem, H36.14–15

cock-crow: Raguel dug a grave about —, T22.1; — is voice of preachers, T22.2

coming: blindness got the better of people of Israel as — of Lord was imminent, T5.11; creator of world on — into world undertook world's way of life, T19.7; faithful await in hope — of glory of heavenly homeland, T34.11; Lord preceded word of preaching in apostles when they announced that good news of Christ's — had already been realized, H12.4; Jews distressed that Lord, detained among Gentiles, is slow in — to save them, T27.2; — of divine visitation an unexpected bow to test kingdoms of world, H21.2; this going forth, i.e. Lord's — into world, not merely for resurrection of faithful, but also for perdition of unbelievers, H28.12

commandments: so great violation of God's — throughout world, T39.4

commentaries of venerable Fathers, T6.7

companion: dog that is a traveller & — of an angel, T30.2

compunction: St Peter's tears of —, H14.2–3

condition of human frailty on earth, H38.2: prophet contemplates — of human race, H33.7; — of present world, H1.4

confess: Tb believing & –ing what Father says. . . , T3.6; believing & –ing that he (Tbs) would commit no sin, T3.10; burning entrails || renouncing Satan & –ing faith in trinity for remission of sins, T20.2–3

confession of true faith followed by remission of sins, T21.1

confidence: (*see* trust)

confiscate: Tb's property to be –ed on account of his good deeds, T4.1

consolation: Christ's promise of —, H37.3

contemplation *versus* action, H35.4: in light of — prophet sees his imperfections, H35.4–5; Lord raises gaze of faithful to — of perpetual light, T40.10; preachers enlightened by — of heavenly joys, H24.16; prophet rapt in — of heavenly mysteries, H35.3

convert: Gentiles wishing to — to (Jewish) way of life, T2.4; those –ed produce streams of doctrine for others, H23.9–10

Cornelius: Lord himself filled home of — with Holy Spirit, T11.3

cornerstone: Church will come in to it (Judea) that there may be one house of Christ supported upon one —, T35.4

correction, fraternal: (devout Jews) correct *erring brethren*, T5.15; cf. words of healing reproof or exhortation, H22.6

creator: Lord — by virtue of his divinity, H8.9; — of world coming into world undertook world's way of life, T19.6

creditor: Gentiles pay back —, T3.15

crime(s): devil & his —, spawned like a wicked brood, T4.5

cross: miraculous happenings around —, H4.8; Son of God had to undergo suffering of —, H1.13

crucifixion: events of — showed Christ's divinity, H4.8

crucify: devil ordered (Lord) to be –ied, T12.12

cure: your — from God is at hand, T8.2

darkness: Egypt || hearts clouded by — of unbelief, T21.7; Lord rescued future children of light from power of —, T14.9; Jewish people from whom black — of error is removed, T34.16; true dawn of faith to come after — of error, T22.2; one deserted by grace of divine light filled by prince of —, T21.6; prince of — found in (Lord) nothing of his own, T12.8; Paul & Silas singing hymn to God amid —, H38.14; Tb sitting in —, T8.2

darts: || Christ's words to pierce human hearts, H26.2; — || words of preachers that overcome perversity of unbelievers, H26.7

daughter: Raguel agreed to give — away, T19.1; Raguel alarmed when asked for his —, T19.1; fate of seven husbands of Raguel's —, T19.1; unclean could not have Raguel's —, T19.1

David T3.5

death: Lord dreaded —, T13.2; Lord washes faithful from sin & —, T12.9–10; destruction of eternal —, T19.4; devil desired — of humanity in our redeemer, T12.3–4; devil tried to cause spiritual — of God's people through idolatry, T4.3; lurking fish

|| invisible seducer of human race held power of —, T12.6; Lord's — destroyed him who had power of — i.e. devil, H3.2–3; dominion of — demolished by (Lord's) —, H9.4; Lord by dying caught the one who wanted to catch him in —, T14.2; departure from world in — was portion of Lord himself, H2.12; (Lord) conquering all — by this kind of —, H10.3; (Lord's) — confirms power of his glory in elect, H10,3.7–8; (Lord's) — promised glory of future immortality, H10.4

decalogue: knowledge of divine law which is contained in —, T3.12

deep: preachers || — i.e. filled with — knowledge of truth, H24.6–7; — || teachers, H24.2.4

delay: Tbs –ing at wedding || Christ –s in Church of Gentiles, T27.1–2

deluge & wiping out of human race, T39.5

demon (*see* devil): — allowed to tempt but not overcome faithful lest they fall away from faith, T21.2; — bound by angel || demon driven out by water of baptism, T21.1

desert: & Egypt || hearts of unbelievers which are deserts i.e. forsaken by God, T21.3–4; — of Saracens to east of Red Sea in Arabia, H18.9

devil: (*see* demon, (ancient) dragon, (ancient) enemy, Satan); (*other designations of* — ; deceiver, T16.3; (ancient) devourer, T12.4; malicious one, T38.4; invisible seducer, T12.6; — head of all wicked & all wicked are his head & members, T14.7; — head of those he allied to himself & made one body with him || Lord head of his Church & Church his body, T14.4–5; — king of all the perverse, T2.2); after renunciation of — follows remission of sins through baptism, T21.1; — allowed by Lord to have dominion over unbelievers only, T21.7; — ancient enemy, T14.4; — came to see if he could find any sin on (Lord's) soul, T12.12; — caught by power of divinity, T12.4; — desired death of humanity in our redeemer, T12.3–4; — not allowed to harm even the wicked as much as he longs to, T21.7; fish || — ancient devourer of human race, T12.4; in (unbelievers) too (Lord) holds — bound, T21.7; — invisible seducer of human race held power of death, T12.6; (Lord) by death destroyed him who had power of death i.e. —, H3.3; Lord dreaded not — but death which resulted from –'s envy, T13.2; Lord smashed to pieces –'s capabilities, T14.9; — master of wicked, T21.7; name of — in white chalk still means deep darkness, T5.4; — overcome & condemned for his crimes, a wicked brood, T4.5; renunciation of — followed by confession of faith in trinity for remission of sins, T20.2–3; — restrained from snatching away faithful, T21.7; –'s cunning, T15.3–4; –'s malicious fury against human race, T15.6; insatiable rage of —, T21.7; –'s wickedness & secret snares exposed by Lord, T15.2–7; Tbs tying up — on instructions & with aid of archangel, T6.4; young men || the strong in faith getting upper hand of malicious one, T38.4; those changed from members of — into members of Christ, i.e. converted from unbelief to faith, T16.2; those who on hearing God's word prefer to remain on as dead & decaying members of their deceiver rather than return to companionship of saviour, T16.1–3; — tried to cause spiritual death of God's people through idolatry, T4.3; — who had ordered (Lord) to be crucified, T12.12

disciples: (Lord) became known to — on mountain (of *Transfiguration*), H4.3

divinity (of Christ/the Lord) H7.16–17: faith in — will accompany him everywhere & accomplish everything at end of time, T8.8; saviour in his — remains with Father incapable of suffering, T6.8; Lord is understood by elect as equal to Father in his —, T36.7; Lord creator by virtue of his —, H8.9; cf. Jewish people in their writings recognize Christ is true God & man, T29.9; Lord our saviour lived as almighty among weak, as God among human beings, H2.3; events of crucifixion showed he (Lord) was God, H4.8; man (Isaac) in Isaac story ‖ godhead (of Christ), T6.9

doctrine(s): (*see* teaching(s)); bondage of worthless & harmful —, H31.6; those converted produce streams of — for others, H23.9–10; true —, H12.5

dog(s): holy preachers ‖ Tbs' —, T11.2; — ‖ Church's teachers, T30.3; — ran ahead ‖ teacher first preaches salvation then Lord, the enlightener, cleanses hearts, T30.5; teachers called — because they defend their founder's home & property, T11.4; Tbs set off & — followed him, T11.1; Tbs' — arriving as if bringing news, shows joy by wagging tail, T30.1; one must not scorn metaphor of this — that is traveller & angel's companion, T30.2; natural to — to repay favour to those kind to them, T30.4; — patrol in vigil for safety of their masters, T30.4

dominion: death's — demolished by (Lord's) death, H9.4

dragon: (*see* devil); ancient — eagerly longed to devour Christ in his passion & was killed for this & lost his members i.e. those he held in thrall, T33.2

earthly: transience of — things, H38.18; preferring — to heavenly things, H27.2; retrenching — appetites, H27.3

egg: denotes hope, T34.10

Egypt: desert & — ‖ hearts of unbelievers deserted by God, T21.3–4; — ‖ hearts clouded by darkness of unbelief, T21.7

elect: all — anointed with grace of Holy Spirit, H28.3; Tb blind & preaching God's word ‖ both reprobate & —, T5.16; — are (Lord's) feet by whose means he walks upon earth, T14.12; enemy instigated persecution against (Lord's) —, T14.12; — enjoy eternal fellowship of their heavenly compatriots, H36.26; — have rest because of their firm hope, H36.25; rest of — consists in renouncing earthly trifles for heaven, H36.5; Lord offered joy of salvation to his chosen ones, H29.2

Elijah: 'Between two living beings' ‖ 'between Moses & — ', H4.2

embrace: Father –d Lord, H38.25; Habakkuk = '-ing', H38.24; his (i.e. heavenly bridegroom's) right arm shall — me, H38.30; if we — God he will clasp us in arms of his love, H38.27

enemy (*see* devil): astuteness & cunning of ancient –'s trickery teach us caution, T15.11; — could not rob them of belief in Lord's incarnation, T4.4; — could not rob them of Synagogue, T4.4; — desired to conquer faithful by tempting but only made them victors by martyrdom, T23.10; — persecuted them with ferocity, T4.4; — instigated persecution against (Lord's) elect, T14.12; Lord on overcoming malicious — exposed him, T14.11; Gentiles who doubted whether Lord had vanquished ancient —, T22.3; our Lord overcame — (i.e. devil), T6.4

entrails: burning of fish's — ‖ renouncing Satan & confessing faith in trinity for remission of sins, T20.3

envy: death came through devil's —, T13.2

error: Jewish people from whom black darkness of — is removed, T34.16; preachers sang of true dawn of faith to come after darkness of —, T22.2

eternal death for those refusing to be anointed with Christ's grace, H29.2: destruction of — death, T19.4; elect enjoy — fellowship of their heavenly compatriots, H36.26; — hills, H16.1; — hills ‖ those converted to humility glorified –ly, H16.3; — hills = hills of Lord, H16.5–6; former teachers of Gentiles had nothing reliable to say on — joys, T19.3; cf. Gentiles without hope of immortal life but for God's word through teachers, T19.3–4; Gentile teachers unable to say anything about

— life, T6.2; people of Israel imploring God's mercy to obtain — life, T5.15; Lord enlightens hearts of those he has predestined to — life, T40.3; Christ answered teachers in temple as God of — majesty, H7.9; — rest welcomes in the just, H36.19; Lord with his whole body the Church enters into — rest at end of world, T41.2; Christ announced to Jews joy of — salvation, T8.4; — tribulation overtakes reprobate, H36.19;

eternity: journeys of Lord's —, H17.3,8–13

Ethiopia H18.1

Ethiopians: tents of —, H18.1; *meaning of* tents of —, H18.13; — Gentile people, H18.2; conversion of — & that of Midianites || conversion of all Gentiles, H18.2; — are at end of earth, H18.7; Candace queen of —, H18.8; Candace's minister first-fruits of Gentiles, H18.8; let — be awestruck at name of Christ that faith in him which is to reach ends of earth may be sealed, H18.10

evils could not happen without God's prevision, H1.8

example(s): Lord gathered from Judea as many as would set good —, T16.8; love & knowledge of truth engendered in us by good —, H7.27; saints by whose — faithful are refreshed, T23.12; Bk of Tb abounds in — of moral conduct, T1.1; prophet reminded by — of Lord's mercy to executioners to bestow kindness on his persecutors, H4.10; (the repentant) water parched hearts of others by — or word so as to bring forth fruits of virtues, H23.10; preachers/teachers sprinkle waters on their ways when they show — of upright living to those whose eyes are always upon them, H24.10

exile: Babylonian — & return from it || our own condition, H36.7,10; earthly — of human race, T2.2; Jews' return from — & restoration of temple & city, H36.8–9; cf. children of deportation, H36.7

faith: after Judea is given light through — Church will come in to it, T35.3–4; — enlightens hearts & renders them worthy of God's indwelling, H12.6; Lord scattered first seeds of — in temple through apostles' preaching, H7.7; Gentile people delighted at — in Christ, T23.2; spirit of —, H38.17; in gospel parable bread, fish & egg || three supreme virtues —, hope, love, T34.12; renouncing Satan & confessing — in trinity, T20.3; young men || those strong in — & getting upper hand of malicious one, T38.4; — in Christ's divinity to accompany him everywhere & accomplish everything at end of time, T8.8; Israel alone served God with true — & acts of virtue, T1.4; Jewish people when converted to — at end of world, T37.3; (Lord's) resurrection bestowed hope & — on world, H9.5; Lord gathered to — from Judea as many as would serve as an example of virtuous living or for ministry of preaching, T16.8; members of Christ i.e. those converted from unbelief to —, T16.2; nourishment & strengthening of — of Church, T10.2; –of believers, T10.3; — of Gentiles, H1.3; one who perseveres in good works never deprived of light of —, T5.6; preachers sang of true dawn of — to come after darkness of error, T22.2; prophet's —, hope & love, H37.5; Tb || unbelievers through blindness & believers through —, T28.5; work of teachers converts to repentance & —, H23.2–3; faithful ask Lord to come among them to gather to his — Gentiles who have not yet accepted mysteries of —, T25.2; that through obedience to — (Gentiles) may give back talent of word, T25.3; cf. belief in Lord's incarnation, T4.4

faithful are members of their redeemer, T21.7: — ask Lord to entrust some of believers with preaching the word, T25.2; — ask Lord to come among them to win Gentiles to faith, T25.2; Christ's coming was for resurrection of —, H28.12; — ones of Jews, H37.33

father: book of holy — Tb of saving benefit to its readers, T1.1; Where did this man whose — & mother we know come by all this? H30.5; (God the) —, T3.6; H21.6; Lord is understood by elect as equal to — in his divinity, T36.7; Lord showing (his people) he is in — & — in him, T36.5; (saviour) in his divinity remains with God —, T6.8; voice of — from heavens, H4.5

Fathers: (i.e. of Church): commentaries of venerable —, T6.7

fat: marrow & — || grace of heavenly love, T23.5

fear (*see* terror): Gentiles' — on hearing gospel, H18.1,3,5–6; — of (God's) punishments, T37.1; (prophet) in — & very alarmed on hearing tidings of (Lord) & pondering on passion, H5.5; (prophet's) — of (Lord's) anger, H6.1,2,4,5; prophet (Habakkuk's) — as he meditated on incarnation, H18.4; H34.4–6; cf. H2.11–13; Tbs who –ed God could have Raguel's daughter, T19.1; spirit of — of Lord, T3.10; cf. trembling over actions of one's frailty, H3.4; Tbs frightened of fish || Lord dreaded death, T13.1–2

feet: teachers || Lord's —, H13.3

fields not producing food || those unable to find truth in scripture, H37.25

fig-tree H37.1,8: — || Synagogue of Jews, H37.8

film: white — obstructing Tb's eyes || folly of self-indulgence, T34.3

first-born: Israel my —, T3.7–8

fish: huge — lurking in Tigris || invisible seducer of human race held power of death, T12.6; — trying to devour Tbs || ancient devourer of human race, T12.3; — trying to devour Tbs || mystery of Lord's passion, T12.2; Tbs frightened of — || Lord dreaded death, T13.1–2; Lord removed entrails of — || exposed devil's wickedness, T15.2; put away gall of — || Lord wanted devil's malicious fury against human race recorded, T15.6

fleeting (*see* transience)

flesh: Lord appeared in —, T10.2; natural frailty of — (in Lord), T13.2; cf. our frail human actions, H34.2; (*see also* bones)

fold (*see* pastor)

footsteps: preachers followed in (Lord's) —, T11.2

foreknowledge: Lord rescued those he foreknew to be children of light, T14.9

forgiveness: Lord's — of executioners, H4.9

founder: the redeemed, i.e. members of their —, T41.3; what life better than to dwell forever in glory of one's — ? T41.7

four servants & two camels || two cows & — rams slaughtered, T26.4: — slaughtered rams || — books of holy gospel, T23.8; — slaughtered rams || — cardinal virtues, T23.8; — slaughtered rams || whole world divided into — quarters, T23.9

frailty: condition of human — on earth, H38.2; those aware of their — & ignorance destined to enjoy light of life in Lord, T34.8

fury: fish's gall put away || devil's malicious — against human race recorded, T15.6; was your — against the rivers (Lord)? H19.1

Gabael Tb's fellow-kinsman who was in need, T3.11

Gabriel announcing good news to virgin mother, H7.16

gall: fish's — put away ‖ devil's malicious fury against human race recorded, T15.6

Gehenna: persecutors of saints undergo torments of —, H36.22

generation: Tbs' — ‖ — of those that seek Lord, T41.5; Tbs' — ‖ — of upright, T41.6

Gentile(s) (*see* nations): calling of — world to God, T23.2; — believers whom enemy desired to tempt but only made martyrs of, T23.10; — acknowledged Christ to be bridegroom of holy Church, T22.6; — admonished by apostles to form Church of Christ from progeny, T19.2; — agitated by preaching, H32.3–4; H33.5; because given to idolatry — all carried off by devil till Lord true bridegroom came, T6.3; — astonished at Lord's & apostles' miracles, H30.9; — by faith & upright living join in wedding-feast of Church, T25.3; — confessed belief in Christ, T19.7; *conflicting responses of — to Christian preaching*, H32.4–6; — delighted at faith in Christ, T23.2; — disavowed gods because of Lord's & apostles' miracles, H30.9; — embrace faith on witnessing miracles, H30.9; — embrace (*Christianity*) only after reliable investigation, T19.2; faithful ask Lord to come among them to win — to faith, T25.2; faith of —, H1.3; H33.4; –' fear on hearing gospel, H18.1,3,5–6; former teachers of — had nothing reliable to say on eternal joys, T19.3; former teachers of — knew about joys of this life alone, T19.3; teachers of — all knew about life in this world only, T6.2; their teachers unable to say anything about eternal life, T6.2; — gladly received Lord's word in great many places, T18.2; people of God entrusted to — knowledge of divine law, T3.12; — entrusting Christ's mysteries to Jews for their salvation, T3.16; in his teachers (Lord) came for salvation of —, T10.5; Jews join Church assembled from — by sharing in heavenly mysteries, T29.11; like hungry person — devour bread of God's word avidly, H31.4–6; Lord deigned to visit — through preachers to take a bride, T16.10; Lord detained among — is slow in coming to save Jews, T27.2; Lord sent to redeem — from bondage of idolatry, T7.2; Lord went to — people through teachers of his word, T18.2; until (Lord) should lay foundations of Church among —, T16.8; — made so much progress in Lord that some became teachers, even martyrs, T23.2; poverty of nations partakes of banquet of God's word, H31.7; preachers chosen from — through whom Lord wins over others, T26.2; Raguel giving daughter away ‖ — accepting faith, T19.2; Raguel stands for people of —, T16.10; — received word of God from Israel through translation, T3.14; cf. nations received letter of law through seventy translators, T25.6; — rejoiced that they were sanctified by his (Christ's) sacraments, T19.7; Sarah ‖ mass of —, T6.1; Tbs delays at wedding ‖ Christ delays in Church of —, T27.1–2; — through obedience to faith to return talent of word received, T25.3; — understood creator of world came into world & undertook world's way of life, T19.6; — unlock for Jews secrets of scriptures, T3.16; when — acknowledged light of truth they overthrew enemy, T22.4–6; when Lord came to save —, T11.2; — who doubted whether Lord had really vanquished ancient enemy, T22.3; — who have merely heard of but not accepted mysteries of faith, T25.2; — who thought it better to conceal belief in (Lord's) name, T22.3

gill of fish T14 *passim*: Tbs taking fish by — ‖ Lord seized hold of devil, T14.1–2

glory (-ies): Lord crowned with — & honour through his resurrection, H8.4; — of Lord, H38.21–22; prophet focusing on Christ's future sufferings & subsequent —, H33.4

God: help of —, H38.3,8; fear of punishments of —, T37.1; holy ancestors of people of Israel who once nobly served —, T5.14; (Lord) lived as almighty among weak, as — among human beings, H2.3; love of —, H38.12; mercy of —, T37.1; people of Israel imploring –'s mercy to obtain eternal life, T5.15; Tb reminding faithful to preach about –'s acts of kindness, T37.1; Tb confessing sternness & mercy of —, T37.1; punishments of —, T37.1; (saviour) in his divinity remains with — Father, T6.8; Son of — had to undergo suffering of cross, H1.13; evils could not happen without prevision of —, H1.8; that — is light written in black ink, T5.3; those who did not know true – would perish, T19.4

golden calves: Jeroboam made himself — || authors of idolatry, T5.3

gold: that God is light would always have been written in bright —, T5.3

good: men's — deeds have a bad meaning & their bad deeds a — meaning, T5.2; temporal affliction of the —, H5.5

good works: Lord takes care of those who continue in health of —, T40.9; one who perseveres in — never deprived of light of faith, T5.6; predestined have by Lord's bounty long been zealous for —, T40.4

goods: shortage of temporal —, H36.24; those who set inordinate store by temporal — suffer pain, H36.24; scorning worldly power through contemplation of everlasting —, H38.5

gospel: Gentiles' fear on hearing —, H18.1,3,5-6; teachers || cattle because they bear light yoke of —, T23.3; those who bear sweet yoke of —, H37.31

grace: divine — goes ahead to enlighten blindness of Jewish people, T29.9; God by whose — (blessed) have been redeemed, T41.9; offer of — by Lord, H37.16; — of heavenly love, T23.5 (*see* marrow); — of Holy Spirit made saints steadfast, H11.3; we attain perfection of holy rest through — of Holy Spirit, T24.2; after Judea receives — of Holy Spirit Church will come in to it, T35.3–4; one deserted by — of divine light filled by prince of darkness, T21.6; progress in virtue by gift of God's —, H23.9; repentance fruit of — not of human preacher's efforts, H13.6; singing praises of God's — here & in life to come, H38.20

Habakkuk = 'embracing', H38.24

hands: horns in Christ's — because he is king of kings & Lord of lords, H10.11

hardness of unbelief worn down by humility, H22.5: teachers by invective break down — of worldly spirit, H24.3

healing: astuteness & cunning of devil's trickery beneficial for — because by investigating we avoid them, T15.11; Raphael means '— of God', T7.1

heaven (*see* heavenly homeland): everlasting bliss of —, H38.18; cf. what life better, than to dwell forever in glory of one's founder? T41.7

heavenly: palm of — calling, H38.9; teachers accustomed to soar to — desires, T22.5; — Jerusalem mother of us all, H20.6; preachers enlightened by contemplation of — joys, H24.16; grace of — love, T23.5; angels assign place in — mansions according to merits, T41.3; preferring earthly to — things, H27.2–3

heavenly homeland (*see* homeland): human race banished from abode of its —, T2.2; in our first parent we were removed from our —, H36.11; (Jesus) opens gate of — to faithful, H37.7; joys of —, T37.3; unbelievers precluded from entry into —, H37.24; various mansions of — assigned according to merits, T41.3; when brought to — people will be acceptable to God by whose grace they have been redeemed, T41.9

Hebrew people (*see* Israel, Jewish people, Jews, Judea): cattle & camels & Sarah's property in abundance || the many virtues of Church incorporated with —, T35.6; — get up from deep sleep unbelief & run with love to Lord, T31.2; — reborn in

Christ & given instruction, T31.3; — stumbling in steps of their actions until they receive full light of faith & good works, T31.2–3

heretics: teachers combat — & drive off wolves from supreme pastor's fold, T30.3

hills: those who are less proud ‖ —, H16.2; eternal —, H16.1; eternal — ‖ those converted to humility glorified eternally, H16.3; eternal — = — of Lord, H16.5–6; — of Lord ‖ holy who spurn temporal things, H16.5–6

holiness: Peter ‖ tree refreshing those hungering & thirsting for —, H7.23–24

holy one: the —, H7.15

holy people: intercession of — shades our frailty against heat of tribulation, H7.21–22; love & knowledge of truth engendered by words of —, H7.28; teaching of — satisfies our hunger, H7.21; — ‖ south, H7.25

Holy Spirit: we attain perfection of holy rest through grace of —, T24.2; after Judea receives grace of — Church will come in to it, T35.3–4; all elect anointed with grace of —, H28.3; grace of — made saints steadfast, H11.3; seven days after Sarah arrived ‖ light of grace of — received in sevenfold form, T35.1–2; those born again through Lord's grace & filled with sevenfold Spirit, T38.3; Lord himself filled home of Cornelius with —, T11.3; — came down upon apostles in vision of fire, T16.5; sending of —, T10.3; — sent by Father, H25.2; they feast for seven days together ‖ they rejoice in gifts & virtues of Spirit, T36.3

homeland: & vision of supreme peace, H36.13; (*see also* heavenly homeland)

hope: elect have rest because of their firm —, H36.25; — of future rewards consoles & sustains, H35.9–H36.3; in gospel parable, bread, fish & egg ‖ three supreme virtues, faith, — & love, T34.12; (Lord's) resurrection bestowed — & faith on world, H9.5; prophet's faith, — & love, H37.5;

horns are in his hands, H10.1–13: — ‖ lofty powers of human mind, for good or evil, H10.10; — ‖ crossbeam of cross, H10.2; — in Christ's hands because he is king of kings & Lord of lords, H10.11; — ‖ kingdoms of this world, H10.9; — of kings i.e. power of arrogant, H11.4

horses: Lord's — ‖ apostles & their successors, H21.3; —, H20.1; preachers ‖ — mounted by Lord, H20.2–6; God's — ‖ holy preachers, H32.2–3

humanity: devil desired death of — in our redeemer, T12.3–4; Lord's — though mortal, excelled heavenly powers, H8.8; ram in Isaac story ‖ — of Christ, T6.9; Lord is of one nature with us in his —, T36.7; cf. Jewish people in their writings recognize Christ is true God & man, T29.9

human race banished from abode of its heavenly homeland, T2.2: (devil) invisible seducer of —, T12.6; Son of God assumed human nature to save —, T7.5

humble: by threatening severe judgement God –s earthly-minded, H27.1–2; Lord will condemn those who disdained being (–d) brought low in this life, H27.4

humility: conversion from pride to —, H15.4; eternal hills ‖ those converted to — glorified eternally, H16.3; hardness of unbelief worn down by —, H22.5; Saul & Matthew converted to — from pride, H15.6; Lord sent enemy force to overthrow proud people not merely of Jews but of all who refused to accept — of Christian faith, H29.9

hunger: poor person (fears) dying of —, H31.3; teaching of virtuous satisfies —, H7.21

husbands: fate of seven — of Raguel's daughter, T19.1; Sarah, Raguel's daughter, given to seven —, T6.1

idolatry: devil tried to cause spiritual death of God's people through —, T4.3; Gentiles all carried off by devil because given to —, T6.3; Gentiles given over to —, T1.4; Jeroboam made himself golden calves ‖ authors of —, T5.3; Lord sent to redeem Gentiles from bondage of —, T7.2

ignorance: those aware of their frailty & — destined to enjoy light of life in Lord, T34.8

incarnation: after Lord's — Gentiles understand God's word spiritually, T3.14; belief in Lord's —, T4.4; Church after Lord's — tossed to & fro like waves, T4.6; prophet pondering Lord's — & passion, H6.9; providential design of Lord's —, H1.11; Christ to reveal mysteries of — to Gentiles & Jews at end of time, T8.7–8; Canticle of Habakkuk gives mystical account of — resurrection & ascension, H1.3; Son of God assumed human nature to save human race, T7.5; world's creator coming into world undertook its way of life, T19.6; God condescended to become incarnate through these (holy) people, H7.27

indwelling: faith enlightens hearts & renders them worthy of God's —, H12.6

ink: that God is light written in black —, T5.3

innocent subjected to daily beatings, H1.5: tears of —, H1.7

intercession of virtuous affords shade from heat of tribulation, H7.21–22

interior life: sustenance & maintenance of —, H33.3

interpretation of Scripture (*see* senses of Scripture)

invective: teachers by — break down hardness of worldly spirit, H24.3

investigation: Gentiles embrace *Christianity* only after reliable —, T19.2

Isaac offered up by his father on an altar & ram immolated ‖ the one person of him who suffered for world's salvation, T6.7: — son of promise, i.e. free people of Church, T16.11; — who came home alive with his father ‖ saviour in his divinity remains with his Father incapable of suffering, T6.8

Israel: (*see* Hebrew people, Jewish people, Jews, Judea); — alone served God with true faith & acts of virtue, T1.4; original happiness of holy ancestors of people of — who once nobly served God, T5.14; God dispenses waters from springs of —, H24.13; Tb's blindness ‖ blindness overcame people of —, T5.5,11; Gentiles received word of God from — through translation, T3.14; Lord will come back to them (i.e. Jews) & all — will be saved, T28.3–4; — my first-born son, T3.8; people of — gave alms of God's word to Gentiles, T2.4; people of — gave their saving knowledge even to Gentiles, T2.6; people of — oppressed by yoke of Roman slavery, T5.11; people of — transgressing divine law by immoral living, T5.11; restoration of land of —, T38.1; Tb denotes people of — faithful to God, T1.4; when all Gentiles come in no one will be able to prevent God from granting salvation to — as well & enlightening blindness that befell part of it, T29.3

Jacob wrestling with angel was both lamed & blessed, T5.17: — by his limping ‖ unbelievers of his nation & by his blessing ‖ believers, T5.17

James: Lord's brightness shone like light in presence of Peter, — & John, H10.5

Jeroboam made golden calves to mislead subjects, T1.5: — king of Israel ‖ authors of idolatry, T1.6

Jerusalem H7.6: get ready for entry into heavenly —, H36.15; heavenly — our mother, H20.6; H36.15; T37.2; that by practising works of mercy in — of present Church we may prepare for entry into heavenly —, H36.14–15; restoration of —, T38.1; temple in — was from trees of Lebanon, H7.2; — = vision of supreme peace, H36.13

Jesus: Son of God had not yet appeared as a man or received name of — from his parents, H37.6; prophet foresaw this name in Spirit, H37.7; amid adversities prophet rejoices in him (i.e. —) who was to come, H37.7; — opens to faithful gate of heavenly homeland, H37.7

Jewish people (*see* Hebrew people, Israel, Jews, Judea): — attacked & defeated by Romans, H29.4; Lord promises believers among — to reveal mysteries of incarnation to Gentiles, T8.7; at end of our times Lord will make mysteries of incarnation known more widely to his own people from whom he had taken flesh, T8.8; by miracles Lord showed — from whom he had taken flesh that he was Son of God, T8.3; — & Synagogue from which (Lord) had taken human origin, T10.4; cf., H7.18; Church's teachers eventually send Christ back, together with Church itself full of riches of virtues, to enlighten by faith & enrich with property of good works — from whom he had taken flesh, T29.6; — ‖ fig-tree failing to bear fruit of virtue, H37.16; — from whom darkness of error is removed will recognize that Christ has already come & redeemed world, T34.16; — persecuted Lord attacked by Roman army, H29.3; — in their ‘writings recognize Christ is true God & man, T29.9; — largely blinded, T8.7; Lord sent to redeem — from darkness of unbelief, T7.2; — still have a veil in front of their heart that they may not understand grace of Christ, T34.13; — suffer blindness in fond hope of a Christ to be born in flesh & free them & give them great kingdom throughout world, T34.15–16; — when converted at end of world will have teachers & prophetic men to set minds on fire with heavenly desires, T37.3; through Christ's labours & journeys both — & Gentiles to attain eternal rest, H17.13

Jews (*see* Hebrew people, Israel, Jewish people, Judea): — anointed worthless with unction of adulation, H37.21; — astounded at Jesus' teaching & miracles, H30.4–5; believers among — know they can rely on Lord's promise to return, T28.4; believers among — sad at blindness of unbelievers, T29.4; converts to faith in Christ among — distressed that he is slow in coming to save, T27.2; stalls of heavenly scriptures abound among —, H37.30; — do not taste food of heavenly meaning in scriptures, H37.31; — embracing true faith join Church assembled from among Gentiles, T29.10; fruits of love not among general masses of —, H37.18; Gentiles receive into unity of Church — who believe, T3.15; — join Church assembled from Gentiles by sharing heavenly mysteries, T29.11; mountain from which holy one is to come = kingdom of — from which (Son of God) took human origin, H7.18; cf., T10.4; Lord detained among Gentiles is slow in coming to save —, T27.2; Lord will come back to — & all Israel will be saved, T28.3; money Tbs received from Gabael ‖ knowledge of scriptures lent by — to Gentiles is returned to them, T35.7; people from among — who now believe, T28.2; prophet reflects on reprobation of his people, H33.4; Synagogue of —, H37.8; Tbs sent off to parents with Sarah & much property ‖ Christ with his Church sent back to enrich — his own people, T29.5–6; unbelief of —, H1.3; — who now believe, & console themselves that a time will come when Lord will come back to them, & all Israel will be saved, knowing that Lord is someone they can trust, T28.2–3; — who believe at end of world, T3.15; Lord sent enemy force to overthrow proud people not merely of — but of all who refused to accept humility of Christian faith, H29.9

John the Baptist H2.9

John (the Apostle): Lord's brightness shone like light in presence of Peter, James & —, H10.5

Joshua H36.7: — type of Christ, H36.12

journey(s) of Lord's eternity, H17.3,8–13: temporal — of Lord, H17.1–2,6; Lord who prospers our — of salvation & life, H2.16; preparations for Tbs' — || preparations for redemption, T10.1–2; Tbs' — || Church's — in this world, T10.1–2; Tbs' — || Christ's appearance in flesh, T10.1–2; Tbs paused by river Tigris for first break in —, T12.1

joy(s): just grounds of prophet's —, H37.38; (Lord) preached — of heavenly salvation & peace, T10.4; saints rest when they share in — of just in heaven, H36.21; Christ announced to Jews — of eternal salvation, T8.4; Raguel welcomed Tbs & angel with —, T18.1; Tb without —, T8.2

Judea (*see* Hebrew people, Israel, Jewish people, Jews) H36.7: after — is given light through faith, after it receives grace of Holy Spirit, Church will come in to it, T35.3–4; Lord gathered adherents to faith from — who would edify & preach, T16.8; — rejoicing that it believes, grieving that it has been so late in reaching Lord, T32.2; Tb welcoming & kissing son || — joining in Christ's embrace, T32.1–2; works of Lord accomplished in —, T10.4

judgement: general —, H36.20; by threatening severe — God humbles earthly-minded, H27.1–2; — prerogative (not of God the Father but) of Son, H21.7

just: afflictions of — (upright), H1.4; — not saddened by loss of creature comforts, H37.2; — have joy of possessing heavenly kingdom promised Christ's poor, H37.3

justice: Lord, sun of — enlightened Church, H25.2

Keturah: Midianite people took origin by — from Abraham's son Midian, H18.9

kindness: God's —, T37.1; prophet reminded by example of Lord's mercy to executioners to bestow — on his persecutors, H4.10

king assassinated by his sons, T4.5: (Christ) — of –s & Lord of lords, H10.11; Lord who is — in heaven over all things, T14.12

kingdom(s): sceptres i.e. — of this world, H21.2; Christ (stone from mountain) crushed — of world, H7.19; — of heaven promised Christ's poor, H37.3

knowledge: people of Israel always gave their saving — (*scientia salutaris*) even to Gentiles, T2.6; — of divine law contained in decalogue, T3.12; preachers || 'the deep' i.e. filled with deep — of truth, H24.6–7; zeal for God but not based on —, T34.4; love & — of truth engendered by words or examples of holy teachers, H7.27–28

lamps: unfaithful bring extinguished — at hour of final retribution, H37.24

land: restoration of — of Israel, T38.1; — of living, T41.11–12

laudes matutinae: morning praises, H1.2 n.

Lauds: (*liturgical hour of* —), H1.2 n.

law made by Moses, H37.16: divine — contained in decalogue, T3.12; Christ has made new wine of water || gives spiritual understanding of —, T25.4; nations received letter of — through seventy translators, T25.6; those bearing yoke of —, H37.12; victim to be offered on (Lord's) account according to —, H7.14

Lebanon highest mountain in Phoenicia, H7.2: Lord's temple in Jerusalem made from trees of —, H7.2; — noted for its tall, incorruptible, aromatic trees, H7.2; Open your gates, —, H7.4

lend: money Tbs received from Gabael || knowledge of scriptures lent by Jews to Gentiles is returned to them, T35.7

licentiousness: slave to — & pride, sleeps beneath a swallows' nest, T5.10

127

life: (Gentiles') teachers all knew about — in this world only, T6.2; — in this world only, which runs course of seven days, T6.2; Gentiles without hope of immortal — but for God's word through teachers, T19.3–4; good things of future — very soon to come, T38.2; holy teachers among God's people provided for their — & salvation, T4.3; Lord prospers our journey of salvation & —, H2.16; Lord enlightens hearts of those he has predestined to eternal —, T40.2; people of Israel imploring God's mercy to obtain eternal —, T5.15; nourishment & strengthening of — of Church, T10.2; Son of God visibly spending — with human beings to save them, T7.5; Lord closes gaze of heart of faithful to enjoyment of present —, T40.10

light: Lord raises gaze of faithful to contemplation of perpetual —, T40.10; Lord rescued from power of darkness those he foreknew to be children of —, T14.9; the — of full faith & good works, T31.3; one who perseveres in good works never deprived of — of faith, T5.6; after Judea is given — through faith, Church will come in to it, T35.3–4; — of life, T8.5; teachers fix — of truth in hearer's heart, H12.8; H13.2; one deserted by grace of divine — filled by prince of darkness, T21.6; Tb cannot see — of sky, T8.2; that God is — written in black ink, T5.3; those aware of their frailty & ignorance destined to enjoy — of life in Lord, T34.8; those who despaired of obtaining heavenly —, T8.5; cf. Lord the enlightener cleanses hearts, T30.5

limp: Jacob by his –ing ‖ unbelievers, T5.17

liver 'cooks out' hidden properties of food eaten ‖ careful consideration to find in what order to carry out what we propose to do, T15.8: fish's — put away ‖ Lord made known through teachers of truth the mischievous maturity of devil's intrigues against us, T15.7; Tbs produced from his satchel part of (fish's) —, T20.1

living beings: (Lord) became known between two —, H4.1–2; 'Between two –' ‖ 'between Moses & Elijah', H4.2

Lord (*see* Christ): — appeared in flesh, T10.2; — bids Church at beginning of its betrothal to renounce Satan, T20.2; belief in –'s incarnation, T4.4; Church after –'s incarnation tossed to & fro like waves, T4.6; dog ran ahead ‖ teacher first preaches salvation, then — the enlightener, cleanses hearts, T30.5; — dreaded death, T13.2; — dwelt among sinners & mortals ‖ Tbs stopped over by Tigris, T12.7; — himself filled home of Cornelius with Holy Spirit, T11.3; — is the one the prophet longed for, T9.3; — is understood by elect as equal to Father in his divinity, T36.7; — lays open wider the gifts of his knowledge, T36.5; — is of one nature with us in his humanity, T36.7; our — overcame enemy, T6.4; our — through faith united Gentiles to himself, T6.4; prince of darkness found in — nothing of his own, T12.8; — sent to redeem Gentiles from bondage of idolatry & Jewish people from darkness of unbelief, T7.2; — showing (his people) he is in Father & Father in him, T36.5; true bridegroom our —, T6.3; water of sin did not touch —, T12.8; — went to Gentiles through teachers of his word, T18.2; — who is king in heaven walks upon earth by means of (elect), T14.12; — will come back to them (i.e. Jews) & all Israel will be saved, T28.3; — gathered to faith from Judea as many as would serve as an example of (virtuous) living or for ministry of preaching, T16.8; — by his death destroyed him (devil) who had power of death, H3.2–3; — is creator by virtue of his divinity, H8.9; departure from world in death was portion of — himself, H2.12; glory of —, H38.21–22; journeys of –'s eternity, H17.3,7–13; — lived as almighty among weak, as God among human beings, H2.3; — mediator between God & men, H7.16; prophet said — would be revealed & become known, H5.3; — prospers our journey of salvation &

life, H2.16; — scattered first seeds of faith in temple, H7.7; chosen ones of — called 'anointed' 29.2; temporal journeys of —, H17.1–2,6; tidings of coming of — saviour, H2.2; anger of —, H22.2; — venting anger upon material-minded, H27.4; —'s wrath against rivers, H19.1; — having abandoned those he knows not to be his own, T40.3

love (*see* marrow): grace of heavenly —, T23.5; in gospel parable, bread, fish & egg ‖ three supreme virtues, faith, hope & —, T34.12; prophet's faith, hope & —, H37.5; carnal rendered spiritual & strong by fire of Christ's —, T16.4; inner fresh growth of —, H7.22; — with which (holy people) are habitually aflame in Lord, H7.26; wound of — caused by darts of Christ's words, H26.2

Maccabees: enemy's ferocious persecution evident in tortures of —, T4.4

man: angel & — ‖ the one person of mediator between God & men, T6.6; — (Isaac) in Isaac story ‖ godhead (of Christ), T6.9; why should not — more aptly ‖ (Christ's) humanity? T6.9

marrow & fat ‖ grace of heavenly love, T23.5

martyrs: Gentiles made so much progress in Lord that some even became —, T23.2; holy teachers & — instruct flock of Christ throughout world, T23.9; holy teachers & — preserve four books of gospel by faith & action, T23.8; — whether by death or mortification ‖ two slaughtered cattle, T23.6; cf. those who hand over body to be killed ‖ two slaughtered cattle, T23.6

Matthew: Saul & — converted to humility from pride, H15.6

meaning: allegorical — of Bk of Tb, T1.2; historical — of Bk of Tb, T1.2; inner — of Bk of Tb, T1.2; superficial — of Bk of Tb, T1.1; men's good deeds have bad — & their bad deeds good —, T5.2

Medes: Rages, city of —, T8.6

mediator between God & men, T10.4: two persons, angel & man ‖ one person of — between God & men, T6.6; H7.16

Mediterranean peoples to be saved by this faith, H18.11

members: the faithful, Christ's — , ask Lord to appoint believers to preach, T25.2

merciful (*see* mercy)

mercy: divine — remembers believing Jews are sad at unbelievers' blindness, T29.4; — of (God), T37.1; craving (God's) —, H21.5; people of Israel imploring God's — to obtain eternal life, T5.15; Lord's — to those renouncing pride, H15.4; trust in God's —, H6.3–5; cf. belief in clemency of (God's) act of pardon, H6.3; clear from his appeal for executioners how merciful (Lord) was, H4.9

merits: place in heavenly mansions assigned according to diversity of —, T41.3

messenger: Christ's miracles showed he was angel, i.e. — of Father's will, T8.3; dog 'bringing news' ‖ every faithful teacher a — of truth, T30.6

metonymy: in Greek — = transference, H18.17

Midian: land of —, H18.1; Abraham's son —, H18.9; *meaning of* tents of land of —, H18.13

Midianites: Ethiopians & — Gentile peoples, H18.2; *their conversion & that of Ethiopians* ‖ *conversion of all Gentiles*, H18.3; let — be awestruck at intimation that Mediterranean peoples too are to be saved through faith (in Christ), H18.11

ministry: Lord gathered to faith from Judea as many as would serve for — of preaching, T16.8; preachers exercise — of word for their hearers, H24.7; cf. word ministered through teachers, H13.3

miracle(s) (*see* works of power): Lord through — showed he was Son of God, T8.3; — our Lord wrought in flesh, T8.3; Jews (in gospel) stunned and astounded at — of Jesus, H30.4; Gentiles dumbfounded at Lord's & apostles' — & disavowed gods, H30.9; — causes astonishment & rapture & inspires belief in Lord, H30.7; brightness of saviour's — & teaching enlighten believers, H9.2; glory of — followed words of light, H26.5; — authenticate the truth of preaching, H26.7; refusal to fear God or be converted despite — of saints, H32.8; Paul & Silas crowned the advance of their deeds with —, H38.15; cf. angel was companion for Tbs to perform wonders for his people, T7.4

money Tbs received from Gabael ‖ knowledge of scriptures lent by Jews to Gentiles is returned to them, T35.7

moon ‖ Church, H25.4

morning praises H1.2

mortify: those who — body so as to become living victim, T23.6; those who for Christ — their body themselves can resist enemy, T23.7; cf. retrenching earthly appetites, H27.3

Moses: 'Between two living beings' ‖ 'between — & Elijah', H4.2; law made by —, H37.16

mother: heavenly Jerusalem our —, T37.2; heavenly Jerusalem — of us all, H20.6; H36.15; God's Son who was to be born of Holy Spirit & virgin —, H1.13; Gabriel announcing good news to virgin —, H7.16; this man whose father & — we know, H30.5

mystery/ies: Gentiles who have merely heard of but not accepted — of faith, T25.2; Jews join Church assembled from Gentiles by sharing in heavenly —, T29.11; Bk of Tb contains — of Christ & Church, T1.3; Gentiles entrusting to Jews — of Christ for their salvation, T3.16; Christ to reveal — of incarnation to Gentiles at end of time, T8.8; Habakkuk writes of future — of Church, H33.9; — of Lord's passion, H1.1; — of ascension, H8.2–3

name: Gentiles who thought it better to conceal belief in (Lord's) —, T22.3; — of devil in white chalk still means deep darkness, T5.4; Tb gave his son his own —, T3.6

nations (*see* Gentiles)

nest: hot droppings from a swallows' — fell into Tb's eyes, T5.1; slave of licentiousness & pride sleeps lying down beneath swallows' —, T5.10

Nineveh: destruction of — near ‖ world already approaching its end, T38.1–2; leave — ‖ turn one's back on worldly desires & seek heavenly things, T39.1

old age: Lord sees in a bad — & passes by those who though living longer are immature in judgement & stooped from burden of vices, T40.5; those who have by Lord's grace long been virtuous in a good —, T40.4

olive-tree H37.1,8: — ‖ Synagogue of Jews, H37.8; yield of — false to its promise, H37.21

origin: people & Synagogue from which (Lord) had taken his human —, T10.4

orthopraxis (*see* example(s)) H24.10: living up to one's own preaching, H33.7

oxen ‖ (devout Jews) preparing to produce fruits of good works, H37.12: — ploughing land of Lord by teaching & chastening hearers, H37.12; — ‖ those (devout Jews) preparing to produce fruits of good works, H37.12

pardon: (prophet) confident he could obtain — for sins, H5.6

parents: Tbs took care of aged & virtuous — ‖ Lord takes care of those he knows to continue in health of good works, T40.8–9

passion: fish trying to devour Tbs ‖ mystery of Lord's —, T12.2; malice of ancient dragon who once eagerly longed to devour Christ in the — 33.2; Lord's —, T10.3; H25.2; mysteries of Lord's —, H1.1; (prophet) alarmed pondering upon events of his (Lord's) —, H5.5; cf. prophet focuses on future sufferings of Christ, H33.4; providential design of Lord's incarnation & —, H1.11; sixth day of week on which this — was accomplished, H1.2

pastor: Tbs' dog ‖ Church's teachers who by combating heretics drive off wolves from supreme –'s fold, T30.3

patience: prophet reminded by example of crucified Lord to bear patiently the pressure of his woes, H4.10

Paul & Silas singing hymn to God amid sufferings, H38.14

peace: Lord preached joys of heavenly salvation & —, T10.4; — enjoyed by sinners, H1.4; homeland & vision of supreme —, H36.13

people of God entrusted to Gentiles knowledge of divine law, T3.12: prosperity returned to — after devil was overcome & condemned, T4.5

penance: graver guilty actions call for greater —, tears & alms, H6.8; (prophet) having done appropriate — for transgressions, H5.6

perdition: Christ's coming was for — of unbelievers, H28.12

persecute: he (the enemy) –d them with ferocity, T4.4

persecution(s) by unbelievers, T10.3: enemy instigated — against (the Lord's) elect, T14.12; — instigated against believers by unbelievers, H33.5; living in Christ entails —, H35.7

persecutors: saints' — undergo torments of Gehenna, H36.22

perseverance in good works never deprived of light of faith, T5.6: Lord takes care of those who continue in health of good works, T40.9

Peter baptized Cornelius' household with water, T11.3: –'s tears of compunction, H14.2–3; — ‖ tree refreshing those hungering & thirsting for holiness, H7.23–24; — ‖ tree which heals ailing by shadow of his body, H7.23–24; Lord's brightness shone like light in presence of —, James & John, H10.5

Philip: when — preached gospel, H18.8

Phoenicia: Lebanon highest mountain in —, H7.2

poor: kingdom of heaven promised Christ's —, H37.3; — person starving eats in secret, H31.1–3

poverty: most abject — being starved of God's word, H31.6

power(s): devil caught by — of divinity, T12.4; Lord smashed to pieces devil's —, T14.9; Lord's works of —, T10.3 (*see* miracles); horns of kings ‖ — of arrogant, H11.4; mountains ‖ people proud because of worldly —, wisdom, wealth, H15.2

praises: morning —, H1.2; singing — of God's grace here & in life to come, H38.20

prayer(s): Lord does not refuse — of petitioners, T25.5; Tb turned to God in —, T5.13; whatever a holy person utters is wholly — to God, H33.11; cf. everything done to please Lord is intercession, H33.12

preach: by –ing they beget & nurture others to bear gospel yoke, T23.3; dog ran ahead ‖ teacher first –es salvation, then Lord, the enlightener, cleanses hearts, T30.5; Lord gathered from Judea as many as would serve for –ing, T16.8; Tb reminding faithful to — about (God's) acts of kindness, T37.1; Tb blind & –ing God's word ‖ both reprobate & elect, T5.16; Christ –ed through apostles to (Jewish) people & Synagogue, T10.4

preachers bring new peoples together into Church with Christ's assistance, T26.5: — ‖ camels because they carry listeners' burdens, T26.3; — chosen from Gentiles through whom Lord wins over others, T26.2; cock-crow is voice of —, T22.2; holy — followed in (Lord's) footsteps, T11.2; holy — ‖ Tbs' dog, T11.2; — sang of true dawn of faith to come after darkness of error, T22.2; — ‖ servants because they serve needs of those they evangelize, T26.3; — enlightened by contemplation of heavenly joys, H24.16; — exercise ministry of word for their hearers, H24.7; holy — ‖ God's horses, H32.2,9–11; — ‖ horses mounted by Lord, H20.2–6; 21.3; — heralds of word, H32.4; — impart their many rich insights according to capacity of weak, H24.8; Lord ever present to — to guide their minds, H32.11–12; Lord follows his —, H12.8; proclamation of — proceeds from fount of wisdom, H24.16; — scattered through world, H32.4; — ‖ 'the deep' i.e. filled with deep knowledge of truth, H24.6–7; voice of — goes forth over entire world, H18.7; — sprinkle waters on their ways when, as well as preaching orally, they show examples of upright living to those whose eyes are always upon them, H24.10

preaching: faithful ask Lord entrust some of believers with task of —, T25.2; Lord gathered from Judea as many as would serve for —, T16.8; first seeds of faith sown in temple through apostles' —, H7.7; — of apostles, H12.3; *effects of* apostles' —, H8.5; living up to one's own —, H33.7; Lord preceded word of —, H12.4; repentance fruit not of human — but of grace, H13.6; — ‖ rivers watering hearts with words of saving doctrine, H22.5

predestine: Lord enlightens hearts of those he has –d to eternal life, T40.2

Presentation of Lord in temple on 40th day after birth, H7.14

prevision: God's —: *evils* could not happen without —, H1.8

pride (*see* arrogant, proud): slave to licentiousness & — sleeps lying beneath a swallows' nest, T5.10; Lord's mercy to those renouncing —, H15.4; horns of kings ‖ power of arrogant, H11.4; mountains ‖ people proud because of worldly power, wisdom, wealth, H15.2; proud ‖ mountains shattered by Lord's gaze, H15.3; Lord lays proud low, H29.9–11; cf. Lord overthrows those who reject humility of Christian faith, H29.9

prison: Paul & Silas singing hymn to God amid — chains, H38.14

promise: angel's –s to Tb ‖ Lord's — to Jewish believers, T8.6–7; Lord –s to reveal mysteries of incarnation to Gentiles, T8.7; Christ's — of consolation, H37.3

property: Tb's — to be confiscated on account of his good deeds, T4.1; all Tb's belongings were restored to him, T4.5; Raguel sending Tbs home with wife & — ‖ Church's teachers, T29.5–6; Church = founder's spiritual home, — & sheep, T11.4; cattle & camels & Sarah's — in abundance ‖ the many virtues of Church incorporated with Hebrew people, T35.6

prophecy: Tb imbued with spirit of —, T37.2; spirit of —, H1.11; — of Habakkuk a prayer, H33.10–11

prophet(s): God will raise up from among your brethren a — like me, T3.4; Lord is the one the — longed for, T9.3; — (Habakkuk's) fear as he meditated on incarnation, H18.4; words of — bear witness to him who was to come, H12.2; writings of —, H12.4; zealous rebuke & exhortation through —, H37.16; — said Lord would be revealed & become known, H5.3

prophetic men: teachers & — make joys of heaven resound in hearers' ears, T37.3; Jewish people when converted at end of world will have teachers & — to set minds on fire with heavenly desires, T37.3

proselytes: Tb gave tithes to — in captivity, T2.3

prosperity returned to people of God after devil overcome & condemned, T4.5

proud (*see* arrogant, pride)

punishment(s) of God, T37.10: (prophet's) fear of (Lord's) anger & —, H6.2; threat of everlasting —, H21.5

providential design of Lord's incarnation & passion, H1.11

rage (*see* anger, fury, wrath): insatiable — of devil, T21.7; in your — you will pull down nations, H27.1,6; (Jewish persecutors) -d against protomartyr Stephen, H29.7

Rages, city of Medes, T8.6

Raguel agreed to give daughter away, T19.1: — alarmed when asked for his daughter, T19.1; fate of seven husbands of –'s daughter, T19.1; unclean could not have –'s daughter, T19.1; — giving daughter away || Gentiles accepting faith, T19.2; — || people who unite themselves & their folk to community of Lord, T16.12; –'s name = 'God is his sustenance' or 'God is ⟨my⟩ friend', T16.12; — sending Tbs home with wife & property || Church's teachers, T29.5–6; –'s servants & camels || preachers chosen from Gentiles, T26.2; — || people of Gentiles, T16.10; — welcomed Tbs & angel with joy, T18.1

ram(s): four slaughtered — || holy teachers & martyrs preserve four books of gospel by faith & action, T23.8; *symbolism of* Raguel's slaughtering of cattle & —, T23.10–11; teachers || — because they are fathers & leaders of peoples who follow them, T23.4; — immolated for Isaac || him who suffered for world's salvation, T6.7; — in Isaac story || humanity of Christ, T6.9

Raphael (*see* angel, archangel): — means 'healing of God', T7.1; — sent to rid Tb of blindness & Sarah of demon, T7.1

recompense (*see also* rewards): he who does not doubt that through his temporal afflictions he will gain eternal joys, rests not only on day of — but also on day of tribulation, H36.2

Red Sea: desert of Saracens to east of — in Arabia, H18.9

redeem: the –ed, members of their founder, T41.3; God by whose grace (the blessed) have been –ed, T41.9; reflection on –ing works of Lord, H3.1–4

redeemer: devil desired death of humanity in our —, T12.4; merciful — grafting faithful into body of his Church, T14.5

redemption: everything concerning — of world made ready, T10.1–2

reflection: hearers open bay of inward — to words of salvation, H22.6; — on redeeming works of Lord, H3.1–4; cf. devout considerations sustain & maintain interior life, H33.3

remission of sins: Lord bade Church at betrothal to confess faith in trinity for —, T20.3

repentance called for, H6.8: — fruit not of human preaching but of grace, H13.6; work of teachers converts to — & faith, H23.2–3

rest: we attain perfection of holy — through grace of Holy Spirit, T24.2; we implore Lord to — in our heart & body, T24.2; eternal — welcomes in the just, H36.19; through Christ's labours & journeys both Jewish & Gentile people are to attain eternal —, H17.13

resurrection: Christ's —, T10.3; incarnation — & ascension, H1.3; Lord crowned with glory & honour through his —, H8.4; — of Lord, H25.2; — of Lord bestowed hope & faith on world, H9.5; — (of Lord) made known on mountain *of Transfiguration*, H4.4

reveal: prophet said Lord would be –ed & become known, H5.3

rewards (*see* recompense): hope of future — reduces & lightens adversities, H35.9–H36.3

riches: devil tried to strip God's people of all — of their virtues, T4.3; Gentiles work at acquiring — of virtues, T3.14; wicked rolling in —, H1.5; cf. mountains || people proud because of worldly power, wisdom, wealth, H15.2 Gentiles getting wealthy on Jewish legacy of God's revelation, T3.13

riding: Lord's — is salvation, H20.1–6; Lord's — into Jerusalem || salvation through apostles, H20.6

righteous (*see* just, upright)

righteousness (*see* justice)

rivers: earth cleft by —, H22.1; H22.5; H23.5–10; earth has veins of water as human body has veins of blood, H23.7; Lord's wrath against —, H19.1; — || hearts of unbelievers, H19.1–2; — || teachers, H24.2–3; — || words of saving doctrine, H22.5

Roman: people of Israel oppressed by yoke of — slavery, T5.11; — army *attacks unbelieving* Jews, H29.4

sacraments: Gentiles rejoiced that they were sanctified by his (Christ's) –s, T19.7

saints: progress, life, suffering & crown of — give joy to many, T23.12; grace of Holy Spirit made — steadfast, H11.3

salt: –ing of fish || Christ taught apostles by word & gave them — of wisdom, T16.7

salvation (*see* save): Gentiles entrusting to Jews mysteries of Christ for their —, T3.16; holy teachers among God's people provided for their life & —, T4.3; Lord prospers our journey of — & life, H2.16; in his teachers (Lord) came for — of Gentiles, T10.5; (Lord) preached joys of heavenly — & peace, T10.4; the one person of him who suffered for world's —, T6.7; Christ announced to Jews joy of eternal —, T8.4; hearers open the bay of inward reflection to words of —, H22.6; — lies in saviour not in ourselves, H37.36; Lord offered joy of — to his chosen ones, H29.2; Lord's riding is —, H20.1–6; Lord's riding into Jerusalem || — through apostles, H20.6

Saracens: desert of — east of Red Sea in Arabia, H18.9

Sarah || mass of Gentiles, T6.1: —, Raguel's daughter given to seven husbands, T6.1; Raphael sent to rid Tb of blindness & — of demon, T7.1; name of — befits Church because of — wife of patriarch Abraham, T16.11; Tbs married — after tying up devil on archangel's instructions, T6.4; Tbs brought into bedroom to —, T20.1

Satan (*see* devil): Lord bids Church at its betrothal to renounce —, T20.2; renouncing — & confessing faith in trinity, T20.2–3

Saul & Matthew converted to humility from pride, H15.6

save (*see* salvation): Lord detained among Gentiles is slow in coming to — Jews, T27.2; Lord will come back to them (i.e. Jews) & all Israel will be –d, T28.3–4; Son of God visibly spending life with human beings to — them, T7.5; when Lord came to — Gentiles, T11.2

saving: Bk of Tb of — benefit to its readers, T1.1; — knowledge, T2.6

saviour: archangel (Raphael) ‖ divinity of our — ‖, T6.5; — in his divinity remains with Father incapable of suffering, T6.8; our Lord & —, T40.9; –'s divinity, T6.8; Tbs ‖ humanity of our —, T6.5; our –'s teaching enlightens believers, H9.2; tidings of coming of Lord our —, H2.2

sceptres: you will surely bend your bow at —, H21.1; — i.e. kingdoms of this world, H21.1

scourging: Paul & Silas singing hymn to God amid —, H38.14

scriptures: Gentiles unlock for Jews secrets of —, T3.16; knowledge of — lent by Jews to Gentiles returned to them, T35.7; fields of divine — producing spiritual food, H37.13; — ‖ extensive fields producing spiritual food, H37.13; — ‖ fields whose nourishment delighted Lord's sheep, H37.14; (Lord) called sun of justice in —, H9.3; stalls of heavenly — abound among Jews, H37.30

sea: Lord's indignation against —, H19.1; — churned up ‖ Gentiles agitated by preaching, H32.3–4; — ‖ hearts of unbelievers, H19.2; — ‖ world, H32.2

secrets: Gentiles unlock for Jews — of scriptures, T3.16; Lord exposed — of devil's snares, T15.2

seducer (*see* devil)

self-indulgence: white film obstructing Tb's eyes ‖ folly of —, T34.3–8

senses of Scripture: superficial, T1.1; inner –, T1.2; historical and allegorical, T1.2; typologically speaking, T5.2; Gentiles spiritually understand God's word, T3.14

Septuagint: (Jews) entrusted divine law to Gentiles through —, T3.12; nations received letter of law through seventy translators, T25.6

servants: Raguel's — & camels = preachers chosen from Gentiles, T26.2; — & camels with Raphael's help bring Gabael to Tbs' wedding ‖ preachers bring new peoples into Church of Christ with his help, T26.5

serve: holy ancestors of people of Israel who once nobly –d God, T5.14; Tb taunted & upbraided as if he had –d God in vain, T5.12

servile actions, sins in body, & wicked thoughts in mind, T24.2

seven days after Sarah arrived ‖ light of sevenfold grace of Holy Spirit, T35.1–2: fate of — husbands of Raguel's daughter, T19.1; — husbands whom demon killed as soon as they went in to Sarah, T6.1; life in this world only, which runs course of — days, T6.2; number — ‖ all, T19.3; Sarah, Raguel's daughter given to — husbands, T6.1; *significance of fact that* sons of Tbs were — in number, T38.4

seventy translators: nations received letter of law through —, T25.6

shade: intercession of virtuous affords — from heat of tribulation, H7.21–22

shadow: Peter ‖ tree which heals ailing by — of his body, H7.23–24

Shalmaneser king of Assyrians, T2.1

sheep || humble listeners to voice of supreme pastor, H37.11: — pine away from pasture, H37.26–27

Silas: Paul & — singing hymn to God amid sufferings, H38.14

silver: Tb gave ten — talents in trust to fellow-kinsman, Gabael, T3.11

sin(s) cannot be put an end to except by destruction of world itself, T39.4: devil came to see if he could find any — on (Lord's) soul, T12.12; Lord washes faithful from — & death, T12.9–10; Lord bade Church at its betrothal to confess faith in trinity for remission of —, T20.3; remission of — follows confession of true faith, T21.1; Tb taught Tbs from infancy to fear God & refrain from —, T3.9; water of — did not touch (Lord), T12.8; indulgence there may be for very smallest —, H6.7; servile actions, i.e., — in body, & wicked thoughts in mind, T24.2; cf. graver guilty actions call for greater penance, tears & alms, H6.8

sinners: peace enjoyed by —, H1.4; when grief of repentance is over — see (the Lord) in life to come & enjoy his blessed vision, H23.4; will Lord's wrath endure forever against all — ? H19.4–5; cf. multitude of perverse is so great, T39.4

sister: dearly beloved — in Christ, H1.1; dearly beloved — & virgin of Christ, H38.26

sixth day of week, day on which passion was accomplished, H1.2

slavery: people of Israel oppressed by yoke of Roman —, T5.11

sleep: Hebrew people get up from — of their unbelief, T31.2; spiritual — neglecting to watch & stand firm in faith, T5.7; Tb —s beneath swallows' nest, T5.1

son: (Tb) fled with his — & wife, T4.4; our Lord through miracles showed Jewish people he was — of God, T8.3; God sent his — born of woman, born subject to law, to redeem those subject to law, H5.2; judgement the prerogative (not of God the Father but) of —, H21.7; — of God had to undergo suffering of cross, H1.13; holy child to be born (of virgin mother) to be called — of God, H7.17; (Lord) recognized as — of God *in Transfiguration*, H4.5

spirit (*see* Holy Spirit): — of fear of Lord would fill him (Tbs), T3.10; those born again through Lord's grace & filled with sevenfold —, T38.3

south: God is from Teman, i.e. will come from —, H7.12; Bethlehem where Lord was born is situated to — of Jerusalem, H7.13; God did indeed come from —, H7.14; — || holy people, H7.25; it is from this — God comes every day, H7.28

stay: Raguel implored Tbs to — with him || we implore Lord to — with us, T24.1–2

steadfast: grace of Holy Spirit made saints —, H11.3

Stephen protomartyr — *upbraids compatriots*, H29.7–8

sternness of (God), T37.1

stone hewn without use of human hands || Christ, H7.19

strangers: Tb gave tithes to — in captivity, T2.3,7

streams: those converted produce — of doctrine for others, H23.9–10

successors (*see* apostles)

suffering(s) (*see* affliction(s)): saviour in his divinity remains with Father incapable of —, T6.8; progress, life, — & crown of saints give joy to many, T23.12; giving thanks to God in —, H38.11–15; Paul & Silas singing hymn to God amid —, H38.14; prophet focuses on future — of Christ, H33.4; — of Christ & apostles, H34.5; Son of God had to undergo — of cross, H1.13; when Lord had suffered on cross, devil came to see if he could find any sin on his soul, T12.12; ram immolated (in place of Isaac) || the one person of him who suffered for world's salvation, T6.7;

Jewish people suffer from mental blindness in fond hope of a Christ to be born in flesh & set them free & give them a worldwide kingdom, T34.15

sun || Christ, H25.2,4: (Lord's) countenance became bright like —, H4.4; (Lord) called — of justice in scriptures, H9.3; Lord — of justice enlightened Church, H25.2

swallows: Tb asleep beneath –' nest & hot droppings from nest fell into his eyes, T5.1; because of swift flight — || pride & volatility of heart, T5.9; uncleanness of — blinds those over whom it holds sway, T5.9; slave to licentiousness & pride, sleeps beneath a –' nest, T5.10

Synagogue: enemy could not rob (people of God) of —, T4.4; — established by Moses with legal ceremonies, T3.2; people & — from which (Lord) had taken his human origin, T10.4; — of Jews, H37.8

tail: (*significance of* —) dog wagging his —, T30.8

teach (*see* teacher(s), teaching(s))

teacher(s): dog ran ahead || — first preaches salvation then Lord, the enlightener, cleanses hearts, T30.5; — accustomed to soar to heavenly desires, T22.5; Judea to be reunited by Lord through –' ministry, T30.9; — called dogs because they defend their founder's home, T11.4; — || cattle because they bear light yoke of gospel, T23.3; — cheer hearers' hearts with promise that Christ's grace will come without delay, T30.10; — combat heretics, T30.3; — drive off wolves from supreme pastor's fold, T30.3; — || dogs defending Church from unclean spirits & heretics, T11.4; — || fat cattle because they are filled with grace of heavenly love, T23.5; (Gentiles') — all knew about life in this world only, T6.2; Gentiles' former — had nothing reliable to say on eternal joys, T19.3; Gentiles made so much progress in Lord that some became —, T23.2; Gentiles without hope of immortal life but for God's word through —, T19.3–4; holy — among God's people provided for their life & salvation, T4.3; holy — & martyrs supported by four cardinal virtues of prudence, fortitude, temperance & justice, T23.8; in his — (Lord) came for salvation of Gentiles, T10.5; Lord made known to us devil's intrigues through — of truth, T15.7; Lord went to Gentile people through — of his word, T18.2; holy — & martyrs instruct Christ's flock throughout world divided into four quarters, T23.9; holy — & martyrs preserve four books of gospel by faith & action, T23.8; — & prophetic men make joys of heaven resound in hearers' ears, T37.3; — & prophetic men to set minds on fire with heavenly desires, T37.3; — || rams because they are fathers & leaders of peoples who follow them, T23.4; — rejoice at results of their work, T30.9; Tbs' dog || Church's —, T30.3; Truth itself teaching within is heard outwardly through —, T19.5; — who were accustomed to soar to heavenly desires, T22.5; first necessary that word of a — be heard, H12.8; — by invective break down hardness of worldly spirit, H24.3; by ministry of — the words of truth became known to world, H26.3; — fix light of truth in hearer's heart, H12.8; at –'s preaching footprints of truth are fixed in hearer's mind, H13.2; holy — children of light, H26.11; — || Lord's feet, H13.3–5; — preach by example as well as word, H24.9–11; — || 'rivers' & 'the deep', H24.2–4; word is ministered through —, H13.3; words & deeds of — shine brightly by Christ's gift, H26.11; work of — converts to repentance & faith, H23.2–3

teaching(s) (*see* doctrine(s)): Christ's —, T10.3; our saviour's — enlightens believers, H9.2; — of virtuous satisfies hunger, H7.21; bondage of worthless & harmful —, H31.6

tears of compunction, H6.8: St Peter's — of compunction, H14.2–3; — of innocent, H1.7

Teman: God is from — i.e. will come from south, H7.12

temple: Christ answered teachers in — as God of eternal majesty, H7.9; Christ first bore witness in — to faith one must have in him, H7.8; Christ questioned teachers in — as young man, H7.9; from — Christ filled world with shoots of his faith & truth, H7.5; (Lord) scattered first seeds of gospel in —, H7.5; — in Jerusalem made from trees of Lebanon, H7.2; presentation of Lord in — on 40th day after birth, H7.14; scriptures designate — by name Lebanon, H7.3–4

temporal affliction of the good, H5.5: hills of Lord ‖ holy who spurn — things, H16.5–6; — journeys of Lord, H17.1–2,6; shortage of — goods, H36.24; those who set inordinate store by — goods suffer pain, H36.24

tempt: demon allowed to — occasionally but not overcome (faithful), T21.2; enemy desired to conquer faithful by –ing but only made them victors by martyrdom, T23.10

temptations: Christ's —, T10.3; all — overcome by God's glory, H38.6–8; *fidelity* proved by — overcome, H38.9

terror: Habakkuk's — at what he foresaw, H34.4–5; prophet's belly trembled with — at his imperfections, H35.6–7

thanks: those who give — to God in suffering are victorious, H38.11,13

thieves & beasts ‖ unclean spirits & heretical men, T11.4: two — on Calvary ‖ the two living beings (of Habakkuk's Canticle), H4.7–8

threat: bent bow ‖ — of God's wrath, H21.5; — of everlasting punishments, H21.5

threaten: by –ing severe judgement God humbles earthly-minded, H27.1–2

tidings of Lord our saviour's coming, H2.2

tiger: because of its swift current, Tigris takes its name from —, T12.5

Tigris: Tobias on his journey paused by river —, T12.1; — because of its swift current, takes its name from tiger, T12.5; — ‖ downward course of our death & mortality, T12.5

Tobias paused by river Tigris on his journey, T12.1: — stopped over by river Tigris ‖ Lord dwelt among sinners & mortals, T12.7; — bade farewell to parents, T10.1; — brought angel in to his father, T8.1; — is brought into bedroom to Sarah, T20.1; — frightened of the fish ‖ Lord dreaded death, T13.1–2; — ‖ humanity of saviour, T6.5; — married Sarah after tying up devil on archangel's instructions, T6.4; –' wedding, T23.1; — produced from his satchel part of (fish's) liver, T20.1; — sent to parents with Sarah & property ‖ Christ sent back to Jews, T29.5–6; Tb taught — from infancy to fear God & refrain from sin, T3.9; no deceit would be found on his lips, T3.10

Tobit: –'s good deeds, T4.1; all –'s belongings restored to him, T4.5; (*significance of* blind –'s giving his hand to a servant, T31.4–5; — blind & preaching God's word ‖ both reprobate & elect, T5.16; — instructed his folk & turned to God in prayer, T5.13; Bk of — contains greatest mysteries of Christ & Church, T1.3; Bk of — of saving benefit even in superficial meaning, T1.1; — gave tithes to strangers & proselytes, T2.3; many people loved —, T4.2; — recovers sight ‖ Jewish people will recover light they lost, T34.1–2; — shared with captive brethren of own kin, T2.3; — taken captive in days of Shalmaneser king of the Assyrians, T2.1; — taunted by relatives & upbraided by wife, T5.12; — took Anna from his own tribe as his wife, T3.1; — ‖ unbelievers through blindness & believers through faith, T28.5; — wearied with burying & blinded, T5.6; —

138

welcoming & kissing son ‖ Judea joining in Christ's embrace, T32.1–2; white film obstructing –'s eyes ‖ folly of self-indulgence, T34.3–8; — with son & wife fled naked & went into hiding, T4.2; — taught Tbs from infancy to fear God & refrain from sin, T3.9

transference: metonymy in Greek = —, H18.17

Transfiguration H4.3–6: , H10.5

transience of earthly things, H38.18: fleeting happiness of wicked, H5.5

translation: Gentiles received word of God from Israel through —, T3.14

translators: through seventy — people of God gave decalogue to Gentiles, T3.12

tree(s): many fruit-bearing –s ‖ many people loaded down with virtues, H7.20–21; Peter ‖ — refreshing those hungering for holiness, H7.23–24; Peter ‖ — healing sick by shadow of his body, H7.23–24

tribulation(s): (*see* affliction(s))

trinity: Lord bids Church at its betrothal to renounce Satan & confess faith in — for remission of sins, T20.3

trust: Jews gave Gentiles divine law in — on condition of repayment, T3.13; — in God, H38.3; — in God not in self, H37.35–36; cf. belief in God's protection, H37.35; cf. (prophet) confident he could obtain pardon for sins, H5.6

truth: dog bringing news ‖ every faithful teacher a messenger of —, T30.6; — itself teaching within is heard outwardly through teachers, T19.5; H26.3; teachers fix light of — in hearer's heart, H12.8; H13.2; footprints of — fixed in hearer's mind at teacher's preaching, H13.2; love & knowledge of — engendered by words or examples of holy teachers, H7.27–28

two: four servants & — camels: ‖ — cows & four rams slaughtered, T26.4

unbelief: Egypt ‖ hearts clouded by darkness of —, T21.7; Hebrew people get up from sleep of their —, T31.2; Jews give Gentiles decalogue to free them from indigence of —, T3.12; members of Christ i.e. those converted from — to faith, T16.2; — of Jews, H1.3; — cuts off Jewish leaders from destiny of faithful, H30.8; hardness of — worn down by humility, H22.5; unbelieving section of prophet's people, H37.32; (*see also* Church).

unbelievers abandoned by God of whose indwelling they are unworthy, T21.4: believers among Jews sad at blindness of —, T29.4; Christ's coming not merely for resurrection of faithful but for perdition of —, H28.12; Jacob limping ‖ — among Jews, T5.17; persecution by —, T10.3; H33.5; Tb ‖ — through blindness & believers through faith, T28.5; Lord's wrath against —, H19.4–5; sea ‖ hearts of —, H19.3

unclean could not have Raguel's daughter, T19.1

unction: (people of Jews) anointing heads of worthless with — of adulation, H37.21

unity: Gentiles receive into — of Church Jews who believe at end of world, T3.15; preachers bring new peoples together into — of Church of Christ, T26.5

upright (*see* just)

veil: Jewish people still have a — in front of their heart that they may not understand grace of Christ, T34.13

veins: rivers ‖ earth's —, H23.7

vicissitudes of people of God ‖ those of Church, T4.6

victim to be offered on (Lord's) account by parents, H7.14

vigil: dogs patrol in restless vigil for their masters' safety, T30.4

vigilance: tired man who neglects — spiritually lies down & sleeps —, T5.7

vine(s) H37.1,8: produce on Lord's –s failed long ago ‖ fruits of love among Jewish masses, H37.18; — ‖ Synagogue of Jews, H37.8

vinegar: (his people) offered Lord — instead of wine when thirsty, H37.19

virgin of Christ, H38.26: God's Son who was to be born of Holy Spirit & — mother, H1.13; Gabriel announcing good news to — mother, H7.16

virgin birth: procreation of Christ without male intervention, H7.19

virtue(s): devil tried to strip God's people of riches of their —, T4.3; Gentiles work at acquiring riches of —, T3.14; Israel alone served God with true faith & acts of —, T1.4; progress in — by gift of God's grace, H23.9

vision: *Habakkuk's — of Christ's coming on earth*, H5.1–6; when grief of repentance is over sinners enjoy blessed — (of God) forever, H23.4

visitation: divine — an unexpected bow to put kingdoms of world to the test, H21.2

wash: Tbs went into river to — feet ‖ Lord embraced to death to — faithful from sin & death, T12.9–10

water: demon driven out by — of baptism, T21.1; — of sin did not touch (Lord), T12.8; Peter baptized (Cornelius' household) with —, T11.3; Christ has made new wine of the — ‖ gives spiritual understanding of law, T25.4; many –s ‖ Gentiles 32,2

wealth/y (*see* riches, pride)

weary: –ied with burying, Tb falls asleep, T5.1; Tb –ied with burying & blinded, T5.6

wedding: Tbs' —, T23.1

wedding-feast of Church at which bridegroom is Christ, T25.4: — at which Christ has made new wine of water, T25.4

week: sixth day of — on which passion was accomplished, H1.2

wicked: fleeting happiness of —, H5.5; — rolling in riches, H1.5

wife: (Tb) fled with son & —, T4.4; Tb's — upbraided him as if he had served God in vain, T5.12

wine: Christ has made new — of water ‖ gives spiritual understanding of law, T25.4

wisdom: fount of —, H24.16; abyss of heavenly —, H24.19; mountains ‖ people proud because of worldly power, —, wealth, H15.2

wise: no truth in people who are — in own estimation, T34.7

witness (*see* example(s), orthopraxis)

woes: pressure of (prophet's) —, H4.10

wolves (*see* pastor)

word(s) (*see* ministry, preach, preacher(s), preaching, teach, teacher(s), teaching(s)): Acts of Apostles testify to welcome Gentiles gave to Lord's —, T18.2; welcome Raguel gave Tbs & angel ‖ welcome Gentiles gave Lord's —, T18.2; Lord went to Gentile people through teachers of his —, T18.2; Christ's — ‖ darts to pierce human hearts, H26.2; — enlightens & renders worthy of God's indwelling, H12.6; first necessary that — of teacher be heard, H12.8; (God's) —, H12.1; — of prophets proclaimed by apostles' preaching, H12.3; heralds of —, H32.4; — is ministered through teachers, H13.3; love & knowledge of truth engendered by — or examples of holy teachers, H7.28; most abject poverty of being starved of God's —, H31.6; poverty of Gentiles partakes of banquet of God's —, H31.7; preachers exercise ministry of — for their hearers, H24.7; — of healing reproof or exhortation, H22.6; — of saving doctrine, H22.5; hearers open bay of inward reflection to — of salvation, H22.6

works (*see* good works): Hebrew people stumbling in steps of their actions until they receive light of full faith & good —, T31.3; daily progress in good —, H36.5; that by practising — of mercy in Jerusalem of present Church we may prepare for entry into heavenly Jerusalem, H36.14–15

works of power: Christ's —, T10.3 (*see also* miracles)

world: adversities of present —, H38.19; allurements of present —, H38.19; condition of present —, H1.4; Christ (stone from mountain) crushed kingdoms of —, H7.19; (Lord's) resurrection bestowed hope & faith on —, H9.5; sceptres i.e. kingdoms of this —, H21.2; — already approaching end & good things of future life soon to come, T38.2; end of — when Lord with Church enters into eternal rest, T41.2; (Gentiles') teachers knew about life in this — only, T6.2; Jewish people when converted to faith at end of —, T37.3; Jews who believe at end of —, T3.15; life in this — which runs course of seven days, T6.2; redemption of —, T10.2; sin cannot be put an end to except by destruction of — itself, T39.4

worldly: mountains ‖ people proud because of — power, wisdom, wealth, H15.2; teachers by invective break down hardness of — spirit, H24.3; the — dismayed when abundance of world's possessions runs short, H37.2; Lord's anger against — minded, H19.5; cf. H27.4

wound of love caused by darts of Christ's words, H26.2

wrath (*see* anger, fury, rage) H22.2: (Lord,) in your — you will remember mercy, H6.1; Lord's — against rivers, H19.1; Lord's — against worldly-minded, H19.5; Lord's look of — shatters proud, H15.3; Lord venting — upon material-minded, H27.4; Lord, do not chasten me in your —, H27.6; threat of — 21.5; will Lord's — endure forever against all sinners? H19.5

yoke: people of Israel oppressed by — of Roman slavery, T5.11; teachers ‖ cattle because they bear light — of gospel, T23.3; those who bear sweet — of Gospel not among Jews, H37.31; those assiduously bearing — of law, H37.12

zeal for God but not based on knowledge, T34.4

Zechariah: saying of — concerning Chaldaean army, H7.4

Zion H7.6

Zorobabel H36.7: — type of Christ, H36.12